Philosophy and Literature

ROYAL INSTITUTE OF PHILOSOPHY LECTURE SERIES: 16
SUPPLEMENT TO *PHILOSOPHY* 1983

EDITED BY

A. Phillips Griffiths

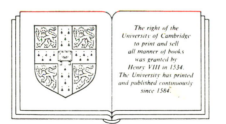

The right of the
University of Cambridge
to print and sell
all manner of books
was granted by
Henry VIII in 1534.
The University has printed
and published continuously
since 1584.

CAMBRIDGE UNIVERSITY PRESS

CAMBRIDGE
LONDON   NEW YORK   NEW ROCHELLE
MELBOURNE   SYDNEY

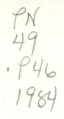

Published by the Press Syndicate of the University of Cambridge
The Pitt Building, Trumpington Street, Cambridge CB2 1RP
32 East 57th Street, New York, NY 10022, USA
296 Beaconsfield Parade, Middle Park, Melbourne 3206, Australia

© The Royal Institute of Philosophy 1984

Library of Congress catalogue card number: 84–5894

British Library Cataloguing in Publication Data
Philosophy and literature—(Royal Institute
of Philosophy lecture series; 16)
1. Literature—Philosophy
I. Griffiths, A. Phillips II. Series
801   PN45
ISBN 0 521 27411 7

Printed in Great Britain by Adlard & Son Ltd, Bartholomew Press, Dorking

Contents

The H. B. Action Memorial Lecture: Solitude in Philosophy
and Literature   I
HYWEL D. LEWIS

Death and Fulfilment, or Would the Real Mr. Dostoyevsky Stand
Up?   15
STEWART SUTHERLAND

Aristotle and Agamemnon   29
RENFORD BAMBROUGH

"Reality" in Early Twentieth-century German Literature   41
J. P. STERN

Literary Examples and Philosophical Confusion   59
R. W. BEARDSMORE

Thematic Concepts: Where Philosophy Meets Literature   75
STEIN HAUGOM OLSEN

Dostoyevsky: Psychology and the Novelist   95
İLHAM DİLMAN

The End of the Road: the Death of Individualism   115
JACQUELYN KEGLEY

The Noble   135
JOHN CASEY

When do Empirical Methods By-pass 'The Problems Which
Trouble Us'?   155
FRANK CIOFFI

Devant la Loi   173
JACQUES DERRIDA

Philosophical Autobiography: St Augustine and John Stuart Mill   189
MARTIN WARNER

Philosophy, Interpretation, and the Golden Bowl   211
PETER JONES

Notes on Contributors   229

Index   231

Preface

Contributors to the Royal Institute of Philosophy Lectures, 1981–82, were asked to consider what were the important issues arising in the relationship of philosophy and literature. The question presupposes or determines hardly anything. If the vagueness of the request needs defence, it may be found in the richness and variety of the response.

Professor Jacques Derrida's lecture, *Devant la Loi,* was first read in an English translation prepared by Dr Paul Foulkes. Having done so, the author felt that Dr Foulkes' version was too English for publication. The article is therefore published in the original French, edited by Dr Foulkes, with some cuts imposed by limitations of space (marked . . .). Many thanks are due to Dr Foulkes for his work.

A fourteenth lecture of the series by Professor Anthony Nuttall has already been published, contained in his *A New Mimesis: Shakespeare and the Representation of Reality* (Methuen, 1983), with further material, between pages 8 and 75.

Solitude in Philosophy and Literature

The H. B. Acton Memorial Lecture

HYWEL D. LEWIS

'I understand that the world was nothing, a mechanical chaos of casual, brute enmity on which we stupidly impose our hopes and fears. I understand that, finally and absolutely, I alone exist. All the rest, I saw, is merely what pushes me, or what I push against, blindly—as blindly as all that is not myself pushes back. I create the whole universe, blink by blink. —An ugly god pitifully dying in a tree.'

These words are from a novel which will be, I imagine, familiar to many. It is by John Gardner and was first published in 1971. Some greeted it with wild enthusiasm, as a modern masterpiece of imaginative writing, others were repelled by the stark horror which the occasional pity does little to relieve as the terrible story unfolds itself. The title of the novel is *Grendel* and it offers a terrifying picture of a modern Beowulf.

The torment of Grendel lies in his inability to communicate. He has grown out of the world of his beast-mother though remaining partly dependent upon her, on her mindless pity and affection as well as her help. But she provides nothing that he needs even though they both move at some kind of supernatural level. But neither can he communicate with men, he makes nothing of their talk; and while he aspires initially to be like them or with them, their total inability to make anything of him, beyond the menace of his power and preternatural presence, drives him to unmitigated hate and destructive malice. An object of pity to itself, he is otherwise the symbol of total evil.

This is the theme, presented in less colourfully fantastic forms, of a great deal of recent literature. On occasion the world of fantasy becomes dominant again, and one is not certain when one is moving in a realm of fable and allegory and when in the community of real persons, as in another much admired and perplexing work of fiction, *Surfacing* by Margaret Atwood. But the upshot, even when not so explicitly stated, is the same rejection of the world as we initially have it, the retreat into a world, sometimes a very hateful one, where we ourselves weave all that matters into some fashion of a projection of ourselves, not simplistically into what we wish but quite often into what we ourselves know to be most repulsively degrading. There is even a craving, but in a horrifyingly sophisticated human way, for animal existence without the unawareness of beasts. We cannot escape our destiny to be human, but we also fail to relate to the world as we ourselves apprehend it in the proper community of our awareness of each other.

When fantasy is not invoked to bring out the full horror of this incarceration in a world that is not fitted to our proper needs and aptitudes, there is a more explicit portayal of essentially the same situation in a more overtly and properly human context. We are dealing with people as they normally are, but in the same appalling situation of a failure of involvement, an estrangement for which there is no easement in outright madness.

Take a novel that moves easily in the normal liberated culture of today. It is *The Instrument* by John O'Hara.[1] The author is, I suspect, a little underestimated by our finest critics. Few would deny that he is a highly gifted and lively story teller. He gets on with his uninhibited, unvarnished story, without pausing to ponder the impact of it or point his moral, obliquely or in any other way. The story is everything. But it is, in its forthright narrative, very profound all the same. The main character, Yank Lucas, is a fine and friendly person, with complete integrity although without any ostentation—there is no parade of virtues. Not all his standards would be widely endorsed. But he is, in a detached and genuinely amused way, interested in people and concerned about them for just what they are. He is fully and perceptively aware that he cannot pass from his fantasies about Anna Phelps, with whom he lodges in the New England village, to which he has escaped from the complications and publicity of sudden fame, as he can flirt and amuse himself with the more wanton girl at the Post Office. His much more serious involvement had been with Zena Gollum, the glamorous star of the play which had brought him instant prominence and assured success. But an affair with Zena, even a deep and lasting one, would make demands upon him not consistent with total commitment to his art and future projects. At all costs these must come first. His break with Zena is savagely ruthless, though kindlier in that way. It is also tragic and prepares for the disintegration of the character of Zena Gollum, already on the way, and her suicide. Lucas returns to New York, grieving but not devastated, his art and his career still untarnished. But he has another deeper tragedy of which he will never be rid, namely that normal vicissitudes will never break him, for he can never be sufficiently involved for them to touch him at the core of his being. Nice fellow though he is he cannot take on the burden of any ultimate care. He never gets properly outside himself.

The story of Yank Lucas is the story of the failure of ultimate involvement, far deeper and more desperate than ordinary destitution, and it is not inappropriate that another character should sum it up himself, in the

[1] Hodder and Stoughton.

closing words of another story[2] with the *sang froid* and simple but frightening detachment of his clear-sighted understanding of himself, and, as he sees it, and rightly in one way, of all others—'What', he exclaims, 'did he know about me?'

> What really, can any of us know about any of us, and why must we make such a thing of loneliness when it is the final condition of us all? And where would love be without it?

It is the same course that is taken in another work of fiction that is much better known, *Memoirs of Hecate County*, by Edmund Wilson. This is usually considered by literary critics in the context of an author's reaction to life and attitudes in America at the time (the book was first published in 1946). But it has importance of a much less transitory kind, and much profundity. The mood for the book is set by the story of 'The Man Who Shot Snapping Turtles', the turtles steadily eliminating the beautiful ducks that were the admiration of a man on whose pond they settled. Evil and ugliness seemed invariably to triumph.

In the main story, 'The Princess with the Golden Hair', the narrator carries on a love affair simultaneously with two very different persons. One of these, the 'Princess' in the title, is the sophisticated, elegant wife of a business acquaintance, the other is the very simple, but not naive, girl he has got to know at the Tango Casino where she works. In both cases there is deep affection and respect, patience and restraint towards the more sophisticated woman in her physical disability, tenderness and practical kindness towards the girl from the Casino caught up in the wretchedness of her background and distressful family relations and her illness. But when various circumstances bring the two affairs abruptly to an end, the lover is not really deprived of anything vital in his own existence. He declares at the close of the story:

> She had given me this vision . . . it was something so strong and instinctive that it could outlive the hurts and infections, the defilements, among which we lived—so organic that it could not be analysed. She had transmitted a belief and a beauty that could not be justified or explained. Nor could they ever be paid for or sold—And what had I been able to give in return? What had I to compare with these? My passion for painting, perhaps. But I had not been able to give her even that.[3]

In all his admiration and concern for the one lovely and superior person, and his tender sharing of the wry humour and trust of the other, a sort of saintliness that shone through the sordidness of their encounters, he had remained inviolable, he had given away nothing that was truly

[2] *Sermons and Soda-Water*, (London: The Cresset Press, 1961), 265.
[3] *Memoirs of Hecate County*, (Boston: Nonpareil Books), 313.

himself, there was no totality in any of his generosity or his pity; at the deepest level he had not been hurt, for his love had not touched him there. He remained confined in the solitariness of his proper existence, radically unaffected but lost; 'I was felled by a sudden glumness as I knew, and found it bitter to know, that I was back now in Hecate County'.[4]

A similar strain runs through much of the work of Iris Murdoch, both in explicit philosophical discussion and in fiction. In *The Sovereignty of Good*[5] we are warned against the false 'consolations of self-pity, resentment, fantasy and despair' and urged to seek help, through art and the world of nature, to pierce 'the falsifying veil' and look at the world as it really is, to 'be realistic, to perceive justly'. In some passages in her novels, Miss Murdoch presents very vividly the horror of the enclosure in one's own inner existence that comes about by failure of involvement: and this becomes the central theme of many of her writings, for example *The Sea, the Sea*[6]. Here we have two young persons deeply and unaffectedly in love with all prospect of a happy life together, but the girl feels the demand of this particular love so excessive that she breaks away from it altogether, and in due course enters into another happy but more commonplace marriage. Many years later the two meet by sheer chance, the man by now at the peak of a fine career, and a celebrity. In fancy at least the flame of the earlier romance is kindled, nothing in all the man's amours and successes having filled the void. He seeks to re-establish their love more deliberately, but the woman feels the force and the depth of it as well; and there ensues in this way a bizarre situation of partially requited love between an ageing and not too obviously attractive woman and almost her opposite in the confident, liberated and much admired person the man has become. Only exceptional literary skill can redeem this. In the end it all comes to nothing, the opportunity for the one involvement that would have been properly fulfilling having been lost and irretrievably abandoned in the first failure to come to terms with it.

In *Nuns and Soldiers*[7] we have the many convolutions of several loves leading, by their desperation again, into near bizarre situations where an almost too determined, cultivated, giving of oneself is frustrated at all crucial points (alike for a young couple—a raffish and rather shiftless young man and his girl-friend determined to wound herself with a rebellious bloody-mindedness which does not seem to be her true nature—and the sophisticated sensitive group into which their lives are strangely drawn) by an equally inevitable drawing away into the security of life as

---

[4] Op. cit., 313.
[5] Routledge and Kegan Paul, 1970.
[6] Chatto and Windus.
[7] Chatto and Windus.

each person seems to see it to be for himself. At the centre is Anne who, having left her bright and talented existence at Oxford to spend many years in a convent, came out to find that the impulse and frame of mind which sent her there is still with her, a need, surviving the loss of her initial faith, to give herself wholly without knowing how this could be done.

> She had been so wise not to tell her love . . . some great necessary integrity, some absolute availability, some eternal aloneness would have been lost by that revelation. She had kept her mouth shut, she had never told her love, and that at least was for her salvation. She was still 'empty and clean', transparent and invisible, although the voice that said this was still the voice of her pride. And she was homeless and free. She had left the convent because it was a home. Foxes have holes, but the Son of Man . . . only now, after the safety of her service to Gertrude, was she facing the void which she had chosen.
>
> But was not the idea of 'void' itself an illusion . . . Or would she perhaps end up after all as a priest in another church? At least she knew that she must now seek solitude, innocence and the silence of being totally uninteresting.[8]

It would be easy to multiply examples in the same vein. Indeed, a most impressive survey has in fact been undertaken by Professor Ben Mijuskovic of the University of Carbondale in his fine book, *Loneliness in Philosophy, Psychology and Literature*.[9] He shows most effectively how prominent the themes of loneliness and inwardness have been in creative literature from quite early times, in the myth of Prometheus, the Odyssey, in parts of Plato and Aristophanes, and in the Upanishads, down to most recent writers of fiction and philosophy. *Robinson Crusoe* recovers the importance it had earlier for speculative thought (the 'History of Robinson and Friday' as we have it in Hegel's 'Outlines of the Phenomenology') and is shown to be part of a concern which continues through Proust to the British novelist Arthur Machen and his frightening portrayal, in his own words, of 'a Robinson Crusoe of the soul'[10] and to Thomas Wolfe's 'We walk the streets of life alone',[11] matched by Conrad's *Heart of Darkness* and Golding's *Pincher Martin*.

Mijuskovic concludes that, on the 'philosophical foundation' of the ability of thought to 'curl back on itself', 'the disciplines of literature, philosophy and psychology have erected a significant and true insight into man's fundamental nature, namely that each of us, separately, exists in

---

[8] *Nuns and Soldiers*, Chatto and Windus 498–499.
[9] 1979, Van Gorcum Press, Assen, The Netherlands.
[10] *The Hill of Dreams*, Richard Press. Introduction, viii.
[11] *Of Time and the River*, Penguin Modern Classics, 185.

isolation, in a state of desolate loneliness, enclosed within the confines of a nomadic prison which we continually strive to escape'.[12]

But, having indicated, if only in outline but, I trust, with some of the starkness of which the subject allows, how persistent and deep is the preoccupation in general literature with inwardness and a radical isolation, it is now time to turn to a more expressly philosophical consideration of the situation which is presented to us in these disturbing works of literature, and to assess its proper significance.

It will, I hope, be evident that the loneliness with which these notable writers are concerned is not just some occasional condition into which some unfortunate persons are plunged by peculiar and distressful circumstances, the old, the deprived, the bereaved and their like. Turns of fortune may indeed highlight a state in which we all find ourselves, and lend it a peculiar bitterness. But we are not all of us cut off from our fellows in these overt ways. Many lead very full lives but are still subject, in the deepest understanding of their state, to the desolation of which the novelists and dramatists write. What is this, and what can the philosopher say about it?

He will not have much, if anything, to say if he subscribes to the prevailing fashion in the philosophy of mind, namely to deny that we have any 'inner' existence or to insist that there is no important sense in which our experiences are private. It has been widely held that mental processes, contrary to what may seem to be obviously the case, are in reality identical with states and changes of the brain. Others, without seeming to endorse an outright materialist view, have sought to dissolve the issue between a corporealist and a dualist view by reducing all our experiences to our public observable behaviour plus the dispositions to behave which are disclosed in our actual conduct. This, in essentials, was the well-known procedure of Professor Ryle; and whatever else may be said about it, it seems to be deliberately contrived to eliminate any significant sense in which experiences are private and exclusive, initially and inherently, to the people who have them.

There could, no doubt, be some ingenious way in which a distinction might be drawn between experiences which are public and those which are private, and some sense of desolate isolation, in terms of a Rylean account of mental existence. Ingenuity can go a long way, as outright materialists have shown from time to time. Misunderstanding could have some place in a Rylean view or its like; and this could be a source of painful isolation and distress. But it would at most be partial and occasional; it would have little to match up to the sense of a despairing imprisonment within oneself, as a constant liability of being as we are, which is so disturbingly vivid in the literature to which I have alluded.

[12] Op. cit., 25.

To appreciate that, we have, I submit, to draw a sharp distinction, in the first place, between mental processes of all kinds and occurrences of a radically different nature in the physical world. Mental events are not extended and locatable. The thoughts I have now, as on-going processes, are radically different in nature from any observable physical processes, and this I know in knowing what thoughts are like in the process of having them. This is true, not only of more severely intellectual reflection, but of all forms of experience, including so-called 'physical' sensation. There is, admittedly, a sense in which pains, for example, are locatable; but, whatever we say on this head, it seems certainly not the case that I can ever observe a pain 'in my tooth', though I may well be able to indicate the cause of it there; the dentist can tell me exactly what is wrong, but he does not see or touch the pain—that is something I feel.

I have presented this view at length, on other occasions and in other writings. I will not recapitulate further here what I have set out fully already. The close interaction of mind and body, and the importance of the body in other ways, is also readily allowed. But this does not make mental existence itself bodily. Nor is there any access to mental existence other than through each person's awareness of what it is like in his own case. This is not to be identified, though many have thought otherwise, with statements about states of mind. It is, on the contrary, a matter of being aware of our own states of mind in the process of having them, as I have also set out more fully elsewhere.

I have also maintained that states of mind, or all experience, 'belong' to, or are had by, a subject which is the same in all experience. This is established not only, as in Kant, by an analysis of what is involved in our having the sort of experience we do have, but also, more unmistakably and firmly, by each person knowing himself as the person he is in having any experience whatsoever. A person is not an 'imaginary focus', or its like, but the actual being that each one finds himself to be. The person, as known in this way, is not any pattern or continuity of the experiences themselves. He remains the one he is whatever the experiences, and in all changes of experience. If my thoughts and perceptions now were altogether different, it would still be me having them. Nor am I merely my dispositions. These may be described, as I may be described in terms of all that has happened to me. But the me who is so described is more than that. But it is known, not by description, but initially by each one in having any experience.

We must, however, avoid the temptation of isolating the self, as known in this way, from the course of the experience or the dispositions and character which it discloses. My thoughts, my likes, my sensations, and so on, are truly me and not just related to me. But in another sense they are not me; if those were different I would still be me. Time will not allow me to go further into the way we must philosophically handle this seeming paradox. I have tried to do so elsewhere. Here I can only insist

7

that there are not two selves, but only the one self who may be identified by description and also, in a more basic way, by each one directly in his own case as the unique being he is—a mode of identity altogether peculiar to persons.

Memory, in the strict form of recalling some event in which we ourselves have figured, including the awareness each one had of himself at the time, provides the more explicit guarantee of continued identity, though much must be filled up further around this. But memory is not constitutive of personal identity, and there is no reason why we should not *be* the same persons, in the basic form noted, in the situations of which all trace of memory is sunk. It is in these terms that we must approach the 'problem cases', as they are called, although this is not the place to pursue that further.

It is for these reasons that I can never be in doubt at the time about my being the subject in any experience. I may be wrong about the causes of a pain I have, but I cannot be wrong at the time about its being me who has it; and so for all experience. But I may be mistaken about many events in my past; for I learn about these in essentially the same way as I learn about other persons—from evidence of one sort or another. I do not, even in telepathy, have or share the experience of another person as he has it. I learn about it from what he says or from his demeanour or behaviour. I do not, even in the most intimate relationships, know another person's experiences, his thoughts or sensations for example, in the same way as his actually having it. I do not know another person properly from within, but only myself. This is where the issue relates very closely to the matters noted earlier.

If my view is sound, there is a very profound and important sense in which every individual is, unavoidably in what it is to be a conscious being, or to have experience, a world to himself. This is not the whole story— far from it. We are aware of the world around us, and we have rich and fulfilling encounters with one another. Life as we know it, would not be possible otherwise. Solipsism is the way of madness, strictly not even that. But it does not follow by any means, as so many of our contemporaries suppose, that the rejection of solipsism commits us to the view that we know one another in the same way as we know ourselves. There is an unavoidable privacy in our being the finite conscious beings that we are. We can never step out of this, and the failure to come to terms with this unavoidable basic feature of the only existence we can have is a prime source of wretchedness and disaster, and the very stuff of tragedy.

The finality of our initial isolation cannot be stressed too much. This is not relative, but total. There is no way, in the nature of what it is to be conscious, by which one consciousness can invade another. This is a hard fact of our finite existence. We can have no one else's experience. There is an awesomeness in this, but it is the price of our dignity as the beings we are, and the condition of all that we find of worth. It is the glory and mystery of how we are made, each in one way his own world, unavoidably and always, but not solely so. If it were all we could not be. But it is not all.

We also apprehend what is presented to us, whatever as philosophers we may say about its status; and from within this general apprehension of the world around us we recognize the items in which there are unfolded, as the obvious explanation of what we find, what other persons are like and intend. This is not infallible, but it also comes about easily and spontaneously and, normally, with all the certainty we need. In reflection it may seem remote and elaborate, and indeed it is elaborate like much else in human existence which comes to seem simple and operates with ease and swiftness. But it makes possible the full and easy communication we have with one another, the warmth and tenderness and intimacy of close personal fellowship. Bodily contact has its part here, though it is never as mere bodies that we meet. The marvel of our essential inwardness is matched by the ease and richness of mediated mutual encounter.

But this has its perils, the risk involved in creating us with such a vast potential. It is only too easy to slide from a world that exists in its own right, a world with which we must come to terms, and from encounters which impose their own requirements and the respect and attention due to persons as real as ourselves, it is easy to slide from this to a more accommodating inner citadel of our own consciousness, the world as we would just like it to be, a world of fantasy and dreams. This does not happen merely in situations of acute abnormality, in madness and delusion. It is prone, in some measure, to characterize all our concerns and attitudes, even in the normal daily round.

Bertrand Russell is a good example. No one would normally think of him as a lonely or solitary person. Even when he was most unpopular he was surrounded by people devoted to him. He was at the centre of much public attention and esteem. He was married many times, he had children in whom he took the closest interest, he had many lovers. And yet he returns, in his autobiography many times to the theme of a 'sombre solitude' by which he was oppressed for most of his life. These are not the terms in which we would normally expect him to speak. His diagnosis of the malaise from which he thought D. H. Lawrence suffered is also significant. Russell wrote:

His thought was a mass of self-deception masquerading as stark realism . . . When he realized that other people existed, he hated them. But most of the time he lived in a solitary world of his own imaginings, peopled by phantoms as fierce as he wished them to be. His excessive emphasis on sex was due to the fact that in sex alone he was compelled to admit that he was not the only human being in the universe. But it was so painful that he conceived of sex relations as a perpetual fight in which each is attempting to destroy the other.[13]

Little is said very explicitly in the contexts to which I have referred about guilt and wrongdoing. But a brooding sense of guilt runs through much of these writings. The authors are not primarily moralists. They do not denounce, they expose; they are more full of pity than condemnation. They have a fair place for genuine goodness and describe it well. All the same there runs through all the dismay and sadness a deep undercurrent of guilt as well. It lies at the heart of the horror, not disentangled from other ingredients, but starkly there. It is not an unhealthy affectation, as in much theology and psychology today; it is not collective but a form of the nemesis to which each one contributes.

This is in line with sound understanding of persons and morals. Much in our lives is shaped for us, though not mainly by sheer pressure from without. We absorb into our own natures the influences which make us what we are. But at the very core of moral accountability is the genuinely open choice between what our main inclinations on some occasions require and opposing moral obligations. Nothing preordains this choice; the person, in the respect which is more than the course of one's life or one's nature, makes it. No one is more lonely than in ultimate moral choice. Here one is wholly on one's own.

But it is for this very reason that failure to conform with what we ourselves feel to be appropriate at the time helps significantly to turn us away from the world as it really seems to the inner world of our own fantasies and wishful thinking. If you betray the world you find it hard to face it, you escape to a convenient world of your own. This is not the only reason for such turning away, but it is a factor which makes for bitterness and hardness of heart. It is in the conflation of these ethical repercussions with others, including a religious sense of desolation, which are not so wholly of our own making, that we find the key to a persistent sense of vileness which is at odds with properly ethical notions of blame and wrongdoing. The part of unconscious repression in these convolutions has been noted and discussed by me elsewhere.[14]

One peculiarly significant form of the misguided ways in which we react to the inevitable inwardness of our existence is when, in frustration and despair, we try to establish an assured contact with others as other by seeking to penetrate directly to their own inner existence. This is bound

[13] *The Autobiography of Bertrand Russell*, II (Allen and Unwin, 1968), 23. The quotation does not mean that Russell had no regard for Lawrence. He despised Lawrence's ideas, and found him impossible personally, but he was fully aware of Lawrence's gifts—'His descriptive powers were remarkable', op. cit., 23.

[14] *Our Experience of God*, (George, Allen and Unwin, 1959) Ch. IV.

to fail; it is, for reasons noted already, inherently impossible. But there is deep in our nature, induced by dismay and misery, an urge, unformulated and not usually reflective, to seek relief and fulfilment in these essentially impossible ways, to push beyond the barrier which finitude itself imposes upon us. This is perverse but understandable.

The most overt and immediately damaging forms of this perversion are found when we force one another into situations where the normal disguises and adaptations are dropped, when we see, as we seem to think, the naked soul. The pretences, the normal conformities, go in extremes of passionate excitation, or in anguish and terror. At last we are truly at one with the other as he really is. In one way this is true: there is some kind of bond between the tormentor and his victim; passion is often stark. But it is also wrongheaded, it provides realism without worth. The impulse which induces it defeats itself. For the inner citadel of the being of the other remains unassailed—as it must be.

How extensively these reactions affect our lives today may not be too easy to determine, and I must leave the matter mainly to the reader. I am well aware of the danger, so expertly exhibited by Lady Wotton,[15] of providing one exclusive explanation or solution of some social malaise. But it seems plain that, all over the world, people are lapsing into various forms of madness and destructiveness. In part this is due to the exceeding rapidity of some of our advances, the ensuing complexities and alarmed reactions; it is helped by the kind of power, and the concentration of power, that can be wielded today. The evil in our lives can also be highlighted and exaggerated, to the disregard of extensive normality and decency, by the threat it poses and its news value. Even so, when all caution is exercised and allowance is made, we seem faced with an astounding upsurgence of violence and barbarism, in our own community and in unbelievably degraded and fanatical regimes all over the world.

My submission is that this may not be accounted for entirely in terms of complexities of our social situation, but rather that the final explanation, the disclosure of the basic factors involved—and with that the ultimate solutions—must be sought deep in our nature and finite existence; and, in this enterprise, we need to heed especially the implications of the limited finite existence we have and the proper way to cope with the inwardness which is an inescapable feature of our being creatures with the sort of potentialities we do have.

What is the proper way to cope? It must clearly be found in the compensating apprehension of the world around us, including other persons, existing in its own right with appropriate claim to our interest and regard. A sickly interest in the world merely as it relates to us will not do.

---

[15] In her *Social Science and Social Pathology*, (George, Allen and Unwin, 1959), and elsewhere.

We have to acquire the right sort of realism. This will involve our own role, in contemplation and action, as well as the impact of the world itself. In the case of persons, there must be the regard which takes them on their own merit, establishing a rapport with them in and for themselves, but which is also distanced. There is a restraint, a holding back, in genuine love, not in the cautious reluctance to enter into total commitment but in the concern not to violate the sanctity of the genuine inner existence of the other. We should not aspire to possess one another, or to be one another, but to love with appreciation and reverence. We have to put off our shoes when we step on the holy ground of the genuine being of others. They are not extensions of ourselves.

Iris Murdoch has taught us much about the way to achieve this kind of realism. I have referred to her work in this vein with warm approval elsewhere.[16] For her, as we have seen, the remedy is found pre-eminently in art. 'Art', she says, 'pierces the veil and gives sense to the notion of a reality which lies beyond appearance.'[17] 'The love which brings the right answer is an exercise of justice and realism and really *looking*. The difficulty is to keep the attention fixed upon the real situation and to prevent it from returning surreptitiously to the self with consolations of self-pity, resentment, fantasy and despair.'[18] A person may be brooding over some hurt to his prestige. Then suddenly he observes a 'hovering kestrel. In a moment everything is altered. The brooding self with its hurt vanity has disappeared. There is nothing now but kestrel.'[19] Miss Murdoch has much to say, in the same vein, in works of fiction as in her essays and I have myself given much prominence elsewhere to the healing power of art. This, in its many forms, available to high and low in diverse ways, has certainly a central place in the restoration of men and societies. But it is not enough.

Or so it seems to me. There is a void which the world made alive and articulate to us in art does not fill, a despair and destructiveness which it cannot wholly correct, a hunger which it does not assuage. In my view, but I can only touch on this in closing, there is only one ultimate solution, the salve in which our distinctness and its dignity remains unimpaired. It is found in our openness to transcendent being, the inexhaustible richness of an ultimate which not only sustains us but keeps us, as it will always keep us, straining after a surpassing holiness which does not crush or overwhelm us or eliminate what we severally are, but which draws us in ever more complete and satisfying ways, measured in the modes in which it may be received of us, to varieties of worth and attainment that do not pall.

[16] *Jesus in the Faith of Christians*, (Macmillan, 1981), 23–27.
[17] *The Sovereignty of Good*, (Routledge and Kegan Paul, 1970), 88.
[18] Op. cit., 91.
[19] Ibid., 84.

The main wonder of this, its crown and glory, is the tempering of what is given to what can be received, in mode as in substance. This is in itself an abiding amazement, and we should not reduce it by belittling what we are or, on the other hand, trying to over-reach ourselves. As we revere one another, there is reverence in the love of God for us. He alone knows from within, and that is an awesome thought. But he does not come with the majesty that obliterates. He comes in the gentle ways of disclosure, of lights that shine peculiarly in our own awareness, the enchantment and triumph of a tender restraint. We may vulgarize this also, as we certainly much distort it, and seek to bring God himself within our possessiveness, we may try to encapsulate him within limited understanding. But he returns, not to be eliminated by rude presumptions, and it is here that we find the triumphant solution to the distinctness, without which we are nothing, and the solitariness ever prone to engulf us and impel to destructive despair. It is a triumph to which the solitariness itself contributes. These are further large issues to which I can only allude. I have resisted, not altogether successfully, you may think, the temptation to preach to you or pass beyond the limits of my assignment. I hope you will not be disconcerted if I venture to add that, in my opinion, the restoration and fulfilment to which I have referred is found finally and supremely in the marvel of the giving of himself, with all that this is known to involve, by God in the man Jesus of Nazareth.

Death and Fulfilment, or Would the Real Mr Dostoyevsky Stand Up?

STEWART SUTHERLAND

Philosophers have devoted much attention to a series of issues grouped under the heading 'the problem of personal identity'. In most of these discussions the focus has been the question of identity over time and the issues confronted have been basically logical or metaphysical. Students enrolled in philosophy classes dealing with such topics often express a sense of disappointment or frustration, for, of course, they belong to a culture in which the jargon of 'self' or 'personal' identity belongs to a rather different intellectual context heavy with the overtones of existentialism or with the suggestion of psychoanalysis. Anglo-Saxon philosophers have tended to bypass these ways of construing questions of personal identity; sometimes for good reason, sometimes not.

While not questioning the importance of established philosophical ways of discussing personal identity. I have some sympathy with those students who suggest that this is not the whole story. There are many directions from which calls emerge for an extension of the philosophical discussion of personal identity, beyond analysis of identity over time. For example, the philosophy of law, political philosophy and medical ethics all pose interesting and important questions here.

In a rather different context, it is my hope that the content of this lecture will impinge upon the question of personal identity as it arises when we begin to talk about moral integrity, moral consistency and consistency of beliefs. The biographer or portrait painter attempt to show us 'the whole man'. In their painstaking detailed creative effort they try to present a unity. My concern is the case of one individual. Fyodor Dostoyevsky. Is there a unity to be found there? If so, what sort of unity? Can anything useful be said about it? Where would we find it? One way of asking such a question which will at least allow us to begin to discuss it intelligibly, is to ask what would count as fulfilment for Dostoyevsky.

Dostoyevsky died on 9 February 1881 (28 January old style). How do we view or assess such a man as Dostoyevsky from the perspective of his death? The temptations of the obituary writer extend far beyond the columns of *The Times*. When a man dies, perhaps for our own sake as much as his, we seek to sum him up, to measure his achievement. In the case of Dostoyevsky such a temptation must be resisted.

15

> The life and work of Dostoyevsky are inseparable. He 'lived in litera-ture'. It was his life's concern and his tragic fate. In all of his works he resolved the enigma of his personality . . .[1]

Mochulsky's comment gives one clue to the magnetic hold of Dostoyevsky's work over the century since the publication of the last section of his final and greatest novel *The Brothers Karamazov* in December 1880, and his death scarcely a month later in 1881. In so many ways his life and his writing were locked together—whether we think of how much of his own personal obsession was beaten on the anvil of artistic form into the story of *The Gambler*, or whether we hear the tense and exhausted cries of his letters:

> From June 15 to October 1, I wrote 20 printed sheets of the novel (*The Brothers Karamazov*) and published *The Diary of a Writer* in 3 printed sheets. And, still, I can't write off the top of my head; I must write artistically. I'm bound in this to God, to poetry, to the success of what's been written and literally to all the readers of Russia.[2]

Life and writing nourished and were devoured by one another. To the very banks of the Styx, to the outer edges of life itself he was inextricably both man and writer. The last pages of *The Brothers* were sent to the publisher on 8 November 1880: a complete number of the *Writer's Diary* was delivered to the printer on 25 January 1881. That same night he suffered from a haemorrhage caused by moving some furniture in his study. Despite further haemorrhaging he was able on 27 January to spend some time with a sub-editor responsible for printing the *Diary*. The next day, in the evening, he died.

The final year of his life brought his greatest literary triumphs. Apart from the completion of *The Brothers* his most ambitious work, within his own time and amongst his own people, the great 'Pushkin Address' of 8 June, was a moment of unique public recognition. He wrote to his wife,

> My speech was this morning . . . . The hall was crowded to the doors. No, Anya, no, you can never imagine the sensation it produced.[3]

And sensation it was: emotionally for those present, intellectually as a bridge between the warring Slavophiles and Westernizers, and in literary terms in the responses and counter-responses which it provoked. Few literary figures can have experienced such climax, such fulfilment, such

[1] K. Mochulsky, *Dostoyevsky His Life and Work* trans. Michael A. Minihan. (Princeton University Press, 1967), xix.

[2] Letter of 15 October, 1880, to P. Ye. Guseva, quoted in *Mochulsky*, 644.

[3] See Jessie Coulson, *Dostoyevsky: A Self-Portrait* (Oxford University Press, 1962), Letter 144, p. 228.

'completion' we are almost inclined to say, in the last months and weeks of their lives. The temptation to look to the Aristotelian and Medieval notion of a *Telos* realized, is indeed great. Dostoyevsky's achievement is immense; it is seminal; it is formative for the generations to come. The life and the literature symbolically came full circle together.

But in such a bewitching picture we slip backwards too easily from the nineteenth century to a world whose death-knell was sounded pre-eminently in the novels of Dostoyevsky. It would be strange indeed for his death to 'round off' his life, *so* neatly and *so* carefully as almost to negate the uncertainty, the ambiguity, the dialectic of his literary presence and creation. The fulfilment, the triumph of the completion of his greatest novel and the impact of his Pushkin address, should not mislead us into looking for a false unity and uncharacteristic singularity of perspective in the thoughts and words of the man who told the tale of the Grand Inquisitor.

Dostoyevsky towers above and defines the nineteenth century in his definition of the multiplicity of the human mind, the multiplicity charted in what Bakhtin refers to as the polyphonic form of his novels. The issue of what constitutes human identity, what gives a human life whole-ness, and unity of form, is a central preoccupation of the novels and is defined simultaneously in both content and form. It would indeed be surprising if his death gave to his life the unity and singularity of a *Telos* fulfilled—a unity and singularity which he could not find for the heroes of his novels. Yet it would be foolish and blind to deny his achievement, his 'success' if you will, both in terms of external recognition, and in terms of artistic creation. One way of attempting to resolve this apparent paradox would be to define the undoubted unity and fulfilment in artistic terms: but such a path would lead us eventually away from Dostoyevsky rather than towards him. Artist as he was, wholeness for him could never be defined in terms of what Kierkegaard called the 'aesthetic'. Indeed his ridicule of degeneration was at least as strong when applied to literary pretension, as when applied to revolutionary fanaticism. The mayhem of dreams of a false political foundation for society is mirrored in *The Devils* in the anarchy of Mrs Lembke's 'festive day'—beginning ominously in 'a literary matinee, from twelve to four o'clock', and ending catastrophically at the centrepiece of the evening ball—'a literary quadrille'.

It would be difficult to imagine a more wretched, vulgar, tasteless and insipid allegory than that 'literary quadrille'. Nothing less suitable for our public could have been devised; the quadrille was made up of six miserable pairs of masks—not really masks even, for they all wore the same clothes as everyone else. Thus, for instance, one short, elderly gentleman in a frock-coat—in fact, dressed like everyone else—and a venerable grey beard (tied on—this constituted the whole of his fancy dress) was bobbing up and down on the same spot as he danced with a stolid expression on his face, working away as fast as he could with his feet without moving an inch. He emitted curious sorts of sounds in a soft but husky bass, and it was that huskiness of his voice that was meant to suggest one of the well-known newspapers. Opposite this mask danced two giants X and Z, and these letters were pinned on their frock-coats, but what the X and Z meant remained a mystery. The 'honest Russian thought' was represented by a middle-aged gentleman wearing spectacles, a frock-coat, gloves and—manacles (real manacles). Under the arm of this 'thought' was a brief-case containing documents referring to some 'case'. An opened letter from abroad to convince the sceptics of the honesty of the 'honest Russian thought' peeped out of his pocket. All this the stewards explained by word of mouth, since it was impossible to read the letter which protruded from his pocket. In his raised right hand 'the honest Russian thought' held a wine-glass, as though he were about to propose a toast. Close at each side of him two short-haired nihilist girls capered and *vis-à-vis* danced another elderly gentleman in a frock-coat, but with a heavy cudgel in his hand, apparently representing a very redoubtable periodical, though not a Petersburg one: 'I'll wipe you off the face of the earth!' But though armed with a cudgel, he just could not bear the spectacles of 'the honest Russian thought' fixed intently upon him and tried to look away, and when he did his *pas de deux*, he twisted and turned and did not know what to do with himself, so much, apparently, did his conscience prick him . . .[4]

The door opened regularly since then, of seeking unity, identity and integrity of life in pursuit of the aesthetic was a door through which Dostoyevsky refused to pass.

Even in his death, it seems, Dostoyevsky has left us with a legacy of ambiguity and uncertainty. Yet even if, to change the metaphor, we cannot see his death as the final line drawn in an account of his life, which, drawn after a year of spectacular achievement and recognition, leaves the bonus or credit which gives unity, identity and meaning to his life, there remains an alternative perspective in which the relation of life to death, for Dostoyevsky, is itself a parable. His death did not come out of season, nor yet, however, did it come at the completion of the circle of seasons from the spring of birth to the atutumn of death. Such a picture of life and death (the latter being 'in season' or 'out of season'), has virtually been lost in our culture, and Dostoyevsky foresaw this is many ways. The rest of this lecture is devoted to discussing one of the most central ways in which he delineated this—in life and in literature— namely in his treatment and expression of religious belief.

4 *The Devils*, trans. D. Magarshack (Penguin, 1953), 505–506.

Those who would see his death as giving completeness to his life, and who thus picture the life as a unity, the race having been run, the battle finished, are paralleled by, and indeed often are, those seeking in his religious beliefs a single, perhaps 'complex', but certainly 'unified', religious outlook. From his writings, his novels, his letters, the journalism of *The Diary of a Writer*,[5] they cull quotations and references and build up *the* picture of Dostoyevsky's beliefs. He is enlisted in, or vilified for belonging to, a variety of religious causes, the one common feature of each of which is the clarity and certainty with which they can be stated. Very often such pictures of his beliefs can be supported by considerable textual evidence, but I believe such pictures to be wholly misconceived. It is not simply that they are overdrawn on this point, or too emphatic on that: rather they misconstrue entirely the issue which they raise. Let us consider two such pictures each of which in its own way has been immensely influential.

In the same year as Karl Barth published the second definitive edition of his *Epistle to the Romans*,[6] his close friend Edward Thurneysen published a short account of Dostoyevsky's religious views.[7] There is more here, however, than historical coincidence, for Barth said of Thurneysen that he

> . . . was the one who first put me on the trail of . . . Dostoyevsky, without whose discovery I would not have been able to write either, the first or second draft of the commentary on Romans.

Thus in discussing Thurneysen's *Dostoyevsky* we are discussing a picture of Dostoyevsky which played a central part in the most significant redefinition of theology to have taken place in this century.

As befits a man whose stimulation Barth acknowledges in the Preface to the second edition of *The Epistle to the Romans*, Thurneysen builds his account of Dostoyevsky round two fundamental general themes. On the one hand he stresses the undoubtedly dialectical character of Dostoyevsky's work, but, as I shall argue he sees only part of the dialectic. On the other hand he insists that what gives his work

> that absolutely conclusive character, that character so superior to Ibsen, Strindberg, Jacobsen[8]

is its foundation upon 'Biblical insight'. Again I do believe that Dostoyevsky had deep insight into the writings of the New Testament, but I also believe that his insights differed in character from those of Thurneysen or the early Barth.

[5] Trans. Boris Brasol (New York: George Braziller, 1954).
[6] Trans. Edwyn C. Hoskyns (Oxford University Press, 1933).
[7] Eduard Thurneysen, *Dostoyevsky*, trans. K. R. Crim (Epworth, 1964).
[8] op. cit., 14.

To be fair, however, Thurneysen and Barth did capture much of what is truly Dostoyevskian. They were right to stress his critique of religion and the church.[9] They were correct in their diagnosis of many of his characters as 'yearning for something that is not accessible to man's grasping';[10] and in their realization and whatever the excesses of his characters. Dostoyevsky's own touchstone of their adequacy is realism; and that for him the extremities of the human spirit point towards rather than away from reality. Thurneysen, however, was wrong, in two crucial respects: he was selective in what he culled from Dostoyevsky, and he misinterpreted the significance of the ending of both *Crime and Punishment* and *The Brothers Karamazov*. The second of these points is contentious and I shall return to it later.

The picture which Thurneysen offers is that of a Protestant, neo-orthodox Christian. It may well be that Dostoyevsky's characterization of nineteenth-century Protestantism is quite congenial to both Barth and Thurneysen:

> Protestantism with gigantic strides is being converted into atheism and into vacillating, fluent, variable (and not eternal) ethics.[11]

Indeed Barth could happily have used such a text as a motto for his *Protestant Theology in the Nineteenth Century*. However what those who see the Protestant principle at work in Dostoyevsky do completely ignore is Dostoyevsky the Slavophile, for whom the notion of a Russian Christian, and at times perhaps a Russian Christ, has more than illustrative or metaphorical force.

This raises the central question of whether there is a unitary single core of beliefs which can be refereed to as Dostoyevsky's religious beliefs. My initial suggestion is that if there is it will not turn out to be the neo-orthodox Dostoyevsky of Thurneysen's reading of the novels. What then of Dostoyevsky the Russian journalist, editor and author of *The Diary of a Writer* or Dostoyevsky the letter writer? This is the Dostoyevsky who contrasts most fiercely at times, in accents both nationalistic and partisan, Western Europe where 'the peoples have lost Christ'[12] with

> . . . *our people* (who) know their Christ God—perhaps even better than we, although they did not attend school. They know, because throughout many a century they have endured much suffering, and in their sorrow, from the earliest days to our time, they have been accustomed to hear about this Christ God of theirs, from their saints who laboured

[9] Ibid., 50.
[10] Ibid., 25.
[11] *Diary of a Writer*, 984.
[12] See *Letters of Fyodor Dostoevsky*, trans. E. C. Mayne (McGraw-Hill, 1964), 219.

for the people and who defended the Russian soil—sacrificing their lives[13] (my italics).

Nor must we be misled by the construction of the sentences. In talking of 'their' Christ God, Dostoyevsky is putting between himself and them the distance of admiration rather than the distance of Westernizing disdain.

Increasingly in the letters of the 1870s and in the *Diary* Dostoyevsky gave voice to a mystical belief in the recuperative and transforming powers of the Christ of the Russian peasant. Of course he had no illusions about the peasants, and he saw all too clearly the way in which some within the Orthodox Church encouraged their superstition—recall Father Ferapont, in *The Brothers Karamazov*, who so envied the saintliness of Zossima. And yet in his letters and journalism, time and again he sets the Russian Christ and the Russian believer over against all the evil and destructive elements brought into Russia from Europe by the intelligent and the fashionable. He selects his targets and pins his colours to the mast in the opening editorial of *The Citizen* in 1873.

> In days gone by . . . the words 'I understand nothing' meant merely ignorance on the part of him who uttered them; yet, at present they bring great honour. One has only to declare with an open air and uppishly: 'I do not understand religion; I understand nothing in Russia; I understand nothing in art'—and at once one is lifted to lofty heights.[14]

He also defines the rules of the game as including irony by adding

> And this is all the more advantageous if one, in fact, understands nothing.

His targets are those intellectuals who are bemused by Europe into believing that no good can come out of Russia (the Russian boys and their professors whom Ivan Karamazov pillories). The strength of his case against them, he believes, is the faith of the Russian peasant appropriated through centuries of labour, toil and suffering. At times it is as if this alone constitutes the providence of God. Of this intensely nationalistic and sectarian response to the spiritual ills of his time, Thurneysen makes no mention.

Which then, if either, is the *real Dostoyevsky*? At times Dostoyevsky himself seems in no doubt and in 1876 he wrote from Bad Ems in Germany to Vsevolod Solovyev (brother of Vladimir the philosopher),

> The June number of the *Diary* pleased you, then. I am glad of that, and for a special reason. I had never yet permitted myself to follow my profoundest convictions to their ultimate consequences in my public writing—had never said my *very last word* . . . So I decided that I

[13] *Diary of a Writer*, 286.
[14] Ibid. 2.

21

would for once say the last word on one of my convictions—that of Russia's part and destiny among the nations—and I proclaimed that my various anticipations would not only be fulfilled in the immediate future, but were already partly realized.[15]

What then is Dostoyevsky's 'final word'? According to Thurneysen the final word of Dostoyevsky the writer is a question—'the questionability of everything human'—but,

> beyond this final word an absolutely final word may be spoken boldly: God would certainly not be God if he were not really the solution.[16]

Or again.

The absolutely final word is resurrection.

On the contrary, however, to Dostoyevsky the journalist and letter writer, the final word says little about 'the questionability of everything human'. He is writing of the dispute over Constantinople between the two great imperial powers of the day, Russia and Britain.

> This would be a genuine exaltation of Christ's truth, preserved in the East, a new exaltation of Christ's Cross and the final word of Orthodoxy, which is headed by Russia.[17]

The exaltation is the unification of all the Slavs under Russia and a Russian garrison in Constantinople!

Ought we to conclude then that Dostoyevsky the Russian nationalist is the 'real' Dostoyevsky, as his letter quoted above, and his journalism throughout, seem to imply?

It seems time to reflect on the course of the argument so far. The question of the 'real' Dostoyevsky is raised by his death and how we see that. Is his death the sign, as in many outward ways it is, of his *telos* fulfilled—his great work written, his Pushkin address re-defining the central cultural argument of his nation and time between Slavophiles and Westernizers? If so, we may set about the question of summarizing and tabulating his views, including giving clear statement to his religious beliefs. The essential difficulties of that view however, are twofold: on the one hand it is to negate all that his novels teach us—of the dualities of the spirit, of the ambiguities of character, and of the uncertainties of the human mind; on the other it is to raise the question of which of the many Dostoyevskys to be found in the interpreters is the real Dostoyevsky—for example Dostoyevsky the neo-orthodox theologian (Thurneysen and Barth) or Dostoyevsky the Russian Christian?

[15] *Letters*, trans. F. C. Mayne, 227.
[16] Thurneysen. op. cit., 43–44.
[17] *Diary of a Writer*, 365.

My contention is that Dostoyevsky's death, as much as his life and writing, forces us to re-assess what we mean by such terms as *'telos'*, 'fulfilment' or 'completion'. As a corollary of this, the issue of what a man 'really' believes is also open to re-definition, in terms of both the nature and the content of belief. The beliefs of a club, or a political or ecclesiastical party may be easily, even if temporarily, summarized in a creed. One of the lessons which Dostoyevsky taught is that this is not equally true of individual human beings. His death, as I shall argue, points to the same truth.

In all outward, or (to use Kierkegaard's term) 'world-historical' ways, one might regard Dostoyevsky's life as embodying figuratively, even if not numerically, the sense of completion of the Biblical 'threescore and ten'. Inwardly, however, the appropriate religious metaphor is *pilgrimage* rather than completion. At the time of his death Dostoyevsky's mind and spirit were not at rest. He had not reached a steady or motionless state. He was still in the process of giving form to possibilities of life and belief. It is perhaps not too strained to suggest that not one but many Dostoyevskys died in February 1881.

The Dostoyevsky we find in Ivan Karamazov, as well as the Dostoyevsky of his brother Alyosha, lived and died together within the one human body. This is true also of the Dostoyevsky we find within the Russian sainthood of Father Zossima, as well as in the energy and spirit of the equally Russian Mitya Karamazov. Neither Dostoyevsky the man nor Dostoyevsky the artist will be confined to the views of one of his characters. What then of Dostoyevsky the journalist? Do we not find portrayed there the *real* Dostoyevsky?

Now perhaps we can see that in the end our question is hermeneutical in character. The issue which confronts us is one which we face in the interpretation of any set of texts: how do we balance one set of writings against nother? (the *Diary* against the novels?) This, I contend, is not a purely technical question for which we can provide a factual or value-free answer. Schopenhauer's comment has much to tell us:

> To estimate a *genius* you should not take the mistakes in his productions, or his weaker words, but only those works in which he excels. For even in the realm of the intellect, weakness and absurdity cleave so firmly to human nature that even the most brilliant mind is not always free of them . . . What distinguishes genius, on the one hand and provides a measure for estimating it, is the height to which it was able to rise when time and mood were propitious and which forever remains unachievable to ordinary talents.[18]

My argument is that in Dostoyevsky's case it is in 'those works in which

[18] *Essays and Aphorisms*, trans. R. J. Hollingdale (Penguin, 1970), 223–224.

he excels' that we find his deepest insights into human nature—those works, that is to say, dominated by the discipline of what he calls 'artistic realism'. This runs much contrary to the biographical fashions of the day; but the post-Freudian assumption that the heart of a man is best seen in the slips and inconsequentialities of his letters or in the indulgences of his unedited journalism is more often assumed than examined.

Time and time again Dostoyevsky reaffirms *not simply his belief in, but his very bondage to* his art. Recall the letter quoted at the beginning of the paper where he talked consecutively of being bound to God *and* to poetry. A very famous example of this bears on all of the central issues at stake. The sixth book of the *Brothers Karamazov* is meant to contain the answer of belief to the atheism of Ivan Karamazov. Ivan's atheism is arguably the most powerfully stated in all literature. Understandably Dostoyevsky was deeply concerned about his ability to provide 'a sufficient answer'. His answer was to be the figure of Father Zossima who both fulfils and re-defines the expectations of Russian sainthood. Dostoyevsky's worry was whether he could make such a figure convincing:

> This is what disturbs me, i.e. will it be understood, and shall I achieve even a part of my aim? And there was the further obligation of art: I had to present a modest but august figure, while life itself is full of the comic, and august only in its interior significance, so that in the biography of my monk I was forced, willy-nilly, by the demands of art, to touch on the commonplace and trivial, so as not to mar artistic realism.[19]

Note that the limits of what it is possible to say by way of response of belief to unbelief are set by the 'obligations of art', but that the art in question is dedicated to 'artistic realism'.

The 'real' Dostoyevsky was bound to the constraints of his art, which in turn were defined by the search for absolute realism. Absolute realism, however, is not to be understood purely in terms of 'social' reality nor in the more parochial concerns of 'kitchen-sink' drama: absolute realism is the portrayal of the inner life and it is at this point that the truth of Mochulsky's assertion that, 'The life and work of Dostoyevsky are inseparable' is most apparent. The concerns of Dostoyevsky the artist and Dostoyevsky the pilgrim are here bound inseparably together. The problem which he faced in giving his Russian saint, Father Zossima, authentic form, *is* the problem of the possibility of belief which is 'sufficient answer' to Ivan' It is also the same problem as those which respectively dominated his portrayal of Sonia in *Crime and Punishment* and Prince Myshkin in *The Idiot*.

In the end he saw the life of faith only as a possibility not as a reality defined. In his novels successively in the characters of Sonia, Myshkin,

[19] Coulson, op. cit., 224–225.

Father Zossima and Alyosha Karamazov, he attempted to define the nature of human goodness, the goodness of the incarnate Christ. But, and here is where I must seriously part company from Thurneysen (and indeed many of Dostoyevsky's 'Christian' interpreters), Dostoyevsky failed, and knew himself to have failed. Both the man and the artist confess this in the very form which he gave to his novels.

The difference between myself and Thurneysen on this point is evident in the following comment:

> And yet the works of Dostoyevsky shine as if illumined from within with the secret, no longer earthly light of a powerful, an ultimate synthesis. Not decline, not contemptuous laughter over men of whom the devil has made fools, but the incomprehensible word of victory 'resurrection', is the last word of his novels.[20]

In the paragraphs adjacent to this Thurneyson refers to *The Idiot, Crime and Punishment*, and *The Brothers Karamazov* to support his view of Dostoyevsky's 'final word' of 'ultimate synthesis' and 'resurrection'. However, he misinterprets these novels quite systematically. There is no 'ultimate synthesis', and the best that is offered is the *possibility* of resurrection, but that possibility remains a hope rather than an established certainty.

Consider the outcome of these novels and what they have in common. What they share is *not* a conception of an 'ultimate synthesis', but Dostoyevsky's inability to portray one. *Crime and Punishment* is a tale summarized by the title of the novel: there is no mention of a novel called *Crime and Rehabilitation*, or *Sin and Resurrection*. The hope of 'the dawn of a new future, or of a full resurrection to a new life', for Raskolnikov the murderer, and Sonia the saint and prostitute, is held out, but note the final sentence of the novel:

> But that is the beginning of a new story, the story of the gradual rebirth of a man, the story of his gradual regeneration, of his gradual passing from one world to another, of his acquaintance with a new and hitherto unknown reality. That might be the subject of a new story—our present story is ended.[21]

And, of course, it *has* ended without giving form to the nature of this resurrected life. The portrayal of goodness, of sainthood, must await a new story.

This was the task which Dostoyevsky undertook in his novel *The Idiot*, a novel in which his hope was 'the representation of a truly perfect and noble man'.[22] He evidently sees this as the attempt to define clearly the possibility of a Christ-like life, but equally evidently he failed. Myshkin,

[20] Thurneysen, op. cit., 12–13.
[21] The translation is David Magarshack's (Penguin edition, 1951).
[22] E. C. Mayne (trans.), op. cit., 142.

the idiot of the title, cannot live in open human society. At the end, like Sonia, he takes his goodness off-stage; he returns to the Swiss sanatorium from which he emerged at the beginning of the novel. The possibility of a resurrected life has still not been defined and, as such, the powers of evil and darkness still reign.

Dostoyevsky's final definition of the problem and his last attempt to solve it come in Books V and VI of *The Brothers Karamazov*. In Book V Ivan states an almost unanswerable case for atheism—based on the suffering of innocent children. In Book VI as we have noted, Dostoyevsky was intent on answering Ivan's atheism by 'an artistic picture', the figure of Zossima. Now whatever his success in the figure of Zossima (and that is much disputed) Dostoyevsky, again by the form of the novel, acknowledges failure. Ivan has not finally been answered. There is no 'ultimate synthesis'. For Dostoyevsky, the true synthesis, the final reply of belief to unbelief can only come in a statement that conforms to the demands of art and reality.

Zossima is not an adequate answer to Ivan, because Zossima still lives within the confines and protection of the monastery. Zossima himself admits this when he tells his disciple, Ivan's brother Alyosha, to leave the monastery, to marry and to live in the community at large, subject to its pressures and temptations. Only if belief survives and defines itself in *that* context has an adequate answer to Ivan's atheism been given. The novel about Alyosha, as indeed a further novel about Mitya, was never written. The task of defining the nature and practice of Christian belief was never completed successfully. There were preliminary sketches, 'cartoons' if you like, in Sonia, Myshkin, and Zossima, but no 'final words'.

That constitutes my case for arguing contrary to the views of Thurneysen (and all those whom he represents), and against those who dismiss Dostoyevsky as ultimately the reactionary Russian nationalist of parts of the *Diary*. My conclusions can be listed under three points.

1. Dostoyevsky offered no final answer to atheism—as he knew, the story which would do that—of Alyosha—remained unwritten and perhaps unwriteable.
2. It is vain then to seek for a 'final word' from Dostoyevsky on the subject of religious belief—the dialectic defined in Ivan and Zossima remained Dostoyevsky's only 'final word' to the grave.
3. Despite the outward signs of success, of fulfilment, Dostoyevsky's own death could not possibly be seen as a moment of completion, or, in traditional terms, as a sign that his *telos* had been achieved.

We find such conclusions foreshadowed in one of his earlier explorations of the notions of 'self' and 'freedom', *Letters from the Underworld*. There the view is canvassed of man as,

. . . a frivolous specious creature, and, like a chess-player, cares more for the process of attaining his goal than for the goal itself. Besides, who knows (for it never does to be too sure that the aim which man strives for upon earth may not be contained in this ceaseless continuation of the process of attainment (that is to say, in the process which is comprised in the living of life) rather than in the aim itself . . .;

. . . he has an instinctive dread of *completely* attaining his end, and so of finishing the building operation. May it not be the truth that only from a distance, and not from close at hand, does he love the edifice which he is erecting? That is to say, may it not be that he loves to create it, but not to *live* in it?'[23]

Dostoyevsky's life and art are testimony to the impossibility of so 'sum-ming-up' a man, and his death did not alter the message of his life one whit. Perhaps in an indirect and re-defined way, that is the only *telos* or fulfilment which since the time of Dostoyevsky, it has been legitimate to expect. As a novelist Dostoyevsky embodied such a conception. He died if not 'with his boots on', certainly with his pen in his hand. His 'achieve-ments' were but stages on the way, for his exploration of human goodness, and of the nature of selfhood was incomplete. The ambiguities remained, the the uncertainties redefined but unresolved. There is in this a form of integrity or consistency, for his writings constitute a profound rejection of precisely those theories of human nature which underpin bad biographies and insensitive obituaries. The self is not like 'all Gaul', a public object divisible into 'three parts'.

[23] The translation is C. J. Hogarth's (Everyman Library, 1964).

Aristotle and Agamemnon

RENFORD BAMBROUGH

My theme is tragical–historical–philosophical.

Though the chief characters are Aristotle and Agamemnon, there are strong supporting roles for Heraclitus and Professor Sir Denys Page, and you will also hear the voices of Aeschylus, Spinoza, J. A. Froude and Professor A. W. H. Adkins.

Heraclitus speaks first: '*dis es ton auton potamon*', he says, '*ouk an embaiēs.*'

Perhaps you fail to understand these words. If so, the failure may be of a more or less fundamental kind. Perhaps you do not know what a *potamos* is, or what *embaiēs* means, or some other Greek word or words. But even if you know all the words you may still be puzzled by the sentence.

If you do not know what *potamos* means you will not understand what Heraclitus means when he says '*dis es ton auton potamon ouk an embaiēs*'. If you do understand what *potamos* means (and *dis* and *embaiēs* and all the rest) you may still fail to understand what Heraclitus means when he says this. And in that case it is not more Greek that you need to learn. Your puzzlement is still about meaning, but in a sense in which you cannot be puzzled about the meaning without first having understood the meaning in the primary sense. The problem is not a problem of *translating* faithfully, or idiomatically, or in the spirit of the original. 'You can't step into the same river twice' is a perfectly accurate, adequate and idiomatic translation, and if it is not, it is not any inadequacy in it that causes the trouble for anybody who, after being provided with this translation, still does not understand what Heraclitus means.

Now one thing that Heraclitus is most certainly asserting, and that you could only suppose him not to be asserting if you had misunderstood the Greek, is that you cannot step into the same river twice. On any view, and quite plainly, he is denying that it is possible for me to step into a certain river today, and then to step into the same river tomorrow or next week. It would be absurd to wonder whether when he says 'You can't step into the same river twice' he may mean to leave open the question whether it is possible to step into the same river twice. The closing of that question is not only something that his remark is meant to achieve; it is what it wholly consists in and amounts to. He might justly and realistically be imagined, if anybody tried to reopen the question whether he envisaged any possibility that I might step once and then again into the same river, to reply impatiently and in emphatic, dogmatic terms. He might reasonably

29

claim that he had 'definitely stated', and in such 'unambiguous terms' that 'it could not be more plainly stated' that you can't step into the same river twice. And if some foolish commentator were to persist in raising the question, he could be reminded that diversity rules out identity, and that he must therefore be construed as meaning that if there have been two or more occasions on which you have stepped into a river, it must follow that you have in your time stepped into two or more different and distinct rivers. If somebody wanted to offer an account of his meaning according to which the assertion that you cannot step into the same river twice might be combined with a recognition that in some sense it is possible to step into the same river twice he might be supposed to declare that he for his part could not 'see how these statements can be reconciled'.

Some of the emphatic phrases that I have used in composing a possible reply from Heraclitus to a foolish commentator are drawn from the replies constructed by Professor Page[1] for Aeschylus to give in answer to other foolish commentators who have persisted in attributing to him any qualification or complication of his plain statement that Agamemnon, in sacrificing Iphigeneia, 'put on the harness of necessity' (line 218). In his note on that line Page writes: '*ananké* here must mean what it says: it is absolutely inconsistent with the idea that Agamemnon had any freedom of choice; what he put on was the harness of *necessity, compulsion*'. He adds that '*ananké* is the last word a Greek would have chosen to describe or refer to a voluntary decision'.

The other similar phrases that I have borrowed for Heraclitus come from Page's Introduction: 'The sacrifice of Iphigeneia, once demanded by Artemis, is an absolute necessity, and necessity is the word by which Aeschylus describes Agamemnon's submission to the will of Artemis; what he bowed to was (it could not be more plainly stated) *compulsion, ananké*' (p. xxiv). But what cannot be more plainly stated can be equally plainly re-stated, and Page adds a footnote on the same page: 'The modern critics say that Agamemnon made a voluntary, however painful decision; Aeschylus says that what he submitted to was *necessity*. I do not see how these statements can be reconciled.' In the question and answer section of the Introduction the point is made again and again. In answer to question (11) 'If it was your purpose to show that Agamemnon had no choice whatever in the matter, could you not have made this very important fact a little plainer?' Aeschylus is made to say '*No: it is definitely stated that he put on the harness of Necessity: a man who acts under Necessity is not acting voluntarily. It is further stated in unambiguous terms that his mind was deranged (parakopa) before the trouble could be begun (protopēmon).*'

Elsewhere in the Introduction Page tells us that there is no philosophy in

---

[1] *The Agamemnon of Aeschylus*, J. D. Denniston and D. L. Page (eds) (Oxford University Press, 1957).

Aeschylus: 'Religion advances hardly one step in these pages. Philosophy has no place in them. Morality is simple and practical: its primary lesson is the rule of Justice, imposed by divine will on human society; it is a lesson which was lamentably forgotten, if it was ever learnt, in the generation to come.'

Philosophers are not so easily disarmed. Even if it were true that there is no philosophy in Aeschylus, it would not follow that the work of Aeschylus could not be illuminated by philosophical reflection. After all, there is no textual criticism in Aeschylus, or literary criticism or palaeography, but studies in these and other fields of classical philology are not therefore assumed to have nothing to contribute to our knowledge of Aeschylus. But in fact the question whether there is any philosophy in Aeschylus is not so straightforward as it is often made out to be, as we can see by considering and answering first the analogous question whether there is any philosophy in Professor Page.

It might plausibly be said that there is no philosophy in Professor Page. Page might say it himself in his own defence, and a critic might say it critically; and though it is possible it is unlikely that the defence and the prosecution would mean the same thing by saying that there is no philosophy in Professor Page. In the sense in which it is true that there is no philosophy in Aeschylus there is very little in Page either; but there is an equally clear and important sense in which there is a great deal of philosophy in Aeschylus and even more in Page.

A man may have ideas without having philosophical ideas, and he may have philosophical ideas without knowing that they are philosophical. Sometimes a man will have good philosophical ideas in these circumstances, but usually, and especially if he is inclined to make much of his refusal to have any truck with philosophy, his philosophical ideas will be partial and confused.

There is no philosophy in Homer, in one very straightforward sense. In the same sense there is no psychology in Homer, or history or meteorology. Equally there is none of these things to be found in the ordinary everyday unsophisticated thought and speech of non-literary and non-philosophic men. This does not mean that our ordinary ideas are not proper objects of philosophical enquiry and examination, or that none of our ordinary ideas relate to philosophical themes and problems, any more than it means that Homer has no ideas about wind and waves and men and women and war and peace and chance and fate.

The same goes for Aeschylus and Page. In the case of Page there is something further. It is not just that he carries into his study of Aeschylus some unexamined ordinary assumptions about action and choice, freedom and necessity, guilt and innocence, and quietly allows them to shape his understanding of Agamemnon's crime and punishment. If he had been content to do that he would probably have come to some sounder conclusions. He goes further, and expresses some of these unexamined assumptions, sometimes in a distorted and confused form, not only explicitly but even (as we have begun to see in some passages that I have quoted) with Johnsonian trenchancy, dogmatism and tireless repetition.

Dr Johnson was at his worst in philosophy just because of the downrightness and forthrightness that stood him in such good stead elsewhere—e.g. in questions of morals or politics or letters. In philosophy emphasis and trenchancy are dangerous tools, and a writer or speaker who uses them too readily will deafen himself to one half of the truth by shouting too loudly about the other half. Johnson was only half wrong when he kicked the stone, or when he said 'Sir, we *know* our will is free, and there's an end on't'. But in philosophy it is not easy to be more than half wrong, and nowhere is it less true than here that *pleon hēmisu pantos*.

When we disinter the philosophy of Page and make it fully explicit it turns out to be confused philosophy.

When we make the philosophy of Aeschylus more explicit we can see that if it is confused that is only because on the same issues we have all always been confused.

The main questions arise in two passages from other authors.

Spinoza is both a severe moralist and a rigid determinist. He urges his readers to aspire strenuously after virtue and tells them that the only freedom they can hope to achieve is a consciousness of the necessity by which they are bound. The charge of inconsistency must therefore be considered in any account of Spinoza's *Ethics*, and the usual verdict is *guilty*. It is usual to make a similar judgment on the similar mixture of determinism and moral rigorism in Stoicism and Marxism and in some forms of Christian theology. But James Anthony Froude,[2] in a long essay on Spinoza in *Short Studies of Great Subjects*, presents an aspect of the matter that is too much neglected:

> The popular belief is, that right and wrong lie before every man, and that he is free to choose between them, and the responsibility of choice rests with himself. The fatalist's belief is that every man's actions are determined by causes external and internal, over which he has no power, leaving no room for any moral choice whatever. The first is contradicted by facts, the second by the instinct of conscience. Even Spinoza allows that for practical purposes we are obliged to regard the future as contingent, and ourselves as able to influence it; and it is incredible that both our inward convictions and our outward conduct should be built together upon a falsehood. But if, as Butler says, whatever be the speculative account of the matter, we are practically forced to

[2] J. A. Froude, *Short Studies of Great Subjects*, I. (London: Longmans, Green and Co., 1895).

regard ourselves as free, this is but half the truth, for it may be equally said that practically we are forced to regard each other as *not* free; and to make allowance, every moment, for influences for which we cannot hold each other personally responsible. If not—if every person of sound mind (in the common acceptation of the term) be equally able at all times to act right if only he *will*—why all the care which we take of children? why the pains to keep them from bad society? why do we so anxiously watch their disposition, to determine the education which will best answer to it? Why in cases of guilt do we vary our moral censure according to the opportunities of the offender? Why do we find excuses for youth, for inexperience, for violent natural passion, for bad education, bad example? Why, except that we feel that all these things do affect the culpability of the guilty person, and that it is folly and inhumanity to disregard them? But what we act upon in private life we cannot acknowledge in our ethical theories, and, while our conduct in detail is humane and just, we have been contented to gather our speculative philosophy out of the broad and coarse generalizations of political necessity.

The inconsistency is on the other foot. As Froude points out, we all do better in practice than our theories would suggest. What is more, we all see straight when our theories are set aside and we look with ordinary eyes, because we then see complications that are simplified away by theories of ethics and philosophy of mind and action. And it is not only philosophers and their critics who simplify and conceal the truth about freedom and action. The study of history and literature, including ancient history and classical literature, provides scope for forgetting what its students and scholars very well know when they are not engaged in their learned pursuits, but are occupied instead in attacking the government or defending themselves. And so the critics of Spinoza (or of the Stoics or Marx or Calvin) are not the only specialists who put down their common sense when they take up their pens. A well-known historian of Greek ethics makes the same mistake. In Chapter II of *Merit and Responsibility*[3] ('Homer: Free Will and Compulsion') Professor Adkins remarks on what he sees as a glaring inconsistency. He finds it 'very odd indeed' that one and the same action can be attributed both to *Moira* and to an individual human agent, and in particular that the Homeric Greeks should attribute all deaths to *Moira* and yet distinguish between 'death from natural causes and homicide of every kind', and regard the responsibility of a murderer as in no way diminished. According to Adkins this is illogical in theory, even if such 'common-sense carelessness' is what we might expect in practice.

[3] A. W. H. Adkins, *Merit and Responsibility: A Study in Greek Values* (Oxford University Press, 1960).

Froude and Adkins are both remarking, even if in different spirits and for different purposes, on some unexamined assumptions which are to be found not only in the particular authors they refer to, but in most people at most times, including our own. And it is a question—a question for philosophers to consider—whether they will bear examination. To suppose that they will or that they will not is to make a philosophical supposition, and nobody who makes such a supposition can consistently plead or assume that he at any rate, whatever follies his colleagues may commit, remains untainted by philosophy.

Adkins would probably agree that he is involved in philosophical controversy. His trouble arises from setting his hand to the plough and then not making the furrow long enough or straight enough.

The assumptions of Page are similar, and even if they are not so consciously philosophical they are equally explicit. Their subject matter is the same as that of the first chapter of Book III of the *Nicomachean Ethics*. That is why I have called this paper 'Aristotle and Agamemnon'. If scholars and critics had *genuinely* avoided tampering with philosophical questions, *or* had dealt with them more fully and adequately, our present discontents would never have arisen. An excellent way of coming to understand the issues better is to mark, learn and digest that chapter of Aristotle.

The main lessons of the chapter, at least for the present purpose, are given in the examples of what Aristotle himself calls 'mixed actions' (*miktai praxeis*). If a tyrant who has power over my parents and children orders me to do something dishonourable, and I do it to save their lives, do I act voluntarily or involuntarily? If I sacrifice a valuable cargo in a storm at sea, in order to save the ship and the lives of myself and the crew, am I acting in accordance with or against my will? These cases are interesting and difficult because Aristotle's criterion for discriminating *to hekousion* from *to akousion* does not seem to settle them one way or the other. An act is voluntary, he says, if the *archē tou kinein*, the source of the movement of which the action consists, is internal to the agent, and involuntary if the origination is external—if the story of the action begins with something outside his control.

It is to the credit of the criterion that it gives such untidy answers in these mixed and borderline cases. Only an artificial neatness could lead us to give an unqualified yes or no to a question about either type of case. The cases are fully described, properly placed in their relation to straightforward cases of voluntary and of involuntary action, only if we look at them alternately from two different points of view, from a narrower and a wider context. The victim of the tyrant's power does something that he would rather not do. He acts reluctantly and in a strong sense against his will. But on the other hand he prefers to do what he does rather than to accept the consequences of refusing to obey the tyrant's order. He prefers obedience to paying the penalty that the tyrant will exact for disobedience. The highwayman's offer is not, as his words imply, a choice of 'Your money or your life': he wants your money in any case, even if it has to be your money *and* your life.

The same general description, with the same dual structure, applies to the ship's captain's decision to jettison the cargo rather than to hazard his ship. If a member of the crew resists the order to throw the cargo over the side, he may find that the captain's determination to enforce his decision is absolute and unqualified, backed by the power of a strong will as well as a strong arm and a code of maritime discipline. And yet when the captain gives an account of himself to the owners and insurers in the Piraeus he will surely and reasonably say that he had no choice, that he was forced to do what he did. If he has a taste for rhetoric and repetition, he may add that the necessity was absolute; that what he had bowed to (it could hardly be more plainly stated) was *compulsion, anankē*. If the chairman of the committee of inquiry suggests that his decision, however painful, was voluntary, could he not with reason repeat that what he had submitted to was *necessity*, and ask how these two statements could be reconciled? 'A man who acts under Necessity is not acting voluntarily'. And surely a Greek would not need to remind the Greek chairman of a Greek committee that '*anankē* is the last word a Greek would have chosen to describe or refer to a voluntary decision'?

If he did, I hope the chairman would notice and point out the mistake. There is one word at least that would have to come *after* what Page says is the *last* word a Greek would choose to describe or refer to a voluntary decision: the word *akousion*—'involuntary'. And yet this is just the word that Aristotle does apply to some voluntary decisions—decisions to which he also applies the word *hekousion*—'voluntary'. If he had the gift for emphasis of a Johnson or a Page or a G. E. Moore he could emphasize equally colourfully and equally justly *both* that he could not have stated more plainly that these decisions are voluntary *and* that he could not have stated more plainly that these decisions are involuntary.

Philosophers are so confusing. No wonder they are the despair of Dr Johnson and authors of introductions to the *Agamemnon* and other straight-thinking plain men who know that what's true cannot also be false and that there is a difference between the way up and the way down or the way forward and the way back. How can a thing be the same as its opposite? How could war and peace and summer and winter be one?

At last we have the key to the maze.

If we can understand almost any remark of Heraclitus we can go on to understand almost any remark of almost any philosopher.

The emphasis on the truth of proposition *p* can be as downright and as forthright as you like, and there can still be equal emphasis on the falsehood of proposition *q* provided that *q* is distinct from *p*. The trouble in philosophy—including the philosophy into which people stray when they are not consciously trying to do philosophy and even when they are consciously trying not to do philosophy—is that it is not always easy to see the distinctness of q from p, especially if one is at a given moment—say in writing an Introduction to the *Agamemnon*—concerned to give great emphasis to p and is not at that moment thinking much or at all about q.

If somebody should then come along and remark that not-q, or that possibly not-q, or still worse, that p and also not-q, you will be liable to redouble your emphasis to the point of breaking into rhetoric. And all the time the position may be that p is true and q is false: that you can allow the newcomer to insist on not-q without conceding that you are thereby reducing your commitment to p.

Heraclitus says that you can't step into the same river twice. Does Heraclitus then deny that on one occasion I stepped into the River Swale to cross to the other side and on another occasion I stepped into the River Swale to pick some hazel nuts that I could not reach from the bank?

It is natural to say that he does.

But it is wrong to say that he does.

It is natural to say that he does because it is natural to suppose that if I cannot step into the same river twice then I cannot step into the River Swale twice. It is wrong to say that he does because it is wrong to assume that it follows from 'I can't step into the same river twice' that I cannot step into the River Swale twice.

What does follow is that stepping into the River Swale twice is not stepping into the same river twice.

Heraclitus is so far from being concerned to deny that I can step into the Swale or the Ilissus twice that he is actually concerned to make me see something of the character of the achievement of stepping twice into the Ilissus or the Swale. And one way of doing this is to say that I can't step into the same river twice, and that the Ilissus is not now the river it was, even a second ago. He is making a point about the nature of the identity of rivers, not saying that there is no such identity.

The same goes for Aristotle on the case of the ship's captain or the tyrant's order and on voluntary action in general. The merit and advantage of Aristotle's account is that it shows both sides of the picture and shows how they come to appear incompatible and how it can be shown that they are compatible. The chapter is a lesson to us all, though some need it more than others.

It is a lesson that Page might have needed less if he had noticed how closely parallel it is to something that he insists on in the same Introduction.

It is approximately true that tragedy is the conflict of right with right, and it is approximately true that philosophy is the conflict of the obvious with the obvious. These two approximations come together when we try to be clear about the relation between tragedy and ethics.

Page is insistent on this view of tragedy. But he has not seen that he is involved in a philosophical dispute in which there is a conflict between two statements of the obvious, and he uses one often-reiterated statement of the obvious in order to rebut something else which, to other commentators, has seemed so obvious that they have rejected the clear evidence on which Page relies for his conclusion.

He is like Moore holding up his hands and letting the sceptic's point slip through them, or Johnson kicking a stone at the spider's web of Berkeley's philosophy and not seeing that the stone goes right through the web without touching.

He is like a reader of a tragedy who says that Agamemnon cannot be right because Clytemnestra is right, or that Creon or Antigone must be wrong because Antigone or Creon is right. He needs to apply once more and in another dimension both the clear apprehension of the obvious that he shows about the tragic conflict and the capacity for grasping the less than obvious that brings him to see that one obvious truth may appear to conflict with another.

Page does obliquely recognize the force of this objection when he rules out the possibility of desertion—*pōs liponaus genōmai?*—as unthinkable. It is unthinkable in the way that matricide is unthinkable for Aristotle. and would therefore be impossible—'for a man of sound mind'—even on the orders of an all-powerful tyrant.

As Hobbes reminded Bramhall, to say that Cato was incapable of living badly is to sing his praises and not to take away from him the credit or responsibility for his virtues. Luther's declaration that he could do no other was not a disclaimer of responsibility for what he did. Stephen Spender points out in *World Within World*[4] that the attachment of his generation to the works and words of Freud did not imply any unwillingness on their part, as their parents' generation alleged, to accept responsibility for their deeds and misdeeds. On the contrary, as he points out, the effect of Freud's work is to widen rather than narrow the scope for self-reproach by tracing to sources within us what we might once have set down to uncontrollable external circumstances.

Here we are reminded again of Aristotle's criterion, and in fact all these examples are germane to Aristotle's discussion. They show how wide is the scope of the questions with which that chapter is concerned—wider even than the range of issues I have touched on here. For Aristotle brings out that there is more than one kind or sense of necessity and in particular that there is at least one kind whose operation is compatible with the exercise of choice and the claiming or admission of responsibility.

Agamemnon would still have been putting on the yoke of necessity if he had not sacrificed Iphigeneia. The necessity of doing evil was in the dilemma that faced him, as in the dilemma that faces Aristotle's captain and the

[4] Stephen Spender, *World Within World* (London: Hamish Hamilton, 1951).

victim of Aristotle's tyrant. The cry *'ti tōnd' aneu kakōn'* is echoed in Aristotle's summing up of the character of mixed actions: they involve a choice of evils, and the things chosen *kath hauta men akousia estin, nun de kai anti tōnde hekousia*. They are not in themselves what the agent would choose, but in these particular circumstances they are to be preferred to the even more unacceptable alternatives.

To think that the stress placed on the necessity excludes the choice is to presuppose the initially plausible but philosophically questionable principle that when there is necessity there is no choice. If we try to apply this principle to the concrete situations of literature and life it will break in our hands unless we are unusually blind or unscrupulous in moulding the concrete into the shape of our abstract expectations.

Page does not fail to see the elements in the play that fall through his net. He faithfully describes the *deliberation* by which Agamemnon comes to the conclusion that he has no choice, and so implicitly endorses my suggestion about what kind of necessity is in question. He recognizes in spite of his schema that we are dealing here with characters, choices, motives; with all the form and matter of life and death in any age or country, regardless of the presence or absence of philosophical ideas about choice and will and destiny. He speaks of temptation, forgiveness, guilt, crime, punishment, blame and revenge; and these notions bring with them most of what he had tried in theory to dismiss from the contexts in which in practice he is constrained to recognize their presence.

Lesky's[5] more untidy statement catches more of the untidy truth: '. . . in human acts both divinely ordained destiny and human will participate. Elsewhere we have seen the daemon as *sullēptōr*, as assisting human passion. Apollo's command, however, makes the act of Orestes one that was largely forced on him from outside. This will ultimately prove the reason for his acquittal. But to make this act fateful for him initially, it must be entirely integrated with his own will' (p. 80).

The tragical-historical enquiry in which I have been engaged leads into some of the main questions of ethics and the philosophy of mind and action, and most of them are questions that apply to the actualities of life and politics and peace and war and the particularities of literature and history as well as to the abstract issues of philosophy in the narrower sense.

We try to understand the causes of crime, and hope that we may be able by schemes of social improvement to eradicate some of them. In this and other ways we try to secure that our children and other people's children will be spared from as many as possible of the influences that might lead them into evil. But we also have courts of law in which the responsibility of sane criminals is assumed in general and established in particular cases.

[5] A. Lesky, *Greek Tragedy*, trans. H. A. Frankfort (London: Ernest Benn, 1965).

Of course there is muddle about these issues, but it is significant that it is the same muddle again: one side emphasizes the causation to the exclusion of the responsibility and the other, as Froude shows, fails to notice that its emphasis on responsibility is in danger of contradicting its recognition that our characters and lives and actions are shaped by teaching and by circumstance.

We try to understand the causes of war, and hope that by schemes of international co-operation we may be able to eradicate some of them. In studying particular wars and other great events we think we can see in some cases how they came about, and in other cases we feel sure that it would be possible if we were wiser and better informed to see how they came about—how one thing led to another so that in the end it was bound to turn out as it did. But we also feel entitled to blame Chamberlain or praise Lester Pearson for what he did or did not do. When Tolstoy suggests or implies that what Napoleon did or failed to do had little bearing on what happened later, or that even if it had an important influence it was itself the product of influences *on* Napoleon rather than an exercise of the influence *of* Napoleon, we feel that he is taking away some of the props of the structure in which we live our ordinary lives; and we notice with satisfaction that he has the common sense and the inconsistency to make judgments on men and events that his official theory might seem to preclude him from making.

But *does* that make him inconsistent?

The question can arise not only in the spheres of crime and punishment and war and peace but anywhere within the wide scope of the proverb *tout comprendre c'est tout pardonner*. Is it inconsistent of us to combine a habit of judging ourselves and others with a habit of explaining the actions and passions that we praise and blame by fitting them into a indefinitely widening context until they are parts or consequences of such a pattern that it seems to have become only a manner of speaking to say that we contribute anything to its unfolding?

We have arrived now at the brink of the philosophical problem of free will, one of the bloodiest battlegrounds in the conflict of the obvious against the obvious. Here I can do no more than raise some of the questions that seem to me to call for further investigation in the light of some of the considerations I have mentioned. The serious difficulties in all of them share their form and much of their content with the difficulties that arise in our effort to be clear about Agamemnon's choice.

There is an assumption made by most contemporary philosophers, though it has radically different effects when combined with different assumptions or conclusions on other points, that if an action of mine is predictable, intelligible and explicable then it cannot be free, responsible, spontaneous or 'authentic'. But it is hard to see how an action can be my responsibility unless it is connected in intelligible ways with *me*—i.e.

with my character, opinions, beliefs and preferences; and it is in that case hard to see how somebody who knew me well could fail to have something useful to offer in the way of a prediction or explanation of the action. My beliefs and character are in turn intelligible in the light of the history of my life and opinions, the story of my upbringing, education and experience. And so it can be made to appear that I can know what I am doing only under conditions that make it false that *I* am doing it, or that I am *doing* it, as opposed to undergoing it, having it happen to me.

Some of the most paradoxical of contemporary philosophical doctrines are responses to this dilemma. Sartre[6] preserves freedom and authenticity at the cost of denying that there is such a thing as human nature, individual or universal. Hare[7] makes all moral debate terminate in arbitrary decisions of principle because he fears that a recognition of the bearing of objective reasons on action and choice would compromise our moral freedom.

Similar problems can be raised about some of Aristotle's doctrines. Surely, it is sometimes said, he represents me as having the character that my training has given me, and hence as not being responsible for what I do? Here again we have the sort of tangle that we are all very good at creating, and Aristotle is very good at sorting out. But that, as he would say, belongs to another enquiry.

6 J.-P. Sartre, *Existentialism and Humanism*, trans. Philip Mairet (London: Methuen, 1948).

7 R. M. Hare, *Freedom and Reason* (Oxford University Press, 1963).

'Reality' in Early Twentieth-century German Literature

J. P. STERN

Among the most striking aspects of modern literature—expecially of modern German literature—are its frequent references to a notion called 'reality'. The philosophical question this raises, 'What is reality?', is to one side of this enquiry, and so is the question whether or not this is a sensible question: this essay is intended as a contribution not to philosophy but to its connections with literary history and criticism. My present purpose, which determines my procedure, is (1) to outline the various closely related meanings of the word 'Wirklichkeit' throughout its very long history; (2) to describe the polarization of meanings which occurred in the course of the nineteenth century, and Nietzsche's part in making the new polarity available to his literary heirs; (3) to illustrate the way German literature became involved in this process in the first decade of our century; and, finally, (4) to point to some of its political implications. My argument is part of a much larger topic, one that is not confined either to the German-speaking countries or indeed to literature. The topic, *the ideologizing of 'reality'*, is relevant to all modern cultures. The present paper offers no more than a sketch of this development in one cultural area of our world.

I

From its earliest uses through the writings of the mystics to the end of the nineteenth century and beyond, the German word for 'reality', 'Wirklichkeit', is marked by a single central connotation which recurs through several fairly well-defined meanings. The word is an abstract noun formation from 'wirken'—a verb in common usage from the first document extant in the language throughout its entire history—meaning 'to effect by acting on'.[1]

---

[1] The word occurs in the opening of the second (prose) part of the 'Wessobrunner Gebet' (*c.* 800): 'Cot almahtico, du himil enti erda gauuorahtos . . .' ('Almighty God, thou hast created heaven and earth . . .') (*Deutsche Dichtung des Mittelalters*, I, M. Curschmann and Ingeborg Glier (eds.) (München, Wien, 1980), 24). The word is cognate with the Greek *ergon* (=work, action, effect) and *ergasomai*, (=to work to be active, to pursue a craft). I am grateful to Fred Wagner and David McLintock for this etymological gloss; to the former I am also indebted for several other fruitful suggestions.

Hence the central connotation of 'Wirklichkeit' is that of an activity in the human world—a being-at-work rather than a static condition or state of things.

In this way it is used in Tauler's sermons (after 1330) as a term for human activity and busyness: 'reality' as action is one of the conditions to which a man's soul is called by God, the other being inactivity or emptiness ('würklicheit' as opposed to 'lidikeit').[2] The author of a famous devotional tract of 1518, *Theologia Deutsch*, sees one and the same will at work ('wirksam') in God and man.[3] But while in man this will is 'active and willing', in God it is 'original and essential, without all works and reality' ('ohn alle werck und würcklichkeit'). We find the connotation again, though within a different religious framework, in Leibnitz's *Monadology* of 1714 (§§ 41–45), where the perfection of God as the centre of the monadic system is designated as 'positive reality'; the monadic system in turn is 'all the reality there is in possibility': the system is 'real' only to the extent that it manifests 'appetitive' energies acting upon 'recalcitrant matter'.[4] At much the same period, that of the early Enlightenment (1720), Christian Wolff defines 'reality' as 'the fulfilment of the possible',[5] while Lessing's friend, Reimarus, describes truth that is visible before our eyes and palpable to our grasp as 'truth in its reality';[6] the opposite, in this scheme, is 'mere appearance'.

With Goethe, the notion of 'reality' is usually opposed to 'possibility', occasionally to 'illusion' or 'chimera'; in Schiller's theoretical writings 'raw', 'barbaric' or 'base reality' is contrasted with a moral or aesthetic 'ideal' which acts as 'reality's' precept and guide.[7] Kant defines 'the real' as 'that which is connected with the material conditions of experience (or sensation)'; and in the chapter on 'Paralogisms of Pure Reason' (in the first edition of the *Critique*, 1781) he adds that, even though space is 'the mere form of our ideas', our ability to perceive objects in space proves that space

---

[2] Quoted from Jacob and Wilhelm Grimms' *Deutsches Wörterbuch*, XIV/2 (compiled *c.* 1930) (Leipzig, 1960), column 582.

[3] *Theologia Deutsch*, ch. xxxi, text and modernized version by R. A. Schröder, (Gütersloh, 1946), 89, 139; see also Grimms' *DWB*, loc. cit.

[4] Gottfried Wilhelm Leibnitz, *Die Hauptwerke*, Gerhard Krüger (ed.) (Stuttgart, 1958), 140–142; see also R. W. Meyer, *Leibnitz and the Seventeenth Century Revolution* (Cambridge, 1953), 117, and note 310. The *Monadology* was written in French in 1714, but was first published in German in 1720, four years after Leibnitz's death.

[5] Grimms' *DWB*, XIV/21, column 584.

[6] Grimms' *DWB* XIV/21, column 583.

[7] In 'Über naive und sentimentalische Dichtung' (1795) (*Sämtliche Werke*, XII (Stuttgart, 1905), 231), Schiller writes: 'Alle Wirklichkeit, wissen wir, bleibt hinter dem Ideale zurück'.

is, or has, 'reality' and is not *merely* 'an invention of our imagination'.[8] The contrast on which Kant relies here, between 'reality' and 'imagination' ('Wirklichkeit'—'Einbildungskraft'), may be as old as Plato's *Republic* (e.g. Book x, 598), but in German thinking it does not seem to go back beyond the Baroque, where it merges with the dichotomy of 'Sein—Schein'.

With Hegel's usage of the word the modern, polysemic part of its history begins. In a famous passage in the *Phenomenology of Mind* (1807), Hegel contrasts the generous human heart (ruled by the law that is valid 'only for itself') with 'reality' seen as a 'contradiction' of that law. Reality 'is thus on the one hand a law which oppresses the single individuality, a violent order of the world which contradicts the law of the heart, and on the other hand it is the humanity which suffers under that order, and which does not follow the law of the heart but is subject to an alien necessity'.[9] In his lectures on aesthetics, however, Hegel refers to the common usage of his time, which ascribes 'reality and truth' ('Realität, Wirklichkeit und Wahrheit') to 'the whole sphere of the empirical inner and outer world', but then goes on to reject that usage. At this point the setting up of an alternative meaning still requires an explicit repudiation of the established meaning. Defending art against the charge of being mere deceptive appearance ('Schein'), he writes: 'Only beyond the immediacy of sensation and of the external objects is genuine reality to be found'.[10] 'Genuine', here, is a tell-tale adjective, it suggests a flexibility and an antithesis—false or inauthentic 'reality'— inconceivable in earlier usage; and Hegel's 'external' connotes 'superficial'. Art is seen as a sphere of 'the Spirit' beyond all contingencies and beyond 'the deception of this bad, transient world . . . of ordinary reality'. Art is a 'Being-in-and-for-itself', and as such 'a higher, Spirit-born reality'.[11]

The two meanings I have quoted from Hegel—the one derived from common usage, the other which is his own—are fairly far apart; the second foreshadows the drastic semantic change we shall note at the turn of the nineteenth and twentieth centuries. If in Plato's philosophy the role of art was merely that of intimating the lower, worldly region to the higher,

[8] Immanuel Kant, *Kritik der reinen Vernunft*, Raymund Schmidt (ed.) (Wiesbaden, n.d.), 461a–463a; the passage is omitted from the second edition; cf. also 458.

[9] G. W. F. Hegel, *Phänomenologie des Geistes*, Johannes Hoffmeister (ed.), (Hamburg, 1952), 268f: 'Das Gesetz des Herzens und der Wahnsinn des Eigendünkels' ('The Law of the Heart and the Madness of Presumption').

[10] G. W. F. Hegel, *Ästhetik*, Friedrich Bassenge (ed.) (Berlin, 1955), 55: 'Erst jenseits der Unmittelbarkeit des Empfindens und der äußerlichen Gegenstände ist die echte Wirklichkeit zu finden'.

[11] Ibid.: 'Den Schein und die Täuschung dieser schlechten, vergänglichen Welt nimmt die Kunst von jenem wahrhaften Gehalt der Erscheinungen fort und gibt ihnen eine höhere, geistgeborene Wirklichkeit.'

timeless realm of the Ideas, Hegel's view of it is entirely historicized. He represents art and the aesthetic as the content of the higher sphere at a certain stage in the development of the Spirit. Hegel's historical consciousness is taken up by the next generation of German writers: Otto Ludwig becomes the chief mediator of the new, antithetical meaning.[12] In his programmatic essay on 'Poetic Realism' (1858) Ludwig argues that 'common reality' is not—or rather, should not be—the concern of contemporary art, and contrasts it with 'the magic world of art', which is said to present a 'truer appearance of reality'; and in a review of *The Mill on the Floss* (after 1860) he praises George Eliot for achieving the highest in art, 'the truth of reality'. Taking Shakespeare as a stick to beat Schiller with, Ludwig decrees that the new dramatic art shall represent 'not an impoverished but an enriched reality', its dialogue shall be 'the conversation of reality impregnated by and reborn in the Spirit'.[13] The contrasts here are less marked (in Hegel, art *is* a certain kind of 'reality', in Ludwig art seems merely to portray it), yet the Hegelian echoes are unmistakable.

Like many other passages in his work, Schopenhauer's definition contains an allusion to Tauler and the mystics generally. In the First Book of *The World as Will and Idea* (1819) he writes: 'Cause and effect are . . . the entire essence of matter: its being is its acting [ihr Seyn ist ihr Wirken]. This is why in German the quintessence of all that is material is called "Wirklichkeit", a word that is much more appropriate than "Realität".'[14] The young Nietzsche may well have Schopenhauer's definition in mind when summarizing Heraclitus's central doctrine: 'The eternal and sole process of becoming', Nietzsche writes, 'the total impermanence of everything *real* [die Vergänglichkeit alles Wirklichen]—which, according to Heraclitus's teaching, only acts and becomes and *is* not—amounts to a terrible, paralysing idea. In its effect it closely resembles the experience we have when, during an earthquake, we lose confidence in the firm ground underfoot.'[15] Hegel's 'ordinary reality' has become 'terrible, paralysing'.

[12] See Pramod Talgeri, *Otto Ludwig und Hegels Philosophie* (Tübingen, 1972).
[13] *Otto Ludwigs gesammelte Schriften*, Adolf Stern (ed.) (Leipzig, 1891), 'Der poetische Realismus', V, 264: 'Das Dargestellte soll nicht gemeine Wirklichkeit sein . . . Diese Zauberwelt, dieser wahrere Schein der Wirklichkeit . . . Wie der Stoff vom Geiste gereingt, wiedergeboren, geschwängert ist, so soll der Dialog vom Geiste wiedergeborenes und geschwängertes Gespräch der Wirklichkeit sein'. '*Die Mühle am Floß* von George Eliot', VI, 172: 'Wir müssen uns an die Wahrheit der Wirklichkeit halten . . .'.
[14] Arthur Schopenhauer, *Die Welt als Wille und Vorstellung*, I, Eduard Grisebach (ed.) (Leipzig (Reclam), n.d.), §4, 40.
[15] Friedrich Nietzsche, 'Die Philosophie im tragischen Zeitalter der Griechen' (1873, published posthumously), §5, in: *Sämtliche Werke: kritische Gesamtausgabe* (*WKG*), I, Giorgio Colli and Mazzino Montinari (eds.) (Berlin/New York, 1980), 824.

2

These remarks come from the young Nietzsche's notes for a history of Greek philosophy, which he abandoned in favour of completing *The Birth of Tragedy* (1872), and with that work, Nietzsche's first published book, we turn to our main theme. The book's anti-Socratic vein is in some ways deceptive. For what Nietzsche undertakes here is a re-interpretation and re-valuation of the Platonic idea of a transcendent 'reality' by making of it the object of art and the content of the highest in art. It is this transformation which decisively influences the generation of young poets and writers at the turn of the century.[16] The influence Nietzsche exercised on every major German writer of this era is unparalleled; no other Western philosopher, with the exception of Plato, has staked out the themes and determined the attitudes of an entire literature so directly, so powerfully, and so widely. There are several reasons for this fact of literary history, though here I must confine myself to one only.

There is no consistency—either in *The Birth of Tragedy* or anywhere else—in Nietzsche's philosophical vocabulary; as often as not 'Wirklichkeit' and 'Realität' are used interchangeably (except where he uses inverted commas round 'Realität', to deride it as the object of 'realist' or naturalistic aesthetics). Moreover there is, as we shall see, no consistency in the meanings he gives to this terminology.[17] Yet this immense flexibility to the point of contradiction, this conscious *and* instinctive refusal to settle on a single terminology, on a single, ideologically determined view of the world, or of experience, or 'reality', is one of the major sources of Nietzsche's influence. In the intellectual climate of the generation following on his death (1899) this flexibility is felt to be a sign of his literariness. Rilke, Stefan George and Hofmannsthal, Thomas Mann, Robert Musil and Kafka, Georg Trakl and Ernst Jünger, Gottfried Benn and Bertolt Brecht all declare (or sometimes unconvincingly deny) their indebtedness to him, all feel that Nietzsche is one of their own, the most literary of philosophers. Given the broad affinity of interests and a general consensus about what matters in the world, a family likeness of *modern*, twentieth-century concerns, these writers believe that they derive from their reading of Nietzsche not a doctrine or an ideology but a stimulus, a reflective energy and a freedom. They see it as the

[16] See e.g. *Nietzsche und der deutsche Geist* ... (1867–1900), R. F. Krummel (ed.) (Berlin/New York, 1974); and *Nietzsche und die deutsche Literatur*, Bruno Hillebrand (ed.), (Tübingen, 1978); Vol. I, *Texte zur Nietzsche-Rezeption* 1873–1963; Vol. II, *Forschungsergebnisse*.

[17]   Looking no further than the first five pages—i.e. section 1—of *The Birth of Tragedy* (*WKG*, I, 25–30), we encounter: 'Traumwirklichkeit', 'diese Wirklichkeit, in der wir leben und sind'. 'Wirklichkeit des Daseins [versus] Wirklichkeit des Traums',' die lückenhaft verständliche Tageswirklichkeit', and 'der Schein [würde uns] als plumpe Wirklichkeit betrügen'.

freedom to take from him, and to transform, whichever of his ideas and metaphors stimulates each writer's creative imagination. And Nietzsche's diffuse and often contradictory notion of 'reality' in its old and new meanings is almost always among the elements of his philosophizing that are so taken and transformed.

As we have seen, except for its usage in Hegelian aesthetics, up to the end of the nineteenth century the word had covered a fairly coherent range of meanings to do with ordinary experience, life in the world, and the like. We know what Thomas Hardy has in mind when, in his Nietzschean poem, 'God's Funeral' of 1912, he speaks of 'rude, uncompromising reality'.[18] These older meanings had been the opposite of esoteric or recondite; and this unemphatic, common-or-garden usage continues from the early nineteenth century into the present day, often in opposition to words like 'semblance', 'appearance', 'Schein', 'Unwirklichkeit' and the like. Jacob and Wilhelm Grimm's *Deutsches Wörterbuch* was begun in 1848; the appropriate volume, from which some of my quotations derive, was compiled sometime in the 1930s. The long-suffering historian of the later era must not be surprised (nor, as I hope to show, is it outrageously irrelevant to note) that this common-or-garden usage is illustrated in that dictionary with a quotation from an autobiographical chapter of *Mein Kampf* (1923), where A. Hitler writes that he 'transformed [his threat to give up going to school] into a reality' ('Ich setzte [diese Drohung] in eine Wirklichkeit um'). Now this to us is no more than a pretentious way of saying that at the age of fourteen the author became a drop-out, and the phrase is in no sense ambiguous or complicated. Yet it illustrates an important step in our argument. To call an expression 'pretentious' is to criticize it for being derived from a different or higher intellectual register than is appropriate to the context in which it is used. A similar shift of register, which may but need not always issue in pretentiousness, accompanies the new, polarized view of 'reality' throughout the age in which Nietzsche's influence begins to spread.

I have spoken of the stimulus to reflection derived from Nietzsche's writings, a stimulus reinforced by several dramatically heightened accounts of his life, which is cast as a symbol in a hazy aura of self-sacrifice and penitential suffering as the very pattern of the heroic intellectual's life in our time. (In Thomas Mann's *Doktor Faustus* this characteristically modern myth receives its fullest fictional form.) Nietzsche's undertaking is seen as exemplary precisely because, being pitched on the philosophical side of the boundary between philosophy and literature, his writings and the very forms in which he cast them give the writers of the modern age the freedom to challenge that division (which, in German literature, had in any event never been very sharp), and to place their writings in some proximity to his,

[18] *Selected Poems of Thomas Hardy*, David Wright (ed.) (Harmondsworth, 1978), 231.

46

on the literary side of the divide. The shift in literary register towards philosophical speculation which now takes place—the immense intellectualizing of literature we now witness—is something quite new. One important sign of this shift occurs in the term 'reality', which, without shedding its characteristic philosophical and theological usages, now fully enters both common discourse and creative literature. At this point an important polarization takes place. Retaining the relative indeterminacy and abstractness of its origins, the word is popularized and down-graded; yet at the same time new and very different meanings loom up, resulting from an opposite process: in literature and in philosophy—and to a more limited extent in common parlance too—the word is elevated to a new, 'higher' meaning. It continues to be used in what we may call its unemphatic meaning, yet it is also made an issue of. And whenever that happens, it turns into the very opposite of the everyday, of the solid, the opposite of being an object of ordinary sense perception: it comes to designate a privileged moment, a state on the margins of, hostile to, or contemptuous of, ordinary experience.

So frequent is the process I have just described—so apt to turn into a cliché—that it is bound to cause us to look more critically at that notion of imaginative freedom which Nietzsche's literary disciples claimed. This freedom is deceptive. From 1900 onwards something like a Nietzschean ideology does come into being. Whether 'reality' is made to connote value (as in 'höhere Wirklichkeit') or non-value ('Realität', 'gemeine Wirklichkeit'), each time it is the centre-piece of a dichotomous, value-related and implicitly total view of the world. It is hardly too much to say that what comes into being is *the ideology and literature of 'reality'*.

Nor is German the only language in which these changes happen: in English too the word, while retaining a curious abstractness and indeterminacy, is both popularized and given a high metaphysical status. Obviously, the term gains currency because it gives expression to some sort of deeply felt *modern* need. Yet one cannot help concluding that the form in which this need is expressed is no better than a contingency, that the terminology of 'the real' is no more than the dispensable cultural option of an era. If proof is needed of this claim, it should give food for thought that the word 'reality' does not occur in the whole of Shakespeare or in the English Bible (nor for that matter in Luther's German Bible); or again, that the word used in the Anglican and Protestant peroration of the Lord's Prayer is 'World without end', and not 'Reality without end'. There *is* a difference. One might describe it by saying that one who speaks of 'the world' (as does St John in the First Epistle) is expressing a necessity of human nature (to be human is to be in the world), whereas one who makes an issue of 'reality' is opting for an overworked though unacknowledged metaphysical metaphor.

Four closely related predicates are attributed to this new notion of 'reality'. First, it is seen as a precarious, problematic state—a state of mind or of the heart, or again (as in *The Birth of Tragedy*) the object and product of the mythopoeic imagination. Above all, it results from a translation of the outside world into a world within. Thus it becomes the opposite of 'reality' in Kant's sense, so much so that in section 4 of *The Birth of Tragedy* Nietzsche can speak—somewhat contemptuously—of the old 'empirical reality' as 'das Wahrhaft-Nichtseiende', that which in truth is (or has) no being.[19] Secondly, it is a state of mind or spirit supremely hard to attain, the fruit of a paramount existential quest, often involving the sacrifice of the endeavouring self and its world. This is what Nietzsche means when he emphasizes the existentially destructive, annihilating, yet artistically fruitful nature of 'Dionysiac reality'. With these connotations of pre-cariousness and even of terror, the word enters common parlance, so that there 'reality' and 'the real' come to mean all those things which are uncomfortable and without comfort—that which hurts, and is 'authentic' because it hurts. And in this sense, too, it has certain important political implications. Thirdly, seeing that it is relative to an individual existential endeavour, the concept of 'reality' comes to have a quantitative connotation. Again the contrast with the old meanings is instructive. They can be summed up by saying that, whatever the *value* of 'reality' to man, it was traditionally seen as something wholly *there*, given in experience. Nietzsche, how-ever, can write of the 'deeper reality' of the Dionysiac view of the world (as compared with the Apolline view), and of our historically determined inability to face it; of the 'greater reality' of music over language, attribut-able to its disclosing a 'greater' truth about the world. With his criticism of our 'belief in the more-or-less real' ('die Mehr-oder-Weniger-Wirklichkeit, die Gradation des Seins, an die wir glauben'[20]), he initiates that deeply familiar outlook conveyed by T. S. Eliot, one of his most attentive readers, when he writes in the first of *Four Quartets*, 'human kind / cannot bear very much reality'.

Finally, and most disconcertingly, the new meaning perpetuates and even deepens the old dichotomy of 'reality' versus language;[21] and again a forceful statement of this peculiar dichotomy is to be found in *The Birth of Tragedy*. For the book criticizes Socratic culture as verbal and 'merely' literary, and therefore a phenomenon of decadence, in opposition to an earlier culture based on the chthonic, Dionysiac and 'musical' grounding of pre-Socratic, true art. Here and in numerous later reflections Nietzsche writes as though (to invert Hobbes's statement) truth and 'reality' were to

[19] *WKG*, I, 39.
[20] *WKG*, XII, 465 (§485 in the posthumous collection *Der Wille zur Macht*), written in 1887.
[21] See e.g. Wilhelm von Humboldt, 'Über Denken und Sprechen', in *Werke in fünf Bänden*, V, Andreas Flitner and Klaus Giel (eds.) (Darmstadt, 1981), 99.

be found everywhere except 'in proposition'. (And placed in this context it becomes obvious that the scorn of language voiced here is one of the signs of Nietzsche's distrust of reason.) However questionable this language–'reality' dichotomy may be, not only in logic but on a commonsense view of things too—and it is difficult to see how it could have been seriously defended for so long—its fruitfulness as a literary theme is immense. But the same is true of all the 'reality' attributes I have mentioned. They illustrate an unsettling paradox concerning the role of general ideas in literature, and perhaps in other arts as well. The peculiar logic of some of these ideas, their contradictoriness and their deeply disconcerting implications alike do not necessarily impair their importance and value as the *données* and themes of the literary imagination.

3

In order now to illustrate the literary consequences of this semantic development let me begin with the work of the greatest German poet of the era. In 1910, aged thirty-five, Rainer Maria Rilke published his only novel, *The Notebooks of Malte Laurids Brigge*. The heavily autobiographical material is fictionalized in the form of a diary kept by a Danish aristocrat of twenty-eight, genteel and almost penniless, a member of what Marx would have called 'das Lumpenproletariat', about to be swallowed up by the anonymous city and its army of the down-and-out. Malte has come to Paris in order (as he says) 'to learn to see': that is, to learn to cultivate his perception and his capacity for creatively experiencing the suffering and decaying city around him, as well as certain pictures, poems, novels and musical compositions closely associated with suffering and decay; and to do all this in order to learn to retrace his perceptions with his pen. In short: his life in Paris is Malte's apprenticeship to the immense, endless, all-consuming task of writing. The pages of his diary, interlaced with prose sketches and letters, record the experience he undergoes, and his gradual defeat by it; the pages of the novel describe the process of learning and exemplify its results. These descriptions are of two radically different though complementary kinds. One kind (which I shall not illustrate here) is supremely concrete and vivid—vividly concerned with (as often as not) details of deprivation, disease and death. The other kind of description is equally vivid, equally telling, yet its lexis is abstract, conceptual and philosophical. Here is an example from one of the many drafts of letters Malte writes home, to his relations in the ancestral castle in Denmark:

But do not imagine that I suffer from disappointment here—quite the contrary. I am sometimes astonished to find how ready I am to give up all that I expected [alles Erwartete] for the real [für das Wirkliche], even when the reality is terrible. My God, if only any of it could be shared!

Ah—but would it exist then, would it exist? No, it *is* only at the price of solitude.[22]

The idiosyncratic emphasis on *sein* ('... wenn etwas davon sich teilen ließe! Aber *wäre* es dann, *wäre* es dann?') as well as the compound verbal noun ('Nein, es *ist* nur un den Preis des Alleinseins') are examples of what I meant by the combination of the vivid with the abstract and, earlier, by the intellectualizing of literature. With the mention of 'das Wirkliche' (in contrast to 'das Erwartete') the old unemphatic meaning is made an issue of, moved into the centre of the perceived experience (or at least of its record), and in the process turned into its opposite:

> The existence of the terrible [Malte's letter goes on] in every particle of air! You breathe it in as something transparent; but inside you it condenses, hardens, it assumes sharply pointed, geometrical forms between your organs. For all the torments and agonies wrought on scaffolds, in torture-chambers, mad-houses and operating theatres, under the vaults of bridges in late autumn: all these have a stubborn imperishability [alles das ist von einer zähen Unvergänglichkeit], all these persist in themselves and, jealous of all being, hang on to their terrible reality [... alles das besteht auf sich und hängt, eifersüchtig auf alles Seiende, an seiner schrecklichen Wirklichkeit].

The opposite of that 'terrible reality' (we read a little later) are 'the sugared water of twilight quietude' and the false, inauthentic security of those who try to exclude that 'reality' from their lives.

These lines could not have been written by Nietzsche, but Rilke is using here in his own, characteristic manner an area of philosophical expressiveness made available by Nietzsche. The fact that this 'reality' is said to be 'terrible' does not make it unwanted; on the contrary, we are intended to see the experience in its full intensity and destructiveness as a hallmark of its authenticity.

Twelve years later, in the tumultuous month of February 1922, Rilke reached the summit of his poetic and philosophical undertaking. The *Duino Elegies*, which he then completed, are a cycle of scenes and images chosen for their particular fittingness to represent the condition of *modern* man, often by throwing a light on that condition from the perspective of other ages. Explicitly as well as by elegiac intimation the poems are expressions of an acute historical consciousness, the consciousness of a change which they register with unparalleled intensity. The tenth and last

[22] Rainer Maria Rilke, *Die Aufzeichnungen des Malte Laurids Brigge*, I, (Leipzig, 1919), 106f. I have only slightly adapted John Linton's excellent translation, *The Notebooks of Malte Laurids Brigge* (London, 1930), 68f. For Nietzsche's influence on Rilke see Erich Heller, *The Disinherited Mind* (Cambridge, 1952), Ch. 5, 97–141.

of them asks the question: What is man's destiny 'under the stars'? If it is a journey, from a *here* to a *there*, how is such a journey to be conveyed? How, in particular, is such a journey to be conveyed in the light of Rilke's conviction, expressed in the First Elegy, 'Aber Lebendige machen/alle den Fehler, daß sie zu stark unterscheiden' ('But the living/all make the mistake of dividing too sharply')? For that notion of a complete, catastrophic break between the two 'realities', of a division conceived by us on the analogy of an absolute division between life and death, is an essential feature of the change I have described, yet it is also an aspect of experience which Rilke's poetry is intent on overcoming.

The journey described in the Tenth Elegy begins in the streets of the anonymous city, 'die Leid-Stadt',[23] the city of distraction and of suffering insufficiently acknowledged and validated, and thus of suffering denied and wasted. The scene moves to a fairground, and there we suddenly find ourselves in the presence of a young man who is leaving the region of the inauthentic city, guided (but this will become clear only in retrospect) by a young girl, perhaps as Dante was guided by Beatrice. Here is a last glance on what he is leaving:[24]

> Von Beifall zu Zufall
> taumelt er weiter; denn Buden jeglicher Neugier
> werben, trommeln und plärrn. Für Erwachsene aber
> ist noch besonders zu sehn, wie das Geld sich vermehrt,
> anatomisch,
> nicht zur Belustigung nur: der Geschlechtsteil des Gelds,
> alles, das Ganze, der Vorgang—, das unterrichtet und macht
> fruchtbar . . .
> . . . Oh aber gleich darüber hinaus,
> hinter der letzten Planke, beklebt mit Plakaten des
> 'Todlos',
> jenes bitteren Biers, das den Trinkenden süß scheint,
> wenn sie immer dazu frische Zerstreuungen kaun . . .,
> gleich in Rücken der Planke, gleich dahinter, ists
> wirklich.
> Kinder spielen, und Liebende halten einander, —abseits,
> ernst, im ärmlichen Gras, und Hunde haben Natur.

> Cheer-struck, on he goes reeling
> after his luck. For booths that can please
> the most curious tastes are drumming and bawling.

[23] T. S. Eliot refers to 'the unreal City' in *The Waste Land*, also written in 1922, in lines 60, 207, 376.
[24] The translation is quoted from Rainer Maria Rilke, *Duino Elegies*, trsl. J. B. Leishman and Stephen Spender (London, 1952), 93.

>   Especially
> worth seeing (for adults only): the breeding of Money!
> Anatomy made amusing! Money's organs on view!
> Nothing concealed! Instructive, and guaranteed
> to increase fertility! . . .
>   . . . Oh, but then just outside,
> behind the last hoarding, plastered with placards for
>   'Deathless',
> that bitter beer that tastes quite sweet to its drinkers
> so long as they chew with it plenty of fresh distractions,—
> just at the back of the hoardings, just behind them, it's
>   *real*!
> Children are playing, and lovers holding each other, —aside,
> gravely, in pitiful grass, and dogs follow their nature.

It is the culmination of the Tenth Elegy, and in some ways of Rilke's poetic oeuvre; it may well be the culmination, too, of the diction and literature of 'reality'.

My second example is taken from Robert Musil's first novel, *Young Törless*, of 1906; the work belongs in some ways to the time-hallowed genre of *Bildungsroman*, the novel of initiation and development. It is a story, again obviously autobiographical in many of its details, of a boy's experiences in an aristocratic military academy, culminating in his reluctant yet fascinated participation, with two other boys, in the blackmail, torture and sexual assault on one of their schoolfellows. 'The reality which one is describing is always only a pretext', Musil writes in his diary at the time,[25] meaning that the outward events of the story are used as a pretext for its psychological and philosophical purport; and this plan, translated into the moral sphere, is intended to justify the main events of the novel. Not that young Törless's actions, or those of his companions, receive any moral condemnation. On the contrary: the point at issue is to show that these events (whose impact on the victim are obviously devastating, though we are not told so) belong necessarily to the adolescent hero's intellectual and emotional development; the harsher and more hideous the events are, the more they show up the 'pretext', the 'unreality' of the school, of his family background, indeed of the whole adult world, as well as of the various kinds of learning with which the adult world world seeks to stifle his intellectual curiosity. (With the help of a flagrant pun a lengthy discussion on the function of the 'unreal' number of $\sqrt{-1}$ is introduced, as an example of the spuriousness of all 'scientific' knowledge.)[26] 'True reality' is to be found in

[25] Robert Musil, *Tagebücher, Aphorismen, Essays und Reden* (Hamburg, 1955), 776.

[26] Robert Musil, *Die Verwirrungen des Zöglings Törleß* (Hamburg, 1959), 74f.; see also *Young Törless*, trsl. Eithne Wilkins and Ernst Kaiser (London, 1971), 97f.

the little secret torture room, its walls draped in red flag cloth and furnished with whips, lamps and a revolver, a hide-out under the rafters of the old monastic building in which the school is housed—the room to which the boys bring their victim and where they torture him. The action turns into a search for those 'moments of almost poetic inspiration' of cruelty from which young Törless will eventually fashion his literary career: 'It was as though something had fallen, like a stone, into the vague solitude of his dreamy imaginings. It was there. There was nothing to be done about it. It was reality.'[27] Törless abruptly leaves when his two comrades decide to denounce their victim for the theft that had enabled them to blackmail him. The episodes of his last months at the school are the 'confusions'—the German title of the novel is *Die Verwirrungen des Zöglings Törless*—which he must go through, regardless of the cost to himself, but above all regardless of the cost to his victim. Giving an account to himself of what happened, Törless 'did not think that [his two companions] suffered as he knew he did. The crown of thorns that his tormenting conscience set on his brow seemed to be missing from theirs . . . The uglier and unworthier everything was that Basini [the victim] offered him, the greater was the contrast with that feeling of suffering sensibility which would afterwards set in.'[28] And again, viewing the events, Törless muses: 'Of course, I don't deny that it was a degrading affair. And why not? The degradation passed off, yet it left something behind—that small admixture of poison which is needed to rid the soul of its over-confident, complacent healthiness, and to give it instead a sort of health that is more acute, and subtler, and more understanding . . . The danger had drawn him into the maelstrom of reality.'[29] The second argument, certainly, is pure Nietzsche.

This then, is the story of the self on its indiscriminate quest for 'true reality' and experience—a quest proceeding without authorial dissociation or criticism: the thorny crown of tormenting conscience is proof of the suffering of an *aesthetic* sensibility, 'eine leidende Feinheit'. And here too we find the language-'reality' dichotomy I mentioned earlier, first in Törless's inability and later in his unwillingness to explain to others what these experiences mean to him, in his deep conviction that to explain them in words is to debase and trivialize them, to deprive them of what later writers will call their 'existential reality'.

Like Rilke's *Malte*, *Young Törless* stands on the threshold of modern German literature. All these ideas, which constitute the moral (but morally unexplored) horizon of the novel, are central to that literature; its major theme is the search for a redemption, a validation and an encompassing meaning of life to which, at its most characteristic, the word 'reality' or

[27] Op. cit., 46; translation 61.
[28] Op. cit., 111f.; translation 148f.
[29] Op. cit., 112, 128; translation 149, 171.

'true reality' is attached. And these are invariably said to be attainable only on the margins of experience—it is the harshness and hardness of that 'reality', the difficulty in the way of attaining the goal, and indeed on occasion (as with Franz Kafka) its radical unattainability, that are offered as proof of the value of the goal. What this early novel of Musil's offers is an uncritical, indeed crude version of the central theme and ethos of modern German literature; a critical and fully conscious—that is, ironical—embodiment of it is to be seen in the work of Thomas Mann.

But as the pursuit of this new, catastrophic 'reality' becomes a common literary theme, so the word itself becomes dispensable. (No history of a word can ever be meaningful without a history of what it denotes—similar conceptual ends are reached by diverse verbal means.) In prose fiction especially, a characteristic pattern develops: action, plot and characterization are carried on a realistic plane all the way to the margins of mundane experience, then that plane is abandoned, and they are validated in anti-worldly, metaphysical terms. Thomas Buddenbrook's discovery of Schopenhauer's meditations on 'the indestructability of our Being as such' is an early example of this practice, and so are the major novels of Hermann Hesse, Alfred Döblin, Robert Musil and many others.[30]

Franz Werfel's *The Forty Days of Musa Dagh*, one of the few explicitly political novels of the inter-war years, provides a transition to the dominant ideology of the age. Conceived during the author's extended tour of the Middle East in 1929, its massive Tolstoyan tableau depicts an episode in the persecution and massacres of the Armenians by the Young Turks in 1914–15; by 1933, when the novel was published, Werfel had become aware of its potential as an allegory of the persecution of the Jews in Germany and Central Europe.

The members of a small Armenian rural community decide to defend themselves against the Turks by setting up an armed camp on Musa Dagh, i.e. Mount Moses, in the coastal mountains west of Antiochia. Extensive study of documents from the archives of the French Ministry of War enables Werfel to tell the story of the Armenians' heroic defence and eventual rescue by Allied warships in convincing realistic detail. Their powerful, religiously motivated racial hatred is presented as a driving force

---

[30] See Thomas Mann, *Buddenbrooks: Verfall einer Familie*, II, (Berlin, 1923), 344ff.; *Buddenbrooks: the Decline of a Family*, trsl. H. T. Lowe-Porter (Harmondsworth, 1975), 505ff.; see also T. J. Reed, *Thomas Mann: the Uses of Tradition* (Oxford, 1974), 79–85. The conclusions of Hermann Hesse's *Das Glasperlenspiel*, of Alfred Döblin's *Berlin Alexanderplatz*, the elaboration of 'the Second Condition' in Robert Musil's *Der Mann ohne Eigenschaften* as well as the notion of 'zweite Wirklichkeit' in Heimito von Doderer's *Die Dämonen* (e.g. part II, chapter 4) follow this pattern.

throughout forty terrible days of siege, attack and counter-attack, whereas the hatred of the Turkish oppressors is more diffuse and more directly political. This complex motivation, as well as the creation of a leader figure (not provided by Werfel's documentary sources), are essential features of the realistic novel, but since this leader is to embody and highlight the Jewish allegory, we end up with a narrative in which racial, national and religious motives coincide.[31] There is no authorial criticism or dissociation from this unholy mixture of motives. Not a sensitive stylist at the best of times, Werfel uses a racialist diction without noticing how close it brings him to the literature of contemporary nationalism.

In the figure of Gabriel Bagradian, an Armenian brought up in Paris, déraciné, with a French wife and frenchified son, 'fate' has united all the traits of a charismatic leader of men. Bagradian happens to be on a visit to his native village when the persecutions break out; he is rich, head of the local aristocracy; and he has received full military training as an officer during the Balkan War of 1908, when the Turks wooed their Armenian minority. While all the other communities surrender cravenly to the Turkish marauders, Bagradian is determined to defend and revenge his kith and kin: a belief in 'Blut und Volk'—mere empty words in the perspective of his life in cosmopolitan Paris—now becomes 'a test of his own reality'. But when at last, after much suffering and great heroism, many deaths in battle, acts of betrayal and adultery, the miracle-like rescue comes, Bagradian is not among the survivors. His spiritual development has moved against the grain of the realistic narrative: 'The reality around him became as unreal as reality always is where its most real concentrations are to be found'.[32] The ancestral religious consciousness he is said to have regained—'the fate of his blood'—leads him out of this world, into death. And in his freely chosen death 'Gabriel Bagradian is more real than all men and all nations'.[33] On any mundane view his sacrifice is pointless, unnecessary, but it fits the destructive ideology of the age. It is an ideology which the oppressors share with many of their victims.

---

[31] Alma Mahler-Werfel's remarkable autobiography, *Mein Leben* (Frankfurt/M and Hamburg, 1963), 178, 198, 216f. gives details of the composition and reception of the novel, which was an immediate bestseller in the USA. The fact that it has to this day remained the main document around which Armenian resistance and terrorism have rallied points to the ambivalence of its nationalist diction.

[32] Franz Werfel, *Die vierzig Tage des Musa Dagh* (1933) (Frankfurt/M 1980), p. 31: 'Blut und Volk! Ehrlich sein! Waren das nicht nur leere Begriffe?'; p. 341: 'Die Wirklichkeit um ihn wurde so unwirklich, wie sie es in ihren wirklichsten Verdichtungen immer ist'.

[33] Op. cit., 867f.

4

I spoke of the quest for a new 'reality' as a cultural option of our age. The need it fulfils, or promises to fulfil, arises in an age of deep bewilderment and unease in the wake of what Nietzsche had called 'the death of God'. This new conception does not and is not intended to bring reassurance and certainty. Indeed, it is characteristic of the highest German literary and philosophical achievements of that age that they reject all certainties and comfort as inauthentic. The heedless enthusiasm with which almost the entire German intelligentsia and almost all German writers—with a very few honorable exceptions—welcomed the outbreak of war in 1914 as a solution to their political, national, cultural and personal quandaries indicates that what they were seeking, at least according to their overt declarations, was an extreme, as it were penitential experience; and the events after 1933 constitute a further radicalisation of that same quest.

The point to be made here is apt to be misunderstood. I am not saying that the quest I have been describing necessarily leads to, or fully explains, or contains a sufficient cause of, Hitler's National Socialism. Obviously, neither political ideologies nor political events ever have single causes. That what I wish to establish here is not a simple causal relationship becomes obvious as soon as we recall that the search for a new 'reality' is, first, a *literary* (and philosophical) search, and that the relationship between literary (or philosophical) insights and achievements on the one hand and political ideologies and conduct on the other is in itself a complex relationship, full of indeterminacies. Secondly, as a literary search, I take it to be part of a European concern. It is a major and, I believe, profound literary theme, confined neither to Germany nor to the age in question, but appearing in that place and at that time in a characteristically radicalized form. And, thirdly, most obviously, other countries, in which similar literary themes have been explored, did not proceed to similar political solutions; the lack of any political consequences of, say D. H. Lawrence's work, which containes similar ideas, is a case in point. The pattern I am trying to describe is best illuminated by a saying attributed to Hippocrates, that 'If one gives to a person in fever the same food which is given to a person in good health, what is strength to one is disease to the other'; or, in his more aphoristic vein, that there are people who fall gravely ill after eating cheese.[34]

All this must be said by way of a caution, against assuming too direct and too facile a relationship between the literary and philosophical quest for a new 'reality' on the one hand, and the political development of Germany

[34] *The Genuine Works of Hippocrates*, II, trs. Francis Adams (London, 1849), 771.

and Austria on the other. At the same time, however, it seems to me obvious that, given the importance of the search I have been describing; given the fact that literature is, after all, a social phenomenon, rooted not only in the individual creative mind but also in the society that encompasses and sustains that mind; and given, finally, the fact that National Socialism was a phenomenon rooted in recent German history—that the National Socialist régime did not descend upon an unsuspecting country as Pizarro and his *conquistadores* descended on Peru[35]—given all these, *some* influence from the literary to the political sphere is undeniable.

The attributes attached to the new 'reality' I enumerated earlier—that it is a precarious and problematic state, the opposite of a safe haven; that it is the product of a paramount existential effort, a condition of being which is full of danger, hurtful and involving sacrifice, attained on the very margins of existence; and even the distrust of language, at all events of language as the faculty of reason and of the process of criticism inherent in what Nietzsche had called the Socratic culture—all these attributes we find present in the ideology and propaganda of National Socialism, and in important aspects of its practice too. The author of *Young Törless* (one of the novels in which the literary–political relationship is most palpably present) was anything but a National Socialist. Nor do I know of any evidence to suggest that the novel was influential in affecting the course of political events in any *direct* way. And the same is true of all the works in the canon of this literature. What I think we can say is that in a certain historical situation—a situation characterized by a discrediting and loosening of institutional restraints, such as happened in 1919 and again in 1933, coupled with a high expectation of order and security—the literary and philosophical search for a new 'reality' of the kind I have described did contribute not merely to the chaos but, in a society singularly frightened of chaos, to the setting up of that new order which was designed to exploit and supersede the chaos. That the historical circumstances which I see as the enabling condition of this process (the circumstances in which, as Nietzsche put it, 'Everything is permitted') were themselves the result of the process to which the quest for 'reality' was a tributary, adds to the complexity of the argument, but it does not, I think, render the argument invalid.

[35] I am indebted for this simile to Chris Waller.

Literary Examples and Philosophical Confusion

R. W. BEARDSMORE

It is by no means unusual in works of philosophy for writers to make use of examples from literature or (like e.g. Peter Winch[1] and Eugene Kamenka[2]) to bemoan the lack of literary examples in the work of other philosophers. Nor is it unusual for philosophers to write substantial tomes without ever mentioning any work of literature or (like R. M. Hare[3] and C. W. K. Mundle[4]) to condemn the use of literary examples as a threat to clarity of thought. This contradiction in practice and principle might lead us to suspect that what we are here dealing with is at least to some extent a philosophical disagreement, and I believe this to be the case. Unfortunately, what is extremely unusual is any direct discussion of the philosophical issues involved, that is to say any discussion of what philosophers are doing when they appeal in their writings to works of literature, and of what if anything is lost by those who fail to do so.

I

As I say, direct discussion of the role of literary examples in philosophy is not common. Nevertheless there *is* one view which, while not often explicitly acknowledged does seem to underlie the remarks of many philosophers on this issue and in particular of those who are most conscious of the (alleged) dangers of a preoccupation with literary examples. Indeed so much is the view in question taken for granted that many may see any discussion of this topic as superfluous. 'Is it not obvious', they will ask, 'that the role of literary examples in philosophy is simply identical with that of other non-literary examples?' Both, so the argument goes, are either illustrations of general philosophical theses or counter-examples to general philosophical theses. It is, for example, a widely held view that all moral reasoning is in the final analysis utilitarian and that what is right or wrong

---

[1] 'The Universalisability of Moral Judgments', *The Monist* **49,** 199–200.

[2] *Marxism and Ethics*, (Macmillan), 35.

[3] *Freedom and Reason*, (Oxford University Press), 183 and *Moral Thinking*, (Oxford University Press), 47–49.

[4] *A Critique of Linguistic Philosophy*, (London: Clarendon Press), 14.

is determined by the consequences of our actions. On the present account, someone who (like myself) found this claim unconvincing might present as a counter-example Sheriff Hampton in Faulkner's *Intruder in the Dust*, who, faced with a demand that he hand over Lucas Beauchamp, a negro accused of murder, to a lynch mob, refuses, though he knows full well that in doing so he faces the likelihood that he and many others will die in a fruitless attempt to protect the man. On the other hand they might equally well point to the example of General De Gaulle's refusal to sanction the use of torture in Algeria in the face of the perfectly plausible claim by his military advisers that the information so obtained was saving French lives. For both the literary and the real-life examples present us with the same problems—whether to sacrifice one's moral values for the sake of beneficial consequences—a problem which according to at least some versions of utilitarianism, should not exist.

Whether, and if so how far, you agree that what we have here are counter-examples to the utilitarian thesis, all this might so far seem pretty unexceptionable. And no doubt, so far as it goes, it is. The main difficulty from my point of view is that it seems to present literature with a rather limited role to play in philosophy. There is, for example, no suggestion that great literature might have something to offer philosophy which what is inferior does not, nor any sense that the distinctively literary qualities of literature might have a role to play in philosophy. For in so far as fictional characters and their problems are regarded as examples or counter-examples, but anyway as examples, they are not being treated in the way we normally treat characters in works of literature. When I read *Macbeth* or *Alice in Wonderland* I do not think of Macbeth or Alice simply as examples. And perhaps we can start to see what literature might have to offer the philosopher by observing that when it is claimed that fictional and real-life examples have the same role to play in philosophy because they can present us with the same problems, the use of 'same' here is by no means unproblematic. It will be so only for a philosopher who wishes to maintain that there are no important logical differences between our responses to fictional situations and to those in real-life, no important differences between the significance which each has for us.

Some of the difficulties here come out in a recent Aristotelian Society symposium, 'How can we be moved by the fate of Anna Karenina?'[5] In his contribution to the discussion Colin Radford emphasizes the possibility of our responding emotionally to purely fictional characters. We are, for example, moved by the fate of Anna Karenina while recognizing that no such person ever existed. And this recognition makes a difference to the nature of our response to her fate. We do not, for example, try to intervene or offer solace. Of course, this is not to say that there are no important

[5] *Proceedings of the Aristotelian Society*, Suppl. Vol. **49** (1975).

similarities between our reponses to Anna and to a real person. Pity for characters in fiction is in some respects similar to feeling pity for people we know. For example we may, if we are prone to tears, cry over the fate of Anna as we may cry over the fate of our sisters or aunts, and whether prone to tears or not, we are likely to be upset by their respective fates, discuss with others how the problems arose and how things might have been different. Nevertheless, as Radford emphasizes, these similarities should not blind us to important conceptual differences. In this Radford seems to me to be right as against one of his critics, Barrie Paskins, who wishes to maintain that our responses to characters in fiction are really to be construed as responses to human beings in the same situation.

> When you are moved to tears by Anna, you are not moved by her, at least not really, but by the similarly awful fate of Mrs Muriel Parsons of Belsize Park . . . who in 1937, etc.[6]

Apart from the wild implausibility of Paskins's claim, which Radford mentions, it is also obvious that Paskins does nothing to explain the sense of 'the same situation' or 'similarly awful fate' and in consequence simply begs the question in what respects the problems of fictional characters *can* be the same for us as those of real-life people.

This is not, of course, to say that the way in which Radford presents this question is always clear or even coherent. Paskins is himself led into confusion partly because he is responding to Radford's presentation of the difference as involving some sort of paradox: 'Given that pity is what we feel for real human beings, how can we feel pity for fictional characters, who we recognize do not really exist'. Paskins's mistake is to attempt to answer this question by suggesting that pity for fictional characters is really pity for human beings, whereas it is clear that granted the truth of Radford's premise the question is unanswerable. Given that pity is what we feel only for human beings, then obviously we cannot feel pity for characters in fiction, and that is that. What Paskins misses is that no answer is needed, since the premise is patently false. Just as it is a matter of fact about human beings that they feel pity for other human beings in distress, so it is equally a matter of fact about human beings they they feel pity for characters in fiction. Radford seems to see this as in some way irrational. But it is so only in the (dubious) sense in which the pity we feel for human beings is irrational. In neither case can the feelings we have be justified, but they are nevertheless an almost universal feature of human life. And in neither case should we know how to deal with people who did *not* react in these ways. When I say to a child 'You'll make Mommy cry if you do that—and you don't want Mommy to cry, do you?', I do not expect the

[6] 'On Being Moved by *Anna Karenina* and Anna Karenina', *Philosophy* **52,** 345.

answer 'Yes, that would be nice' except from a child precocious in its use of
sarcasm. And if I were to come across a child who *genuinely* did not feel
pity for those in distress, I should be at a loss to know how to speak to the
child about morality or indeed human relationships generally. In the same
way, I shall be amazed to come across a child who when presented with the
story of Rumpelstiltskin finds the plight of the princess amusing. Certainly,
unless a child reacts in certain ways—laughs at funny stories, cries over
sad ones, shudders at what is horrible—we shall, in the absence of special
circumstances, simply conclude that it does not understand the stories
we tell it. And then we shall certainly not present it with more sophisticated stories, but rather simpler ones in the hope of eliciting the appropriate response—'the appropriate response' being here the response which
would be normal where we are not dealing with fiction. What Radford
seems to ignore is that it is a *precondition* of understanding literature
that we should react to certain fictional situations in partly the same ways as
we do to their real-life counterparts.

Where he is, I think, right is in his emphasis on the differences. With
real-life problems we do not expect people merely to be upset or indignant.
We also expect them to meet problems with compassion, try to help (or
sometimes tactfully to refrain from helping), offer advice, ask for explanations and so on. But it would be a confusion about the logic of fiction
to suppose that any of these responses were appropriate with literature.
Still it does not follow, except with the most unsophisticated reader or the
most unsophisticated forms of fiction, that people's responses are limited
simply to emotional responses. With *Anna Karenina* or *Macbeth* interest
and enlightenment occupy the place which in real-life problems is occupied
by advice and help. A work of literature is presented as an object of contemplation in which we may find profundity and originality, whereas a
situation in real life can only be unexpected or different.[7]

Now if you hold the sort of account of the role of literature in philosophy
with which I opened this paper, you are not likely to attach much importance to these differences. True, on any account fictional examples will have
advantages and disadvantages over real-life examples. On the credit side,
since the novelist, unlike the historian or biographer, is not bound to
recording what actually happens, he is likely to furnish us with a wider
range of problems, situations, possibilities with which to illustrate and test
our philosophical theories. 'In a good work of fiction', it has been suggested,
'the reader enters imaginatively into actions and experiences for many of

[7] I am not, of course denying that the sort of enlightenment which characterizes fiction, can sometimes be found in the description of non-fictional events—
for example, in great journalism. I have in mind, for instance, Orwell's account
of a hanging or the shooting of an elephant in Burma. But it would be important
to note here that Orwell does not just state what happened, but tells a story.

which no opportunities occur in real life and which he could not actually perform.'[8] But there is a price to be paid. For:

> story-books, though they help to stimulate our imaginations, do not by themselves help us, very much, to separate what is really likely to happen from what is not, nor to assess the probable frequency of its occurrence. For this, some experience of actual moral perplexities, and of the actual consequences of certain moral choices, is a necessity.[9]

Given the assumptions which Hare and Ducasse appear to share, then reason would seem to dictate that, like Hare, we err on the side of caution. For, if the value of literature to philosophy lies simply in its ability to present the novel or the fanciful, problems and dilemmas which are merely *different* from those we encounter in real life, then it is so far unclear why the variety it offers should be of interest to philosophers. For, on the face of it at least, to imagine the application of a familiar concept in a wildly fanciful context is more likely to blind us to those features of our lives which give that concept its sense, than to illuminate them. Certainly, some of the examples used by philosophers do fit just this specification.

> Imagine a Robinson Crusoe asleep on an island about to be wiped out by a tidal wave, he is ignorant, experiences no suffering, can do nothing about the outcome . . .[10]

Gombay uses the example to show that there are cases where knowledge is unarguably a bad thing, and its artificiality stems from its having been set up in such a way as to provide a case which excludes any other possible view of the matter. Of course, deciding what we want to say about imaginary Robinson Crusoes is part of the modern philosopher's stock in trade. But it is, I think, worth comparing Gombay's Crusoe with Defoe's. I take it that a major part of Defoe's difficulty in writing the novel would have been to present us with a picture of an unusual situation, that of a man removed from his normal background of social relations, which while unusual is nevertheless convincing. But since Gombay is not writing a novel but merely engaging in an exercise of philosophical fancy, he does not even have to bother about such things. We see the difficulties if we ask now the episode he describes might be incorporated into Defoe's story. Obviously, since *Robinson Crusoe* is written in the first person, it cannot be. Crusoe cannot know that unbeknownst to him nothing can save him. But

---

[8] S. Ducasse, 'Taste, Meaning and Reality in Art' in S. Hook (ed.) *Art and Philosophy*, (New York: University Press), 190.

[9] Hare, op. cit.

[10] A. Gombay, 'What You Don't Know Doesn't Hurt You', *Proc. Arist. Soc.* (1979), 244.

perhaps this point is trivial, for there might be someone else in the story who knows it, for example Man Friday. Remember, however, that what we are being asked to imagine is not a situation of the sort which is familiar to us (and which might be expected to be familiar to Man Friday), where we might say 'nothing short of a miracle can save him'. For here there is still room for the man who believes he ought to fight against hopeless odds, die with his boots on, and hence room for the man who says 'Better for him to know'. If there is to be no argument that he should have been kept in ignorance, then it has to be known that whatever he does (hiding in the caves, climbing the mountains, putting his affairs in order) can make no difference to anything—even to the way in which Crusoe views his own life and death. So what is needed is not Man Friday but a narrator possessing divine ominiscience, that is to say a device whose artificiality is such that it guarantees that we shall be unable to take this aspect of a novel seriously. It is this, for example, for which Sartre once condemned the work of Mauriac. The central fault in Mauriac's style, Sartre suggests, lies in the introduction of God's standpoint into the narrative.

To be able to take Defoe's *Crusoe* seriously, we do not have to believe that he is describing actual events. It is more a matter of knowing what we are supposed to be imagining, being able to respond to the characters and see their problems as real ones. Whether we are able to do this or not will in part decide whether what we are presented with is a work of stature or, for example, mere escapism. But obviously, if like Hare and Ducasse you think of fiction (at least in so far as it is relevant to philosophy) as simply a source of novel situations, you are not going to be able to see the importance of this distinction. For there are novel situations in both the *Iliad* and *Tarzan of the Apes* or *From Russia with Love*. 'As a consumer of fiction', Ducasse remarks, the philosopher 'does not and should not attend to and contemplate aesthetically the technique of the story, since this would to a greater or lesser extent distract from the content of the story.'[11] And Hare also thinks it important to draw a firm distinction between the pursuit of artistic perfection and the pursuit of clarity of thought.

Commonly, of course, the practice of philosophers does not cohere with this principle to ignore literary qualities in favour of content. For it is not, I take it, mere coincidence that their examples tend to come from the work of people like Tolstoi or Shakespeare, rather than that of Edgar Rice Burroughs or Ian Fleming. And this seems to suggest that in practice at least they recognize the difference between the profound and the merely fanciful, between the original and the merely novel. But I believe that the most illuminating discussion of the principles behind this difference is to be found in the writings of Wittgenstein.

[11] Ducasse, op. cit.

II

A central theme, perhaps *the* central theme of the notebooks now translated under the title *Culture and Value* makes its appearance in one of Wittgenstein's earliest entries where he speaks with approval of Tolstoi's claim that the significance of the greatest art lies in its being universally understood. In his *Memoir* Norman Malcolm mentions how impressed Wittgenstein was by this theme in Tolstoi's writings. But on the face of it Tolstoi's views seem not only paradoxical, even stupid, but also inconsistent with Wittgenstein's repeated observations both in the *Lectures and Conversations* and in *Culture and Value* that we may appreciate the art of one culture and yet be *completely* at sea with that of another. And Wittgenstein himself remarks that Tolstoi's claim is 'both true and false'.[12] The falsity is apparent even in Tolstoi's own favoured examples. For instance, everyone, he says whatever their social background, can understand the story of Abraham and Isaac. But far from this being the case, it is in fact extremely difficult for a member of our own society to understand this story. What, for example, is it for a man to sacrifice his own child to God? If I were to take my daughter (or even my dog) for a walk, with the expressed intention of making a sacrifice to God, the reaction of most people would be to call the police and try to get me committed. They would regard my conduct not as the expression of religious dedication, but as symptomatic of mental disturbance. Or again, why was it so important that Isaac was Abraham's first-born son? Except in rather special circumstances (among the Royal Family, for instance, where questions of title and inheritance are involved) we tend no longer to attach a greater importance to our first child than to our second, nor to sons rather than daughters. So it appears that Tolstoi's claim that what is important in art can be understood by everyone is not only false, but obviously false. Where another culture, its standards and values are sufficiently remote from our own, we are likely to have difficulty in understanding the art of that society. And it is the possibility of such a lack of knowledge as understanding which Tolstoi tends sometimes to deny.

What Wittgenstein sees, however, is that there is a deeper truth in Tolstoi's claim. To appreciate this we need to remember that Tolstoi's claim is specifically a claim about *great* art. In this it differs from the point I have been making so far which is a general one. When I find difficulty in understanding the art of another society it will not be only work of their finest artists, but also of those they regard as mediocre, which puzzles me. I remember once reading of a Chinese mandarin in the last century, who on

---

[12] *Culture and Value*, (Blackwell), 17. I am grateful to the editor of the *British Journal of Aesthetics*, Dr T. J. Diffey, for permission to quote extensively from my review of this work.

observing the painted shadow on the face in a Gainsborough portrait asked whether it was the custom of English ladies to wash only one side of their faces. The mandarin would have faced the same difficulty presented with the work of any British portrait painter of the period, good, bad or indifferent. For his problem was, at least in part, that he was ignorant of the standards and conventions of British portrait painting. By contrast what Tolstoi sees is that the puzzlement which any of us may face when presented with a *great* work of art, is not a matter of knowledge, of the intellect at all (and in that sense not a matter of the understanding) but as Wittgenstein says, of the will—not a matter of what it is hard to see in the sense of 'requiring intelligence or specialized knowledge', but of what it is hard to see in the sense of 'requiring courage'. Courage, the courage of the great creative artist, or the courage required of an audience in coming to terms with his work is emphasized by Wittgenstein throughout. What he had in mind here is not a matter of holding on to one's views in the face of powerful opposition as when, for example, Kenneth Tynan once used a certain old English verb on television. For though what Tynan did was different from what had been done before and perhaps (in one sense) required courage, it would be simply absurd to suggest that he had done anything profound or even original. The courage of which Wittgenstein speaks is not the courage to go against received opinion (though it may certainly involve that), but the willingness to question what is simply taken for granted, even by oneself. An artist who is profound or original will be difficult to understand not because we lack the intellectual capacity, but because in order to do so we shall be forced to throw over what is dear to us, because it will appear to us as a threat.

I think that this is what Wittgenstein has in mind when he says that the difference between Mendelssohn and Brahms is that 'there is perhaps in Mendelssohn no music that is hard to understand' or 'difficult'.[13] The conflict which gives rise to the difficulty here is a conflict between what the music can bring us to see and 'what most people want to see'.[14] But unlike the difficulty facing the mandarin in my previous example it has nothing to do with taste, with an education in or understanding of the standards of one's own or any other culture. Reviewing the first Impressionist exhibition of 1875, Albert Wolff, critic of *Le Figaro*, remarked that it would be as difficult to explain to Renoir that a woman's torso is not a mass of green and violet patches as to explain to a madman that he is not the Pope. Wolff's difficulty with Renoir's work was not an intellectual difficulty, a lack of education in art. On the contrary, he was a man of highly cultivated taste. But he had been faced with a conception of representation, a new artistic style, which questioned the very principles on which his taste

[13] Ibid., 28.
[14] Ibid., 17.

rested, and, unable to accept this questioning, he was forced to represent it as a fraud. Again, it was only by having the courage to question the principles of the French schools that Renoir had himself been able to reach the conception of nature as patterns of light and colour which Wolff condemned. As Wittgenstein says, 'The faculty of taste cannot create a new structure, it can only make adjustments to one that already exists',[15]

I have illustrated the point by referring to music and painting, but it is more to my purpose, and I think even more obvious, that in literature the difficulty of appreciating an original style is bound up with the difficulty of questioning our most deeply rooted ideas. It is, for example, clear that the problems faced by many of his contemporaries in coming to terms with what they saw as the brutality and disagreeable nature of D. H. Lawrence's style cannot be separated from Lawrence's emphasis on the instincts and passions as opposed to the life of reason. For instance it is no coincidence that a writer of the previous generation like John Galsworthy with his emphasis on reasonable thought should have found *The Rainbow* aesthetically detestable, nor that T. S. Eliot, while remarking that Lawrence 'can reproduce for you not only the sound, the colour and form, the light and shade, the smell, but all the finer thrills of sensation' should nevertheless comment, 'This is not *my* world, either as it is, or as I wish it to be'.[16] For the power of Lawrence's style lay precisely in its ability to question the current ideas of what the world is like.

Now it is evident that if what I have been saying about the relationship of style and content in art and literature is correct, then those writers who I discussed at the beginning of this paper will be forced to say that there is a fundamental difference between literature and philosophy. For, as we saw there, many writers hold questions of style to be irrelevant in philosophy and if so this difference would be important. What is interesting is that the philosopher I have been discussing does not appear to have held this. For throughout his writings, and especially in *Culture and Value*, there are comparisons, both explicit and implicit, between the originality or profundity of an artist and that of a philosopher, between the difficulty of finding (and understanding) a new form of artistic expression and that of solving a philosophical problem. Of course, in itself this proves nothing. Wittgenstein could simply have been wrong. But let us begin by asking whether in saying that in literature a new mode of expression may bring about a change in the way we see things, we are describing something which is wholly unfamiliar in philosophy. I think that it is obvious that we are not. Consider for example F. H. Bradley's claim that 'Time is

[15] Ibid., 58.
[16] From 'The Contemporary Novel' quoted in *D. H. Lawrence: The Critical Heritage*, R. P. Draper (ed.) (Routledge), 276.

unreal'. In his article 'The Conception of Reality', G. E. Moore says of this claim:

> If Time is unreal, then plainly nothing ever happens before or after anything else; nothing is ever simultaneous with anything else; it is never true that anything is past; never true that anything will happen in the future; never true that anything is happening now; and so on.

Here as elsewhere Moore held such claims to be preposterous, held that when they had been expressed in this way they would be claims which we should wish to reject. Still, I should not be surprised to learn that Bradley was not too impressed by Moore's response to his theory. For the attraction of the claim that Time is unreal and the arguments which led Bradley to it cannot be recaptured by a list of claims about whether so and so had breakfast before lunch, or whether such and such happened at the same time as the clock struck three. Again, I have discovered that one philosophical thesis which seems to hold a great deal of attraction for my students is the paradoxical claim that two people can never really know when they look at physical objects whether they see the same colours. Expressed in this way the claim strikes them as both true and exciting. Unfortunately, what they soon discover is that it is impossible to express the claim in any other way, and still preserve its appearance of embodying a fascinating insight. For if you *ask* any two people what colour they see when they look at a sample door or lampshade, they will, except in special circumstances, agree in calling it 'red' or 'blue' or 'green'. So it appears that they *do* generally see the same colour, and the thesis is false. And if the student then replies (as he or she usually does), 'Yes, but it's just that we've been taught to call it "red" or "blue" or "green" ' (with the implication that they do not really believe it to be so), then one has only to ask 'So what colour do you *really* think it is?' to elicit the response 'Well, "red" (or "blue" or "green")'. So again the thesis turns out to be false. In the long run, of course, the student will normally be forced to some claim which does express a truth, for example, 'Whenever I see a colour, it is always *me* and not another person who does the seeing'. But the trouble is that this claim turns out to be as completely boring as the claim that it is always me and not another person who nods my head. True, this is not normally how the student sees it. He or she is likely to feel that when translated in this way, the point of the philosophical thesis has been lost. And of course in one sense this is true, just as the point of a joke will be lost if we try to explain it in other words, or just as a poem will lose its force when translated into prose. For the fascination of the original claim lies in part in the language in which it is expressed.

If this were not so, if the attraction of general philosophical theses owed nothing to the way in which they were expressed, then one would find it difficult to understand why apparent counter-examples do not always seem to destroy this attraction. One would, for example, expect F. H. Bradley to have retracted his claim that Time is not real when presented with the known truth that G. E. Moore really had breakfast before dinner. Or to return to an earlier example, one would expect De Gaulle's refusal to sanction the use of torture while recognizing its socially beneficial consequences to destroy the utilitarian claim that what is held to be right or wrong is determined by its consequences. But anyone who does expect this has obviously little acquaintance with philosophical discussions. For notoriously what generally happens is that the alleged counter-example is explained in terms of the theory, so that the theory remains intact and the philosopher holds on to the form of language which embodies the original confusion.

Nevertheless what does not follow from this is the sceptical conclusion that counter-examples can never be effective in philosophy. For what I have been (purposely) ignoring is that the examples may themselves have a force, that they may be expressed in language whose power is such as to break the hold on us of other ways of expressing ourselves. And just as I said in literature a new mode of expression may bring about a change in the way we view the world, so it may have the same function where the way we view the world is one which has been distorted by philosophical confusion.

As an examples of a view distorted by philosophical confusion let me return to the case of utilitarianism. Though it is an over-simplification, it is only a slight over-simplification to say that the attraction of utilitarianism is the attraction of the idea of a calculation. This is apparent in the very terms in which writers like Bentham and Mill express their fundamental task, i.e. as that of finding the 'measure' of virtue, or of founding a 'science' of morality dealing in generalizations (that is, in amounts).[17] So it is not surprising that what the theory 'measures' is numbers, nor that the generalizations which it discovers should state *how often* such things as honesty or murder harm or benefit people and *how many* people they harm or benefit. Of course, numerical considerations may make some difference on any account of morality. That my actions will harm more people rather than less may make *some* difference whatever my moral viewpoint. But in the various versions of utilitarianism, these considerations have become all-pervading. For the utilitarian *all* moral decisions are in the final analysis calculations. 'That it be made a matter of reason and calculation, and not merely of sentiment is', according to Mill, 'what renders argument or discussion possible.'[18]

---

[17] It may be said that Mill breaks decisively with this aspect of his introduction of qualitative considerations. But it is worth noting that in the last resort Mill is forced to explain even this aspect as a matter of what *most* qualified judges would choose, i.e. as a matter of numbers.

[18] 'Essay on Bentham', in *Utilitarianism* (Fontana), 120.

Given that you do think of morality in mathematical terms, it will of course appear to you that only *certain* judgments, *certain* viewpoints are possible, even intelligible. For the language in which you have chosen to describe morality (or rather, feel obliged to do so) will determine for you which aspects of our lives make sense. Suppose that the question is whether it is permissible to torture or even kill a terrorist in order to save, let us say, 100 lives. The inclination will be to present this as a sum and then to subtract from the 100 lives the one terrorist's life, thus ending with a credit balance of 99 lives in favour of this particular atrocity. So that the man who like De Gaulle refuses to permit the sacrifice will appear to be ignoring one element in the calculation, the 100 lives, or supposing that somehow one life is more than 100, and hence to be guilty of an error in calculation. The only way out of this absurd conclusion is to pretend that De Gaulle had really got the right answer, but to a different sum. What he had done was to subtract the 100 lives from the net total of lives saved by a general ban on the ill-treatment of terrorists. And so the argument continues.

What the man gripped by this theory needs to be brought to see is that numerical considerations *need* play no part at all in someone's moral deliberation, or to put it another way, that many of the considerations which are central in morality have no numerical aspect. And I suggested earlier that one way of combating utilitarianism would to be appeal to a work of literature like Faulkner's *Intruder in the Dust*. Faulkner's novel is not, of course, his greatest, and it is not always convincing, particularly in the later chapters, where he employs long polemical speeches by the lawyer Gavin Stevens to preach to the reader. What *is*, in my opinion, convincing (as in most of Faulkner's writing) is the portrayal of individual characters and their relationships. And it is such portrayals which can help break the hold on us of the abstract and mathematical account of human relationships embodied in the theory of utilitarianism. Thus we are presented with the picture of Will Legate, the hunter who is willing to risk his life to protect Lucas Beauchamp, because he has been paid to do a job, or the jailor who has taken an oath of office and will not be able to live with himself if he lets a 'passel of no-good sonabitches' take a prisoner away from him, or the young narrator who will prevent the lynching if he can 'not because he was himself, Charles Mallinson junior . . . but because he alone of all the white people Lucas would have a chance to speak to between now and the moment when he might be dragged out of the cell and down the steps at the end of a rope, would hear the mute, unhoping urgency of the eyes . . .'[19]

Unlike the relationship of a man's actions to the happiness of the greatest number (or some other variant), none of the relationships by which characters are impelled to act in Faulkner's novel, a man's relationship to

[19] *Intruder in the Dust* (Chatto & Windus), 68–69.

his job, or to a particular human being (father, mother, friend), has any numerical or mathematical aspect, and this is why utilitarians have traditionally had difficulties with these aspects of morality and have often been forced simply to deny their reality.

Whether, when we read Faulkner, such relationships do strike us as real, whether we are capable of responding to the characters in the novel, is, as I have tried to show earlier, a literary and stylistic question. But it is not, however, a question which is irrelevant to philosophy. For it may be that by seeing how Faulkner writes and thinks of human beings we are brought to think of them in that way ourselves, and in this way to see the artificiality of the utilitarian preoccupation with quantities. In this respect the relation between counter-examples and philosophical thesis is comparable to the relation between one artistic style and another which I discussed earlier.

III

'But now', someone may say, 'are you not in danger of blurring the differences between literature and philosophy. For, whatever its faults, one merit of the account of the relationship between the two which you have criticized is that by claiming that literary qualities are philosophically irrelevant, it does at least make clear why we distinguish the two subjects in the first place. Whereas on your account this becomes quite mysterious, so that it now appears as though one way of doing philosophy is to write novels and plays.'

There is certainly a danger that by rejecting the mistaken idea of a conflict between literature and philosophy we shall fall into the opposite error of over-emphasizing the similarities. This seems to me to have happened to some extent in the writings of Renford Bambrough and especially in his paper 'Literature and Philosophy' where he is concerned to emphasize the unity of the two subjects. According to Bambrough this is necessary because of an artificial separation of the two subjects which he lays at Plato's door.

> His struggle to separate them would have been unnecessary if he had not recognized that both in principle and in ancient practice, philosophy and literature were modes of one substance.[20]

We see this unity in their subject-matter. For both subjects centre around the same range of topics:

> Man, God, Nature, Arts, Will, Fate, Necessity, Chance and Freedom; Knowledge and Ignorance; Truth and Falsehood, Good and Evil.[21]

[20] In *Wisdom: Twelve Essays*, (Blackwell), 274.
[21] Ibid., 275.

Since it seems impossible to imagine *any* problem which could not plausibly be subsumed under one of these categories, or indeed the first four, one might be forgiven for thinking that it is Bambrough's unity, rather than Plato's separation, which has been artificially imposed. But it would be premature to suppose that Bambrough's thesis is merely vacuous, for he claims to detect not simply a unity of subject-matter, but also of method. In both 'the understanding moves in dialectical paths'.[22] That is to say, in both we find a procedure aimed at removing paradox and confusion engendered by generalities through an examination of particular cases, by 'a process of examining more minutely and particularly the minute particulars concerning which the opposed generalities are in conflict'.[23]

This is similar to what I have said about the way in which a study of examples may break the hold on us of abstract philosophical theories. And of course Bambrough is right to say that the problems, puzzles, paradoxes which torment philosophers are also to be found in literature. But there is a difference which may be expressed by saying that though works of literature may involve such problems, philosophy *starts from* them. Wittgenstein once remarked[24] that in his later life Russell had lost his sense of philosophical problems, so that everything now seemed simple to him. And he identified this process with the trivialization of Russell's thought. Whether or not one agrees with Wittgenstein's assessment, it is, I think, clear that he was right to equate the two things. For without a sense of puzzlement, there is no philosophy.

Unfortunately, when Bambrough speaks as if problems had the same part to play in literature, he is in danger of over-intellectualizing our responses here. I said earlier that it is among the most general feature of human beings that they tend to respond to certain portrayals in fiction. Given this response, then through his characters a novelist may present us with general problems and ideas. But we can still speak of a work as literature even where there are *no* problems. In a well-known essay Ford Madox Ford recounts his reactions on receiving the manuscript of Lawrence's 'Odour of Chrysanthemums' for publication in the *English Review*. He read, so we are told, the first few sentences and knew that he was in the presence of a great writer. Yet these sentences present us with no problems, indeed nothing of any generality at all. They describe a train pulling into a station, watched by a woman on the platform. Ford recognized literary talent in Lawrence's ability to outline character and situation with 'a casual word here and there', because in a few lines he could bring people to life. But where the characters are mere abstractions, where we

---

[22] Ibid.
[23] Ibid., 276.
[24] *Zettel*, (Basil Blackwell), 82.

are unable to respond to them as living things, the problems and the ideas will lack force for us.

> Take *Everyman* where the hero, Everyman, threatened by death, first asks Fellowship for help and Fellowship deserts him. Then he goes to Kindred, and Kindred also backs out. At last he falls back on Good Deeds, who finally saves him from Hell . . . The failure of *Everyman* is a defect of characterization. How are we to take any interest in such lay figures as Good Deeds and Kindred? But we don't object to Christian and Faithful Byends or Giant Sloth in *Pilgrim's Progress*, or to Sir Wilfull by Congreve. These are like real people subject to whim and moods, but the characters of *Everyman* are mere conceptions.[25]

It should be clear from what I have said so far that in so far as I understand it, I believe Plato's characterization of literature as a device which bewitches the intelligence by appealing to the emotions to be simplistic. Even so, by assigning drama and poetry to the realm of the feelings and philosophy to that of reason, Plato was at least pointing to an important difference which Bambrough with his emphasis on unity is in danger of blurring. For a problem presented in a work of literature can be made real to us, only if we are first capable of responding to the characters there, that is to say, if our feelings are involved. In this sense it is the feelings which are fundamental in our appreciation of literature. My aim in this paper has been to show that it is by making problems and ideas real to us in this way, that literature can be of service to philosophy. But it will do this only if we feel the force of the problems in the first place. Without the problems there would be no philosophy. And so, in this sense, it is the problems which are fundamental in philosophy.

[25] Joyce Cary, *Art and Reality*, (Cambridge University Press), 154–155.

Thematic Concepts: Where Philosophy Meets Literature

STEIN HAUGOM OLSEN

I

In Euripides' *Hippolytus*, Phaedra, wife of Theseus, king of Athens, falls in love with the unsuspecting Hippolytus, Theseus' son by the amazon Antiope. Phaedra's passion is the work of the goddess Aphrodite, who wants to revenge herself on Hippolytus because he has rejected her and devoted himself to the chaste Artemis. Through Paedra's nurse Hippolytus is made aware of her love and invited to her bed. He emphatically rejects her offer and violently abuses Phaedra and her nurse. To save her honour Phaedra commits suicide and leaves a note accusing Hippolytus of raping her. Theseus, confronted on his return from an expedition with the suicide and the note, banishes Hippolytus and prays to his father, the seagod Poseidon, to fulfil one of the three wishes he has granted him and kill Hippolytus. Leaving Troezen, Hippolytus is killed when his horses are frightened by a monster thrown on shore by Poseidon from a giant wave. Theseus is brought to realize his mistake by the goddess Artemis who appears to him and reveals the truth. The play ends with the reconciliation of Theseus and the dying Hippolytus. This, in bare outline, is what happens in the play. It is what might be called its subject. The play is about these events and characters. Now it is also possible to give another type of description of Euripides' play. For the play does not merely have a subject but also a theme. While it is straightforward and unproblematic to give a description of the subject of the play a statement of its theme presents difficulties. The subject is, in an obvious sense, given for any competent speaker of the language in which the work is written. The theme, on the other hand, emerges from the subject in conjunction with other features of the work, and it emerges through the reader's constructive labour. There is no theme for the reader who is unwilling or unable to engage in this constructive labour.

One possible point of departure for an analysis of the theme of *Hippolytus* is the fact that the play is framed by a prologue and an epilogue spoken by two different goddesses: Aphrodite speaks the prologue and Artemis the epilogue. These goddesses represent supernatural forces beyond human control and influence and Aphrodite determines the outcome of the action. At the beginning of the play she initiates a sequence of actions which will destroy Hippolytus, her reason being that he has sinned against her. Being a goddess, she knows that her initial action is sufficient to ensure that Hippolytus is destroyed and she displays her knowledge about the future to the audience by giving a brief summary of what will happen in the play. Noticing this deterministic framework it would be reasonable to suggest that the play raises the problems of free will and responsibility. The play cannot, however, be construed as presenting a simple and crude form of determinism. For each of the main characters have weaknesses which are necessary for the tragic outcome of the action. If the characters had not displayed these weaknesses, Aphrodite's initial action would not have led to tragedy.

Phaedra's weakness is one of will. She fails to control her naturally amorous disposition:

We know the good, we apprehend it clearly.
But we can't bring it to achievement. Some
are betrayed by their own laziness, and others
value some other pleasure above virtue,

Phaedra says (ll. 380–383);[1] and it soon becomes clear that Phaedra values some other pleasure above virtue. For though her passion for Hippolytus is the work of Aphrodite, she not only fails when she tries to resist it, but the very form of the attempted resistance is a kind of indulgence. In his first speech to Artemis, Hippolytus draws a distinction between 'those who by instruction have profited/to learn' and those 'in whose very soul the seed/of Chastity toward all things alike/nature has deeply rooted' (ll. 79–82), and as the audience becomes acquainted with Phaedra, it becomes clear that her virtue is a result of instruction, of nurture rather than nature. She is born amorous rather than virtuous and she bemoans this inheritance: 'Mine is an inherited curse. It is not new' (l. 343). Her mother, Pasiphaë, conceived an unholy passion for Poseidon's white bull and gave birth to the Minotaur; and her sister Ariadne was Theseus' helpmate when he entered the labyrinth to kill the Minotaur, and later his mistress before he left her on the island of Naxos where she became the bride of Dionysus.

Hippolytus and Theseus have weaknesses which complement that of Phaedra's and which promote to an equal degree the tragic outcome. Hippolytus is one of those 'in whose very soul the seed/of Chastity toward all things alike/nature has deeply rooted', but his total devotion to Artemis and chastity excludes him from society. Socially he is an outsider: Theseus' bastard son with the amazon Antiope. He has been sent to Troezen, to his grandfather Pittheus, in order not to compete with Theseus' legitimate children for the throne of Athens. His religious

[1] Trans. David Grene in *Euripides I. The Complete Greek Tragedies*, David Grene and Richmond Lattimore (eds) (Chicago, 1955). All quotations from this edition.

attitude reinforces his position as an outsider. His attitude is exclusive. He sees himself as one apart. Consequently he is resented by other members of society; also, as it turns out, by Phaedra and Theseus. When Hippolytus rejects Phaedra's offer and abuses her, Phaedra's reason for striking back at him is 'that his [Hippolytus'] high heart/may know no arrogant joy at my life's shipwreck' (ll. 728–729). And Theseus refusal, in his rage, to listen to Hippolytus' defence is partly motivated by a resentment of what he considers excessive and hypocritical chastity: distancing himself from others in his virtue, Hippolytus is misunderstood and arouses resentment. As a man apart, he also fails to recognize that he is arousing resentment. His exclusiveness prevents sympathetic insight into other people's attitude to him. Thus he bears responsibility for those adverse human reactions which are instrumental in his destruction.

There is finally Theseus himself. He can function as Aphrodite's instrument because he has little or no control over his emotions. His reaction to his wife's death is a sentimental indulgence in grief and despair. His reaction to her suicide note is an uncontrolled outburst of rage. If Phaedra is incontinent when it comes to amorous passion and Hippolytus is the incarnation of continence, Theseus is incontinent in his grief and rage.

The two pairs of concepts freedom/responsibility and continence/incontinence can be used by the reader in his constructive work to grasp the point of the play as a work of art. However, the reader's constructive work must go further and further concepts must be brought in. For the play brings about the defeat of human happiness and this defeat is ultimately accidental: 'The care of God for us is a great thing', sings the chorus,

if a man believe it at heart:
it plucks the burden of sorrow from him.
So I have a secret hope
of someone, a God, who is wise and plans;
but my hopes grow dim when I see
the deeds of men and their destinies.

For fortune is ever veering, and the currents of life are shifting,
shifting, wandering forever.

(ll. 1102–1110)

Man hopes that there is a divine order, but his hopes are vain. The gods act not in accordance with a plan but for their own private reasons, to satisfy their own whims. The defeat of human happiness in *Hippolytus* cannot be construed as serving any higher purpose as it can in, for instance, *King Oedipus* where Oedipus' discovery of his own identity and guilt, and his consequent suffering, can be seen as confirming a divine order where accidents have no place. Aphrodite nourishes an ill-founded grudge against Hippolytus and makes him suffer out of all proportion to the alleged offence. And the action she initiates involves innocent people in the acutest suffering: it requires the death of Phaedra and brings Theseus the deepest misery. There is no reason for the suffering of these people. There is no divine order or purpose which confer meaning on this suffering.

The lack of a divine purpose in a world where human beings are at the mercy of forces beyond their control combine in *Hippolytus* with human weakness to produce tragedy. The tragedy is not merely one of loss and physical suffering, it also has an ethical aspect. It involves two of the characters in *miasma*, pollution, and it involves the destruction of the pure, the unpolluted character. Through their actions Phaedra and Theseus become 'unclean' or 'stained'. 'My hands are clean: the stain is in my heart', Phaedra answers when the nurse asks, 'There is no stain of blood upon your hands?' (ll. 316–317). However, the stain later spreads to her hands when she leaves the suicide note accusing Hippolytus of rape. She also contaminates Theseus by getting him to stain his hands with his son's blood. 'And so you leave me, my hands stained with murder', Theseus says to the dying Hippolytus. But the tragedy does not end there. 'No, for I free you from all guilt in this', (u.1448–1449) is Hippolytus' answer to Theseus, and the blame for the tragedy is placed firmly on Aphrodite. This is not merely a matter of placing the blame where it belongs, it is also a positive act of forgiveness and Theseus and Hippolytus are reconciled. The play thus distinguishes morally not only between man and man, but also between man and god. Whatever weaknesses man may have, at least he has the ability to forgive. There is no such virtue among the gods. At the end, man stands superior to the forces that break him in his sympathy and charity.

II

This brief and simplified description of the theme of Euripides' *Hippolytus* is built up by help of a number of general concepts through which the different features of the play are apprehended and related to each other: freedom, determinism, responsibility, weakness of will, continence/ incontinence, sympathy, guilt, human suffering, divine order, purity, pollution, forgiveness, charity, reconciliation. These concepts can suitably be labelled *thematic concepts* since they not only are employed to identify the theme of the work but are also constitutive of the theme as identified through the above analysis. Now theme is of the essence of literature and literary appreciation necessarily involves the recognition of theme. Assume that a reader failed to attempt, or to make any headway with, a thematic analysis of Euripides' *Hippolytus*. Such a reader might notice the two goddesses and their influence on the action but would not attribute any further significance to them and the influence they have. He might notice

Hippolytus' distinction between the naturally pure heart and those who must restrain their desires to remain pure. He might notice Phaedra's distinction between recognizing what is good and acting in accordance with this insight, and he might notice her explicit comment on weakness of will. However, he will not take these passages as having any further relevance for his apprehension of the play. For such a reader the passages will have a local relevance in the immediate context where they occur, but this reader will not take them out of this immediate context and try to understand them as contributing to the definition of the author's artistic purpose. Such a reader may also recognize Phaedra's essential weakness, her amorous nature and inability to master it, Hippolytus's exclusiveness and Theseus' repeated over-reactions, but he will not be able to see these weaknesses as together defining a general type of human weakness, as manifestations of continence/incontinence, nor to see them as qualities which contribute in their different ways to a tragic outcome. A reader, who for some reason fails to pursue the further significance in the play of Aphrodite's control of the outcome of the action and the weaknesses of the main characters; who fails to see the wider application in the play of the thematic concepts introduced into the speeches of Hippolytus, Phaedra and the chorus; and who could offer no way of seeing the play which would confer thematic significance on its various features, would fail in *appreciation* of the play as a literary work of art. His failure would be a failure to identify those features which make it a worthwhile object of appreciation and his failure would have consequences: either he must question the adequacy of his own appreciation of the play or he must dismiss the play as trivial. The identification of the theme of the play is not incidental to the apprehension of the play as a literary work. It does not constitute a further judgment coming in addition to the appreciation of the work. It is a judgment fixing the very nature of the particular work in question. Phaedra, described as the woman who falls in love with her stepson, invites him to her bed, is rejected, commits suicide and falsely accuses Hippolytus of rape, is the Phaedra of the myth and of many plays. Thus described she has no work-specific qualities. Euripides' Phaedra gains her individuality, her uniqueness among such other literary and mythical Phaedras as we know of, through the use to which Euripides puts her, through the relations in which he places her, through the perspective which he provides. And this use, these relations, and this perspective is apprehended through thematic concepts. A minimal description of Phaedra devoid of thematic concepts is by necessity a limited description: it represents a lack of perception of what the play presents to the reader.

Consider next a very different example:

O rose, thou art sick:
The invisible worm

That flies in the night,
In the howling storm,

Has found out thy bed
Of crimson joy;
And his dark secret love
Does thy life destroy.

Superficially it may seem that a short lyric poem like this does not offer the same opportunity for the application of thematic concepts as a tragedy. Clearly, it is in the nature of the genre that it cannot display the same complexity as the vastly longer works belonging to a genre like tragedy. The images presented in this poem do not function in a larger context including action and character, but address themselves directly to the reader in their concreteness. And the experience of these concrete images does not require thematic analysis. 'The Sick Rose', and any lyric like it, may seem to require a different mode of apprehension from a work like *Hippolytus*.

Not so. Here is a typical critical response to the poem

> . . . it is immediately apparent that the rose which sickens is a mortal rose. The human rose is attacked by a worm which possesses a *dark secret* called *love*, and it is an evil power which destroys the life of the rose. The flower is attacked in its *bed of crimson joy*, and this last imageric phrase can only stand for the sexuality of the mortal rose. The argument of the 'Sick Rose' differentiates between *love* and sexuality. Love here is destructive, it is a night-force, one of the links in the chain which binds delight in the 'Earth's Answer'. But sexuality, the experience in the *bed of crimson joy*, is the very centre of the life of the rose. When it is attacked the flower sickens and dies. What then is the *love* which destroys it? Blake uses the word deliberately, and if we think of it as a counter in a commonly played game of communication we shall more clearly see his intention. He uses a personal expression to convey the experience of sexuality because it is a something which he has discovered, as it were, for himself. But if he has discovered it, it is in spite of *love* as it is commonly called. Blake is concerned in this short poem with an incredible area of experience. In it sexuality is revealed as the basis of life, the social concept of love, as something destructive to life. Love in its social definition is a negative creed of secretive joyless forbidding; love in Blake's experience is a vital matter of joy, open and sensuous.[2]

Here the critic links together the images and symbols of the poem by

[2] Wolf Mankowitz, 'The Songs of Experience', *Politics and Letters* (1947); reprinted in Margaret Bottrall (ed.), '*Songs of Innocence and Experience.*' *A Casebook* (London 1970), 127–128.

bringing them together under different thematic descriptions which he interrelates in statements about the theme. Leaving aside the question of the correctness of this particular interpretation, it is clear that the same type of argument can be applied in connection with the apprehension of this poem as in connection with the apprehension of *Hippolytus*: failure to provide thematic concepts through which the poem can be apprehended, constitute a failure of appreciation of the poem. To construe the rose and the worm literally only, to concentrate on the concreteness of the imagery, is to rob the poem of purpose and meaning.

It is of course possible to reject the suggestion that theme is of the essence of literature simply by insisting on the irrelevance of the considerations brought forward in connection with the two above examples, for the question concerning how literary works are recognized and appreciated. It may be admitted that these considerations do indeed support the assumption that it is possible to extract a theme from perhaps most literary works, even from such types of work which superficially seems unpromising candidates for extracting themes. But, it may be argued, even if it was possible to interpret all literary works by help of thematic concepts, this kind of intellectualist approach is irrelevant to the appreciation of the work as literature. The suggestion that theme is of the essence of literature, it may be argued, gains its plausibility from a prevalent but misconceived and distorting intellectualist critical practice which has arisen as a result of the professionalization of literary studies. Such an argument has necessarily a limited appeal in an age where the professors and the critics have taken over as authorities on literature,[3] but apart from that it is possible to deploy yet another example which suggest that it is necessary for a piece of discourse to invite construal in thematic terms if it is to merit the label 'literary work'.

Consider Ezra Pound's 'In a Station of the Metro':

The apparition of these faces in the crowd;
Petals on a wet, black bough.

These two lines appear under their title as a separate poem in editions of Pound's poems. The 'poem' has only these two lines: two descriptions coupled together by the poet to form a unit. Apart from attending to the two images themselves and the juxtaposition in which they are placed there does not seem to be much one can do with the 'poem'. It does not invite construal in thematic terms. No clue is provided in the poem which may indicate that the details of the images and their juxtaposition have some significance, some function beyond that of presenting a juxta-

---

[3] I have recently come to suspect that this argument has a much more powerful appeal than I have so far believed: I have repeatedly been under fire for relying too much on academic practice for examples and paradigms.

position of images. Nor was the 'poem' meant to invite or yield to construal in thematic terms. It is an imagist 'poem' written in accordance with a programme for literature which holds that it is a legitimate, important and independent function of literature to convey directly a fresh impression.[4] Despite the fact that Pound's lines have rhetorical merit, or what one could call literary merit in a wide sense (the images are precise and the juxtaposition is striking), one would, I think, hesitate to call them a literary work, a genuine poem. Considered as a piece of literary discourse, the lines give the impression of incompleteness: if a reader had no knowledge of their origin or of the fact that they are presented under an independent heading in collections of poems, these lines would naturally appear to him as a fragment, as needing completion; that is, if indeed he construed them as piece of literary discourse.

As a contrast consider the following two lines:

Swiftly the years, beyond recall.
Solemn the stillness of this spring morning.

These lines do not leave an impression of incompleteness, of being fragmentary. Cut off from independent generic information about these lines it is still possible for a reader to justify construing them as an independent poem: they do have a point beyond that of presenting a juxtapositions of two descriptions conveying a fresh impression, and it is a point which is captured in thematic terms:

Two experiences, two concretions of emotions, are
juxtaposed to yield the proportion, 'My feelings of
transience are held in tension with my desire to
linger amid present pleasures, as the flight of time
is in tension with the loveliness of this spring morning'.[5]

This poem has obvious limitations which are due to its brevity: the contrast *passing time/present moment* remains undeveloped and it is unclear what the poet might have intended to make of it. But this is a defect of a complete poem where the poet has tried to deal with too large a theme in too small a format. Unlike these lines or any conventional poem like 'The Sick Rose', 'In a Station of the Metro' does not yield to thematic interpretation and it is not unreasonable to suggest that the impression of incompleteness which it gives is due to this.

The incompleteness of Pound's lines together with the imagist intention that these lines should convey directly a fresh impression rather than yield a theme, explain the hesitation to call them a genuine poem, a literary work. If it had been part of the imagist intention that the lines should

[4] See T. E. Hulme, *Speculations*, 2nd edn. (London, 1936), 162ff.
[5] Hugh Kenner, *The Poems of Ezra Pound* (Norfolk, Connecticut, 1951), 90.

yield a theme, then a reader would have to approach these lines as he approaches Blake's 'The Sick Rose' or any other poem. That is, no question about the logical status of the lines would then arise for him, only questions of value and success. A failure to find a theme would then lead to a negative evaluation of the poem, but there would be no reason for the reader to hesitate about what he is faced with. The intention is constitutive of the logical status of the lines if the intention is unambiguous. However, the imagist intention is not unambiguous. The intention is that these lines should 'convey directly a fresh impression'. This intention is accompanied by a claim that to convey directly fresh impressions is a characteristic function of literature. If one accepts this claim, Pound's lines must be seen as a genuine poem complete in itself because they serve this function. Now if Pound's lines had yielded to thematic analysis there would have been no reason to deny them the status of an independent poem which the imagists claim for them by presenting them in a collection of poems under an independent heading, though one might have taken issue with the reason for seeing the lines this way. However, since these lines do not yield to thematic analysis and thus appear incomplete, and since the primary intention is the specific one that they should 'convey directly a fresh impression' rather than the general one that they should be construed as a literary works to be dealt with by the reader accordingly, the status of these lines is left uncertain. If this argument has force, then theme is essential to the very definition of what literature should be, and the hypothesis that theme may be universal in literature but not essential to it must be rejected.

III

If theme is of the essence of literature and literary appreciation always and necessarily involves the recognition of theme, then thematic concepts are constitutive of literary appreciation, and the nature of thematic concepts becomes a central problem in literary aesthetics. A superficial look through the literary classics and the standard works of the critical tradition leaves no doubt about the diversity of thematic concepts. Such concepts seem to come from most areas of human experience and to represent various perspectives. A useful preliminary move in any attempt to achieve some sort of general characterization of these concepts is to distinguish them from other types of interpretative concepts. There exist today fairly powerful theoretical 'schools' in literary criticism which recommend that literary interpretation should employ conceptual frameworks which are not only not generally known to an educated public, but which are dependent for their significance on special theories about the human mind, society, language, etc. Since any one of these conceptual frameworks require special knowledge which in principle cannot have been available to all interested readers of literature (literature has a vastly longer history than any of these theories) they cannot be constitutive of literary appreciation. Such *esoteric interpretative concepts* do not contribute to the diversity of *thematic* concepts which is in question here. They are not logically on a level with thematic concepts which are constitutive of appreciation, and they pose problems of a different order from the problems under discussion here.[6] With regard to thematic concepts themselves, it is possible, despite their diversity, to introduce a general distinction between *topical* thematic concepts and *perennial* thematic concepts. Topical thematic concepts define problems and issues of interest to a group of people (a society, a class, a religious group, etc.) for a certain period. These problems and issues are related to a specific situation in which that group of people find themselves at that particular time. Problems and issues of this type are often of burning interest to the group and may involve a conflict between subsections of the group. When, however, the situation changes, the problems disappear and interest in them vanishes. Consequently, a literary work which can only be interpreted by help of topical thematic concepts has a limited interest. It has an interest only for a limited group of people at such a time as they find the issues with which the work deals important, and for such people as for some reason are interested in this group, its history, its opinions, etc. A theme of such limited interest is an artistic weakness in a work. It constitutes a certain type of artistic failure. Elizabeth Gaskell's *Mary Barton* was one of several novels written on the 'Condition of England' question. John Barton, George Wilson, and their families, the Carsons, etc., are all representatives of the parts in the conflict between rich and poor, the parts in the confrontation between the two nations. 'Mrs Gaskell's strength in *Mary Barton*', says Stephen Gill in his introduction to the Penguin edition,[7] 'is that she manages to capture within a limited range of effects some sense of the really fundamental issues of the social situation in the 1840s'. On the other hand, Stephen Gill maintains, comparing Mary Barton with Dickens' *Bleak House*, 'Mrs Gaskell does not have the intense imagination which could see in the *fact* of a disease an emblem of essential truths about society'.[8] The thematic concepts which are sufficient to characterize adequately the 'fundamental issues of the social situation in the 1840s' are not those in which 'essential truths about society' can be expressed. To see in a fact

[6] I have tried to deal with some of these problems elsewhere. See my articles 'On Unilluminating Criticism', *British Journal of Aesthetics* **21** (1981), and 'Criticism and Appreciation', in Peter Lamarque ed., *Philosophy and Fiction. Essays in Literary Aesthetics*, (Aberdeen, 1983).

[7] Harmondsworth, 1970, 21.

[8] Ibid., 13.

the emblem of a general condition and to shape that fact so as to create a profound characterization of this general condition, is what Dickens does in most of his novels. In *Bleak House* the dominant fact is the Court of Chancery and the description it is given involves necessarily social comment on this institution in Dickens' day. 'I mention here', says Dickens in his preface to the novel, 'that everything set forth in these pages concerning the Court of Chancery is substantially true, and within the truth.' However, today this social comment seems incidental to the Court's general significance as a metaphor for the society which civilized man has created for himself. There is nothing like this in *Mary Barton*. Mrs Gaskell's descriptions of social facts do not have this deeper significance. And this lack of a deeper significance affects the novel's stature as literature. *Mary Barton* 'survives', says Walter Allen, 'largely as an historical document illustrating early Victorian attitudes to a social problem and the early Victorian fear, which amounted almost to hysteria, of the poor'.[9] *Mary Barton* fails as literature because it is exclusively topical. A work with a theme which can be formulated only in topical thematic terms is *artistically* or *aesthetically* weak.

Perennial thematic concepts define what, borrowing the title of Thomas Nagel's recent book, may be called *mortal questions*. Mortal questions are concerned with 'mortal life: how to understand it and how to live it'.[10] They are permanent foci of interest in a culture because they are unavoidable. The concepts which define these mortal questions are the fingerprints of the culture. They identify the culture and they are permanent. When they change, the culture itself changes. The questions they define may change, and the application of the concepts will develop with changing circumstances, but the concepts themselves remain the same. In Kingsley Amis' *Lucky Jim*, Jim is at one stage described in this way:

> He felt more than ever before that what he said and did arose not out of any willing on his part, nor even out of boredom, but out of a kind of sense of situation. And where did that sense come from if, as it seemed, he took no share in willing it? With disquiet, he found that words were forming in his mind, words which, because he could think of no others, he'd very soon hear himself uttering (Ch. 18).

It is unnecessary here to put a name to those forces which determine Jim's words and actions. They are impersonal forces which he feels he does not control and which push him towards a life in submission to those he admires least and those he positively hates. But these forces do not win. Jim is saved from a tragic fate by luck, but not by luck only. When the millionaire Gore-Urquhart offers him a job as his private

[9] Walter Allen, *The English Novel* (Harmondsworth, 1958),185.
[10] Thomas Nagel, *Mortal Questions* (Cambridge, 1979), ix.

secretary and thus an escape from 'the situation' which Jim feels controls him, Gore-Urquhart gives a reason for picking Jim:

> It's not that you've the qualifications, for this or any other work, but there are plenty who have. You haven't got the disqualifications, though, and that's much rarer (Ch. 23).

Jim is saved by his personal qualities. He does not have the weaknesses which will make him an unavoidable victim of those forces which he feels control his life. He can be understood as being the opposite type of character to those the reader meets in *Hippolytus* where the weakness of each character promotes the tragic outcome of the action. In *Lucky Jim* luck is still luck in the sense that Jim attains happiness through a series of accidents. But it is *Jim's* luck. If his personal qualities had been different, if he had had the normal disqualifications for the job as Gore-Urquhart's private secretary, he would not have been *Lucky* Jim. Jim is shown to be ultimately free to break out of the situation which he feels controls him, but it is accidental that he is offered opportunity to escape and it is accidental that he has the personal qualities to make use of the opportunity.

Though this may be a simplification of the way *Lucky Jim* handles the issues of determinism, luck, accident, weakness of will, responsibility, etc., the interpretation suggested above still makes the point that a case can be made for interpreting *Lucky Jim* in almost exactly the same terms as *Hippolytus*. Of course, these two works give wholly different applications to these concepts, but the thematic concepts are the same: these are perennial thematic concepts.

Literary appreciation is an effort to recognize the qualities making a literary work a worthwhile object of appreciation. It must therefore be an effort to see a text as expressive not of just any theme, but of such a theme as maximizes the aesthetic reward it offers to the reader. An interpretation of a literary work employing perennial thematic concepts is superior to one employing merely topical thematic concepts exactly in that it defines a richer and more rewarding experience of the work than the latter. It is possible to see *Lucky Jim* as a novel of class-conflict within an academic setting, or as being simply about 'the boorishness provoked by an insufferable sham culture in a provincial backwater',[11] but it gives the novel another dimension and a deeper significance if one concentrates on the perennial thematic concepts indicated in the title of the novel and in the descriptions of Jim's thoughts, and tries to apprehend the novel as a whole through these concepts. Literary appreciation thus always involves an attempt to apprehend the theme of a work using such thematic concepts as come closest to being perennial thematic concepts. Topical thematic concepts can function as stepping stones in a hierarchy of descriptions

---

[11] W. W. Robson, *Modern English Literature* (Oxford, 1970), 154.

leading up to a more general description in perennial thematic terms But a formulation of theme which does not go beond the level of topical thematic concepts aborts the aesthetic significance of the work and is therefore unsatisfactory.

IV

Perennial thematic concepts, it was suggested above, can be characterized as the fingerprints of the culture. Questions about how to understand and how to live 'this mortal life' are inescapable, but the concepts which are used to form these questions are peculiar to a culture. And they are not only peculiar to a culture: they also have a special importance in the culture. They do not merely have an everyday use (indeed, many perennial concepts have no everyday use) but they are also interpreted and developed in practices and forms of discourse which the culture has evolved specifically to deal with mortal questions. The list of concepts employed in the thematic analysis of Euripides' *Hippolytus* can be divided in two parts. The first half of the list comprises concepts like 'freedom', 'determinism', 'responsibility', 'continence', 'weakness of will', 'sympathy', which play a key role in the formulation of central philosophical problems. They have been the foci of philosophical controversies for more than 2,000 years, and as these controversies have developed, the concepts have been interpreted and re-interpreted. The second part of this list comprises concepts like 'divine order', 'purity', 'pollution', 'forgiveness' and 'charity' which have received a significance over and above that which they have in everyday use through the role they play in religious belief, ritual, and in theological discourse. These concepts define central theological issues and all of them have been with us for more than 2,000 years. Each of the concepts have gone through transformations, but it is still reasonable to see them as defining the same issues, as being the same thematic concepts: for example, pollution as it is defined in Greek culture and religion is different from the Christian notion of sin, but they are both interpretations of a more general notion of human corruption.

I now want to suggest that perennial thematic concepts are typically philosophical or theological concepts if one understands both the term 'philosophical' and the term 'theological' in a broad sense. This is not to suggest that perennial thematic concepts receive their definition in philosophical discourse or through the role they play in religious practice and are then borrowed by the reader of literature who wants to appreciate a literary work of art. On the contrary, I would suggest that perennial thematic concepts achieve the importance they have within the culture and receive their content both from the role they play in philosophical discourse and religious practice, on the one hand, and, on the other, from the role they play in literary appreciation. The philosophical or theological use does not have logical priority over their use in literary appreciation. Philosophical concepts like 'freedom', 'determinism', 'weakness of will', 'responsibility', 'sympathy' and the like are interpreted and developed not only in philosophical discussion about the nature of the reality to which they refer, but also through their application in the appreciation of works of art like *Hippolytus* and *Lucky Jim*. This is not to suggest that philosophy and literature 'do the same thing' only in different ways, or that literature could, as Matthew Arnold says it will,[12] replace religion. It is not to suggest that literature offers the *exemplum* to philosophy's concept or religion's ethical precept. It *is* to suggest that in a literary culture like the civilization of the West which traces its origins back to ancient Greece, concepts defining mortal questions are filled with meaning beyond that which they have in everyday discourse and in application to everyday situations by being the focus of interest in literature as well as being constitutive of philosophical discourse and religious practice. It is the role which these concepts play in literature, philosophy and religious practice which make them perennial thematic concepts, and they have become perennial thematic concepts because they are fruitful foci of both, on the one hand, intellectual discursive interest or religious practice, and, on the other, imaginative creative interest.

If perennial thematic concepts are typically either philosophical or theological concepts, then it follows that there is a special connection between literature and philosophy and literature and religion. Looking back to the birth of Western literature in ancient Greece, there is nothing surprising in such a special connection: literature, philosophy and religion all developed in their different ways from myth. And looking at the important position literature occupies among the values of our culture, it is unsurprising that literature should work with themes which are central also to spiritual activities with much the same cultural importance as literature. And with regard to the contrast between topical and perennial thematic concepts, the special connection between literature and philosophy/religious practice, mediated through perennial thematic concepts, explains how an interpretation employing perennial thematic concepts defines a richer and more rewarding experience of a work than one employing merely topical thematic concepts, and in what sense a literary work which yields to analysis in perennial thematic concepts has a deeper and more universal interest than a work which can only be interpreted by help of topical thematic concepts.

However, there is a difficulty about the suggestion that there is a special

[12] 'The Study of Poetry' in *English Literature and Irish Politics. The Complete Prose Works of Matthew Arnold*, IX, R. H. Super (ed.) (Ann Arbor, 1973), 161–162.

link between philosophy and religious practice on the one hand, and literature on the other: there seems, in fact to be a large number of thematic concepts employed in literary appreciation which are certainly not topical thematic concepts, which do seem to define questions concerning how to understand and live this mortal life, but which one could not call philosophical or theological concepts without stretching these terms beyond the limit of their usefulness. In the critical analysis of Blake's 'The Sick Rose' quoted above, the central statement of the theme of the poem runs: 'In [the poem] sexuality is revealed as the basis of life, the social concept of love as something destructive of life'. The concepts employed here to state the theme are not immediately recognizable as philosophical or theological concepts. They seem to be ordinary common-sense concepts which receive new significance from their literary application, and the interpretation of 'The Sick Rose' is none the worse for that. Consequently, it may be argued, it is impossible to maintain that perennial thematic concepts are necessarily foci of general interest in the culture, that they necessarily define either central philosophical problems or are constitutive of central aspects of religious practice.

There is, however, less to this argument than meets the eye. For while it is certainy true that there is a broad range of thematic concepts which at first glance seem to play no role in the definition of philosophical issues or religious practice but which seem to mark out important areas of common human experience, these thematic concepts will nevertheless be closely related either to such issues as define an area of inquiry which is in a broad sense philosophical, or to such concepts as are constitutive of religious belief and ritual. A thematic interpretation of a literary work is a description of it. This description will build up a network of concepts which generalize the significance of the several aspects and elements of the work and tie these aspects and elements together: this is the way in which the artistic design of the work is apprehended. The description will move from the particular to the general and will have different levels of generality. It will naturally employ concepts which are not themselves philosophical or theological, but which form the basis for the application to the work of such concepts. What gives the theme, identified in the quoted critical comment on 'The Sick Rose', of the conflict between sexuality as the basis of life and the social concept of love as being destructive of life, a deeper significance, is that it is an instance of the more general theme, popular in romantic writings, literary and philosophical, of natural individual spontaneity versus artificial social constraint. Related to *this* theme is the still more general theme of the conflict between individual interest, individual needs, and individual satisfaction, on the one hand, and, on the other, the interests of society, protected through constraints imposed on the individual. This theme is as old as Plato and has always been central in moral philosophy. So the theme identified by the quoted critic in 'The Sick Rose' has a clear relationship to a family of concepts which also receive an interpretation in philosophy and define a perennial philosophical problem. A total absence in the culture of interest in the general theme of the conflict between individual interest and social constraint, would mean that the interpretation of 'The Sick Rose' quoted above would make little sense since one would not then see the contrast individual sexuality/social concept of love as particularly worthy of interest and attention.

In this discussion it is important to keep in mind that the general theme of the conflict between individual interest and social constraint does not exist prior to the treatment it is given in philosophy and literature. It is through this treatment that the theme is defined, and given its importance and that the concepts defining the theme become perennial thematic concepts. It is important to keep this in mind because it focuses attention on the fact that literary appreciation does not involve understanding a literary work as an *exemplum* of a general concept. Rather, apprehending the various aspects and elements of the work through a network of concepts, as the reader does in literary appreciation, involves a mutual interpretation of work and concept. 'The Sick Rose' is an irreducible metaphorical presentation of an aspect of the general conflict. Through the symbols of the worm and the rose and the characteristics they are given, the poem defines natural individual sexuality and its opposite, conventional love (that is, this is what the poem does if one accepts the interpretation quoted above). At the same time these concepts organize the poem for the reader and enable him to bring its elements together and to see it as a metaphorical presentation of this general conflict. As a last addition to the network of concepts which constitute literary appreciation, may come the perennial thematic concepts which have given direction to the interpretation and which guarantee both that the work has universal interest and that the interpretation has explained why this is so. However, this last step is often in itself of little importance in appreciation and sometimes it may even be undesirable. Literary appreciation is the appreciation of how a work interprets and develops the general issues which the reader identifies through the application of thematic concepts. *Little Dorrit*, says Lionel Trilling in his introduction to that novel,

> is about society in relation to the individual human will. This is certainly a matter general enough—general to the point of tautology, were it not for the bitterness with which the tautology is articulated, were it not for the specificity, and the subtlety, and the boldness with which the human will is anatomized.[13]

[13] Lionel Trilling, 'Introduction', *Little Dorrit* (Oxford Ill. Dickens) (Oxford, 1953), vi. I have found occasion to quote this before. See my 'Literary Aesthetics and Literary Practice', *Mind* 90 (1981), but it bears repeating.

The perennial thematic concepts are, by themselves, vacuous. They cannot be separated from the way they are 'anatomized' in literature and philosophy. And in literary appreciation it is the 'specificity', and 'subtlety' and 'boldness' of the artistic vision, the vision which is apprehended through thematic interpretation, which is the focus of interest. The focus of interest in literary appreciation is on the description of the work leading up to the application of the perennial thematic concepts. Of course, successful appreciation presupposes that the implied perennial theme is recognized, but to state it is often to state the obvious, and sometimes a statement using perennial thematic concepts will simply draw attention away from the interpretation which gives these concepts content. So literary appreciation does rely on, and literary criticism is full of, concepts which are not topical, which do mark out important areas of common human experience, but which are not philosophical or theological concepts. But these are concepts which figure in the interpretative argument on levels below that where philosophical and theological thematic concepts are brought in, and their presence is justified only if they do form the basis for the application to the work of philosophical and theological thematic concepts.

V

There is one conclusion which to some may seem natural but which cannot in fact be drawn from the present argument, that is, that literature in some way deals with the same issues as philosophy and religious belief. It does not. It is of the essence of philosophical discourse that it is about issues. These issues are defined through thematic concepts, and philosophical discourse is concerned with the nature of the reality to which the concepts refer. Thus these concepts are constitutive of philosophy as an intellectual activity. The situation for religious belief and religious ritual is analogous. Relgious belief is formulated by help of concepts which cannot be removed or changed without changing the belief, and the nature of religious ritual is defined through concepts which, if changed, changes the nature of the ritual. And the interpretation of theological concepts is aimed at increasing the understanding of the reality which they purport to describe. Now literature is attached to thematic concepts only indirectly. The theme of a literary work emerges from the subject it has, the way in which the subject is presented, the rhetorical features used in its presentation, and the structure it is given. Sometimes thematic concepts suitable for formulating the theme of a work can be found in the text of the work itself, but mostly it is the reader who has to bring these concepts to the text. The connection between the thematic concepts and the literary work is established through his creation of a network of concepts enabling him both to tie together the different elements and aspects he recognizes the work as having, and to establish what and how thematic concepts can be applied to the work. It is this constructive labour which is literary appreciation. Literary appreciation is concerned with the application of a set of thematic concepts to a particular literary work. It is not concerned with any further reality to which these concepts may refer in their other uses. Literary appreciation mediates the connection between the work and thematic concepts; it does no more. Literature offers its own alternative realm of application for thematic concepts. It offers an imaginative rather than a discursive interpretation. And this possibility of applying thematic concepts in literary appreciation does not contribute to philosophical or theological insight. It constitutes its own form of insight, its own kind of interpretation of thematic concepts. The nature of this insight can be analysed by giving a description of how thematic concepts is attached to literary works. But one can do nothing further to throw light on it.

The independence of literary theme from philosophical and theological theme can be illustrated with a final example from *Hippolytus*. Central to a thematic analysis of this play is the concept of pollution. But the particular view of the nature of human corruption defined by the concept of *miasma* is no longer theologically interesting. The concept of human corruption has been re-interpreted and the view of human corruption as a stain which can spread, as pollution which can contaminate like a disease, today appears as a metaphorical way of construing human corruption which makes no claim to literal truth. However, the concept of pollution still has interest as a thematic concept in literary appreciation. Interest in this concept is sustained by the fact that it is applicable in appreciation of works like *Hippolytus* which draw on a religious practice where the concept of *miasma* is central, as well as in the appreciation of a host of modern works where the *image* of human corruption as pollution, as disease is central: 'There is not a drop of Tom's corrupted blood but propagates infection and contagion somewhere', says Dickens in his description of Tom-all-Alone's in *Bleak House* and he is speaking of moral corruption; Oswald in Ibsen's *Ghosts* inherits his father's moral corruption in the form of syphilis; and examples like this could be multiplied. The interpretation of human corruption as pollution is still with us, but as a literary rather than as a theological or philosophical interpretation. Literary interpretation of human corruption is thus independent of the way in which it is interpreted in religious practice or philosophy.

If the present argument is correct, then the *dulce et utile* dichotomy which has provided the framework for every discussion of the relationship between philosophy and literature since Plato, is inadequate. Literature must be worthwhile, but its value does not consists in its being either *dulce* or *utile*. Literature exercises the intellect rather than the emotions, but it does not instruct in the sense in which philosophy can be said to instruct. Literature does not compete with philosophy, nor does it complement it. Literature and philosophy meet in thematic concepts, but it is not a meeting which leads to marriage or even to holding hands. The relationship is a more distant one: literature and philosophy are neighbours in the same important area of a culture.

Dostoyevsky: Psychology and the Novelist

İLHAM DİLMAN

I

In a lecture on 'Science and Psychology' Dr Drury distinguishes between 'a psychology which has insight into individual characters' and 'a psychology which is concerned with the scientific study of universal types', one which comprises 'those subjects that are studied in a university faculty of psychology'. The former, and not the latter, he says, is psychology in 'the original meaning of the word'. 'We might say of a great novelist such as Tolstoy or George Eliot (he goes on) that they show profound psychological insight into the characters they depict . . . In general, it is the great novelists, dramatists, biographers, historians, that are the real psychologists.'[1]

In another paper, 'Philosophy, Metaphysics and Psycho-analysis', Professor Wisdom compares and contrasts Freud and Dostoyevsky. Freud's 'scientific terms (he writes) give us a wider but too distant view of reality—so distant that we no longer feel the sorrow and the joy. And as the detail of the concrete diminishes one loses grasp of what it is that is being talked about.'[2]

Freud, despite his scientific pretensions, is a clinical psychologist, and not an experimental one, and as such he too gives 'insight into individual characters'. It is true that he is concerned with the distortions of emotional life and the arrests in its development; but so was Dostoyevsky. Unlike Tolstoy who painted a moving picture of the normalities of life,[3] Dostoyevsky was primarily interested in what is often concealed in these normalities: 'What most people regard as fantastic and lacking in universality (he wrote to Strackhov), *I* hold to be the inmost essence of truth'.[4] The fact remains that Freud dealt with and wrote about real people, whereas the characters in Dostoyevsky's novels are a product of Dostoyevsky's imgination. But, in that case, how, and in what sense, can they give

[1] *The Danger of Words* (Routledge and Kegan Paul, 1973), 37, 41.
[2] *Philosophy and Psycho-Analysis* (Basil Blackwell, 1953), 261.
[3] See Lionel Trilling, 'Anna Karenina', *The Opposing Self* (Secker and Warburg, 1955), 72.
[4] Letter, 26 February 1896, quoted in Miriam Allott, *Novelists on the Novel* (Routledge and Kegan Paul, 1959) 68.

us insight into individual characters and advance our knowledge of mankind?

Freud's case histories are descriptions of actual people; they are records of Freud's observations of individual patients. Dostoyevsky's novels, on the other hand, are works of imagination. Yet they are studies of the human soul in a sense in which Freud's case histories are not. The case histories are records of the material for a different kind of study. Whereas the novels are themselves an exploration of the soul in the sense in which a sculpture or drawing may be a study of the human form, of the human body in its visible aspect. In contemplating it we get an understanding which our direct experience has not been able to give us. Thus Camus said that Dostoyevsky had revealed to him 'la nature humaine'. Nietzsche said that Dostoyevsky was the only psychologist from whom he had anything to learn about the psychology of the criminal, the slave mentality, and the nature of resentment.[5] And in an interesting piece on *The Brothers Karamazov*, Eliseo Vivas says that 'it is a commonplace that Dostoyevsky anticipated Freud . . .; all the insights that have become commonplaces since Freud were clearly his own'.[6]

Let us try to see what this comes to in the particular case of Dostoyevsky's portrayal of Raskolnikov in *Crime and Punishment*. How does this portrayal embody psychological insight which contributes to the truth contained in the novel? Philip Rahv says that 'the story is almost entirely given over to detection—not of the criminal, though, but of his motive'.[7] I think that there is more in the novel that this; though that this is part of the novel is undeniable. The novel is a study of crime and punishment, as its title aptly suggests, of the evil that enters into the soul of a man who consents to kill another human being, and of the way he can find his way back to the good through the acceptance of punishment.[8] Dostoyevsky is interested in the conditions that make the soul vulnerable to such an evil.

He is interested in the *ideas* which turn Raskolnikov towards the crime he commits and give it the aspect under whicn he sees it. The ideas, of course, like the characters of a novel, are part of the *content* of the novel, so that just as the novel examines the characters it also examines these ideas, and does so critically. This gives the novel a *philosophical* aspect. Dostoyevsky is equally concerned to understand what in Raskolnikov makes him a prey to these ideas. This gives it a *psychological* aspect. Put it like this. The ideas have an appeal to certain kinds of individuals because of what they are

[5] See René Wellek, 'Introduction', *Dostoyevsky* (Prentice-Hall, 1962), 3.

[6] 'The Two Dimensions of Reality in *The Brothers Karamazov*', Wellek, op. cit., 74.

[7] 'Dostoyevsky in *Crime and Punishment*', Wellek, op. cit., 20.

[8] For a discussion of this question see Dilman, 'Socrates and Dostoyevsky on Punishment', *Philosophy and Literature*, **1**, No. 1 (Fall 1976).

like themselves, I mean the ideas, and so a critical interest in their content is partly philosophical and partly moral in character. But they are attractive to certain individuals also because of what these individuals are like, and a critical interest in the individuals is partly psychological and partly moral. So Dostoyevsky is certainly interested in the *psychology* of his hero and in his state of soul.

These two, psychology and state of soul, are not the same thing, though they overlap. Raskolnikov's psychology involves his character, the form of his relationships, the frustrations which these impose on him, the way he reacts to these frustrations, the compensations he seeks, what he does with his anger and resentment, how he responds to other people's expectations of him. His state of soul brings in the dimension of his relation to good and evil, and the portrayal of this, in turn, involves the moral perspective of the novel. Dostoyevsky is interested in both and in the interaction between them. He is interested in the way pride, humiliation, anger and resentment can turn into a force for evil and feed on each other, and in the way they lend their energy to ideas that inspire the desire for grandeur in the self and contempt for other people. He is equally interested in the way the ideas which Raskolnikov adopts—the utilitarian, socialist and Nietzschean ideas which were prominent among the young radical intellectuals in Dostoyevsky's Russia—reinforce Raskolnikov's pride and anger, and organize his destructive tendencies by giving him an aim which he would not have had without them.

This is one half of the two-way interaction, the side of evil, at any rate that is what Dostoyevsky would have called it, the side in which the self is engaged in a struggle to gain power, prominence, recognition and gratification at the expense of other people, a struggle to turn away from passivity and guilt, to seek compensation for humiliations, real and imaginary. The other side is the side of good, the side from which forgiveness arises, hatred is mitigated, grudges are given up, guilt is acknowledged and paid for, depression worked through, and an interest is born in other people through which the self is transcended and the person becomes himself. Dostoyevsky is interested in the way such good can come into a person's life from outside, through contact with other people and new ideas—thus Sonia and the way she turns Raskolnikov to her faith—as well as through the mobilization of what is already there though it has been kept at bay and put into cold storage.

As far as Raskolnikov's motive for the murder goes what is in question is the first half of the interaction between his psychology and his radical ideals. Even then Dostoyevsky gives us an insight into the other side of Raskolnikov's nature, the side which constitutes the good in him from the novel's perspective. He shows us how it constitutes a threat for Raskolnikov, a threat to his defences against exploitation. There is the suggestion that he has been manipulated by his mother, and still feels vulnerable to it, and that the morality which she has transmitted to him spells out danger to his autonomy. He doesn't know how to turn away from that danger and achieve autonomy without rejecting his mother's morality which is part of him. His attempts to achieve autonomy at its expense, therefore, are doomed to failure. They take a particularly extreme and destructive form because of the guilt and rage that have built up in him, each reinforcing the other. But he finds that the supreme destructive act in which he counts on achieving freedom only brings him into conflict with that side of him he has succeeded in denying. The very extremity of this act, paradoxically, makes the denial more difficult to maintain. The novel gives us a fine portrait of the way it is gradually undone and hints at the way Raskolnikov is finally able to find salvation and achieve freedom in accepting this other side, in giving up the pursuits in which he has sought autonomy, and in paying for the guilt he has collected in the process.

I think that it is for this reason that W. D. Snodgrass, in a very perceptive essay on the first part of the novel, an essay entitled 'Crime for Punishment',[9] argues, with some plausibility, that the murder was Raskolnikov's way of seeking punishment for the selfish and destructive way in which he has treated those close to him both in his feelings and in reality. He quotes some words by Simone Weil which shed light on what he means: 'A hurtful act is the transference to others of the degradation which we bear in ourselves. That is why we are inclined to commit such acts as a way of deliverence'. In my reading of the novel, Raskolnikov had certainly invested the pawnbroker Alyona Ivanovna with all the qualities he hated in himself and exaggerated in his mother. No doubt, what she was like in herself, a moneylender, capitalizing on other people's needs, thriving on their poverty, made her a suitable foil for his projective phantasies. This, so far, is the transference which Simone Weil speaks of, though only in phantasy. Being thus built up into a hateful figure the pawnbroker attracts Raskolnikov's hatred and rage. In her he wants to obliterate what, without recognizing it clearly, he finds hateful in himself. It is in this way that the hurtful act is undertaken as a means of deliverance.

It does not, however, succeed in this aim. It only entrenches Raskolnikov further in the self from which he wants to be delivered, uncontributing, parasitic, withdrawn, suspicious; and it makes him more like the moneylender. So it heightens his own inner condemnation of the side of his personality from which he had hoped to be delivered. This, in turn, opens the way to a different form of deliverance—through repentance, reparation and forgiveness, to be worked out in the acceptance of punishment.[10]

[9] *The Hudson Review* **13** (Spring 1960).

[10] This theme of paying in punishment not only for the crime that one has committed, but for everything in one which creates an inclination towards it, whether one in fact commits the crime or not, is one that receives prominence in *The Brothers Karamazov*.

If my analysis is correct and the murder was Raskolnikov's way of seeking deliverance from the evil which his identification with his mother represented for him, does it follow that it was also, for him, a way of seeking a more constructive rejection of this identification, one which does not involve a turning away from his mother, one in which he is prepared to nurse her infirmities and make amends for the pain he has inflicted on her? In short, does it follow that the murder was a way of seeking a reintegration with the good through punishment for his destructiveness and selfishness? I do not think so. The most I feel I can say for this is that the good in Raskolnikov which he had kept at bay and from which he had largely succeeded in dissociating himself gained strength by being outraged. So once the crime was committed this part of him did really begin to crave for punishment, as Porfiry the investigating magistrate, well recognized. I don't think, however, that we could say that Roskolnikov committed the crime in order to find punishment and, through it, a reintegration with the good.

We could, perhaps, say, with Snodgrass, that the murder was a desperate attempt on Raskolnikov's part to provoke the good to declare itself. In this respect Snodgrass compares Raskolnikov to a child who 'deliberately disobeys to find out if the rules really exist, if behaviour has limits, if his family lives inside solid walls'. The punishment he receives gives him an assurance that this is so (op. cit., 246). But, again, this is not the same thing as saying that Raskolnikov committed the murder for the sake of the punishment he unconsciously hoped it would make inevitable.

I have characterized the murder as an extreme act in which Raskolnikov misguidedly seeks freedom and autonomy. Especially in the first part of the novel Dostoyevsky paints a vivid picture of Raskolnikov's immaturity and lack of direction, and of how little he feels a person in his own right. He has given up supporting himself, left the university, has fallen behind with his rent, feels at the mercy of his landlady. He even forgets to eat his meals and daydreams of getting rich all at once[11]—that is (as it is put in the book later) he 'wanted something for nothing, quickly, without having to work for it' (p. 170). Here we have an expression of that side of him which emulates what he hated in the pawnbroker. The long letter he gets from his mother and his reaction to its content shed much light on his immaturity and the way it has been shaped in his relation with his mother.

It is interesting that there is little mention of Raskolnikov's father in the book who, we are told, died when Raskolnikov was very young: 'Remember, dear (his mother writes in her letter), how as a child, while your father was still with us, you used to lisp your prayers on my knees and how happy we all were then?' (p. 57). In the letter we are given a glimpse

---

[11] *Crime and Punishment*, trans. by David Magarshack (Penguin Classics, 1956), 47.

of his mother's subtlety. Under the guise of innocent motherly concern she tries to manipulate Raskolnikov's thoughts and to play on his feelings. Emotionally she has got him just where she wants him to be: 'You are all we have (she says more than once) and our only hope of a better and brighter future'—'we' being his mother and his sister Dunya.

The letter shows her as taking on herself to arrange Raskolnikov's life for him without so much as even consulting him and, on top of this, binding him with the sacrifices involved in the arrangement. What is in question is Dunya's marriage to Mr Luzhin: 'There is of course no special love either on her side or on his (she writes with studied casualness), but Dunya is a clever girl and as noble-minded as an angel, and she will consider it her duty to make her husband happy, and he too will probably do his best to make her happy, at least we have no good reason to doubt it, though I must say the whole thing has happened rather in a hurry' (p. 53). Note the manipulative character of this sentence—'probably', 'at least no good reason to doubt it', 'though the whole thing happened in a hurry'. Its intended effect is carefully measured and also hidden in the tone of simple-minded motherliness which she adopts. She continues further down: 'He may, therefore, Roddy dear, be very useful to you, too, in lots of ways; in fact, Dunya and I have already decided that even now you could start on your career and regard your future as absolutely settled. Oh, if only that were so! . . . Dunya can think of nothing else. . . . (She) is terribly excited and happy to be able to see you so soon, and she even told me once, as a joke, of course, that she'd gladly have married Luzhin for that alone. She is an angel!' (pp. 54–56).

The letter is so written that it both draws Raskolnikov's anger and prevents him from giving direct expression to it, making him feel impotent. And although Raskolnikov sees through it, the letter touches all the right stops in him. He cannot go along with the marriage, but he feels that were it not for the way he has sulked and bungled his affairs his mother and sister would not have contemplated it. He feels guilty and at the same time he resents the way this proposed marriage and his mother's interest in his life double-bind him: 'And what about me? And who asked you to think about me, anyway? I don't want your sacrifice, Dunya! I don't want it, mother! It shall not be, so long as I live!' (p. 62). To accept the sacrifice would only add to his burden of guilt and increase his dependence. He cannot, therefore, accept it and call his soul his own. But neither can he reject it; he does not feel he has been man enough for his mother and sister to have the right to forbid the marriage: 'What can you promise them in return, to lay claim to such a right' (p. 62). It is not that he does not love them; he does. But he doesn't know how to care for them without becoming vulnerable to manipulation and exploitation; he is unable to give without feeling emasculated.

Dostoyevsky tells us that the problem which his mother's letter brings to a head for Raskolnikov is one of long standing: 'All these questions were not new, nor did they occur to him just at that moment; they were old, old questions, questions that had long worried him' (p. 63). Raskolnikov's way of dealing with them had been to try and beat his mother at her own game: he complied by abdicating the management of his life, remaining dependent on her, and thus frustrating her hopes and expectations for him. 'You, Roddy (she says), are all we have in the world, our only hope of a better and brighter future. If only you are happy, we shall be happy' (p. 57). He sees to it that he will not be; but he collects a lot of guilt in pursuing this goal.

He both complies with his mother's wishes and defies her at the same time; he accepts her offer of a dependent relationship in order to spite her. Because his guilt and resentment have kept him from acting differently he cannot respect himself. Consequently he cannot admit to being in the wrong and so make any reparation for the guilt he feels. Instead his bad conscience drives him to be more defiant, his sense of worthlessness drives him to seek compensation in delusions of grandeur, his grudges keep him from forgiving his mother and all those in whom he sees her reflection, and the rage which has built up within him seeks to lash out at those he blames for this situation, including part of himself.

In the pawnbroker Raskolnikov finds a grotesque exaggeration of everything he hates in his mother. The Nietzschean ideas he adopts point to the possibility of proving to himself that he is not what he takes himself to be, that he is in fact its very opposite. The contempt he feels for those he regards as 'ordinary' is the self-contempt he projects on them. If he is to be protected from its sting he feels he must be different from them—'extraordinary', 'above their conventions'. The ideology which gives him the framework for this contempt also sanctions the pent-up violence within him, gives him a unifying aim and justifies its pursuit. The utilitarian ideas which he tries to integrate into this ideology give the means he adopts in this pursuit an aspect under which they evade the vigilance of his conscience. He can thus think of ridding the world of the pawnbroker as a benefit to mankind.

The murder of Alyona Ivanovna is thus meant to obliterate what he hates, to free him form the indebtedness that shackles him, to defy and deny the feelings of guilt that weigh him down. By means of it he hopes to break loose from and turn his back to everything in himself that is dependent, compliant and passive. In the midst of the turmoil caused in him by his mother's letter, he thought that 'he had to make up his mind at all costs, to do something, anything, or renounce his life altogether . . . for ever give up the right to act, to live, and to love' (p. 63). It is at this point that the drift of his thoughts lead him to some words of Marmeladov:

'Do you realize, do you realize, sir, what it means when you have nowhere to go?'

'Suddenly he gave a start: a thought flashed through his mind, a thought that had also occurred to him the day before . . . Now it came to him no longer as a dream, but in a sort of new, terrifying, and completely unfamiliar guise, and he himself suddenly realized it. The blood rushed to his head and everything went black before his eyes' (pp. 63–64). What strikes him is how much like Marmeladov he is underneath. This is not explicitly stated in the novel, but strongly suggested, as Snodgrass points out very perceptively: 'This comparison of himself to Marmeladov is so anguishing that his mind must blot it out, must replace it with something at least less painful. That less painful thought is the murder . . . Raskolnikov replaces the image of himself as Marmeladov with the image of himself as murderer; and finds a relief in that . . . He nearly faints trying to escape the mere thought of the murder; yet, the more horrible that thought, the better; for his mind must use this violence both to discharge his accumulated rage and to refute his own cruellest accusation of Marmeladov-like passivity and nothingness' (op. cit. 222–223).

The murder, however, does not solve Raskolnikov's problems, it only exacerbates them. The question of whether he is a louse or an extra-ordinary man does not go away, but continues to torment him. Now he has to prove that he is worthy of the 'extra-ordinary' act he has committed; otherwise he is still a louse. Only he finds that something in him he had not reckoned with offers him the greatest obstacle, it repudiates the act. He gradually finds that the act which was supposed to be a supreme expression of freedom was nothing of the kind. He had forced it on himself to avoid facing his own feelings of guilt and fears of worthlessness. He had forced it on himself; he had not been behind it. Raskolnikov fights this realization but eventually fails, and out of this failure is born the wholeness and autonomy which has so far evaded him. Dostoyevsky shows us how Raskolnikov is to find these in the opposite direction from the one in which he had sought them—in confessing his crime, admitting he has been a louse, giving up his grudges, taking on responsibility for his guilt, repenting and making amends for it. The novel takes us as far as the confession, and in the epilogue we are given what is no more than a sketch for the subject of another novel: the spiritual and psychological transformation of Raskolnikov—spiritual, I mean his reintegration with the good; psychological, I mean his development towards autonomy. These are two aspects of what Dostoyevsky calls his 'regeneration'.

I have dwelt on his 'degeneration' or 'degradation', and I offered an analysis of his motives for taking an action which further divides him from himself, from the good, and from contact and communion with other people. This is an articulation of what Dostoyevsky has put into the novel. It is not a statement of what according to some psychological theory must be the case. It is a reading of the novel, not an inference, and it can be further substantiated with reference to the details of the narrative. When I speak of Raskolnikov's *motives* for the murder I mean: what led up to the murder, what moved Raskolnikov to such a drastic action and how. I have in mind the significance for Raskolnikov of the incidents leading up to it and the way they affect him. I have in mind, too, the different aspects under which he sees the murder and so the different sides of his personality that come into play in planning and executing it.

The novel explores all this and represents Raskolnikov's motives by painting a picture of the relevant aspects of Raskolnikov's external circumstances, by depicting significant scenes, actions and incidents through which we are given glimpses of his character and inner state. Out of these glimpses emerges a mosaic pattern. We are given further glimpses which confirm and elaborate this pattern in the dreams Dostoyevsky gives to Raskolnikov and in the comparisons he suggests with secondary characters. The letter from Raskolnikov's mother and Raskolnikov's reaction to it, the later reference to Raskolnikov's article 'On Crime' and his discussion of it with Porfiry, Raskolnikov's own subsequent analysis of his motives and that of Svidrigaylov all contribute to this elaboration. As Dostoyevsky himself puts it in *The Idiot*: 'Don't let us forget that the motives of human actions are usually infinitely more complex and varied than we are apt to explain them afterwards, and can rarely be defined with certainty. It is sometimes much better for a writer to content himself with a simple narrative of events.'[12]

If I were to try to sum up what led to Raskolnikov's murder of the pawnbroker, I would mention the way in which his external circumstances interact with his inner state and bring certain pressures on him to the boiling point, and I would single out the following aspects of his personality for comment. I would first mention Raskolnikov's passivity and what sustains it. It is important to see it as a defensive response to his mother's attempts to control him through self-sacrifice and indirect accusation. Its consequences are guilt, an inability to do good and to feel he exists in his own right. Raskolnikov wishes to get away from these consequences without giving up what sustains the passivity. He wants to prove to himself and the world that he is somebody that counts and he uses the violence that has accumulated in him to break away from this passivity—what Freud would call a 'reaction-formation'.

Secondly, I would mention the bad conscience which persecutes him and the excessive guilt he feels. He responds by defying it and behaving badly. He does so because he lacks the self-confidence to be able to tolerate guilt. The hatred he feels for anyone who makes him feel guilty is used in his defiant attitude—another reaction-formation—while his inability to do good in any sustained way keeps him facing in this direction.

[12] *The Idiot*, trans. by David Magarshack (Penguin Classics, 1955), 523.

Thirdly, I would single out the way Raskolnikov accepts things: he feels weighed down by debt instead of feeling gratitude. For what he was given by his mother had strings attached to it. Consequently what he is given does not become his and leaves him with a feeling of inner destitution. Since what he has been given leaves him feeling under an obligation he cannot be his own man. This contributes to his inability to give and do good. It also turns those to whom he feels indebted into tormentors towards whom he has phantasies of violence which appear in his dreams and nightmares. Yet he puts himself into debt as part of a policy of passive destructiveness. It is his way of throwing his mother's sacrifices back in her face.

Fourthly, I would mention his withdrawal from other people and his sense of failure and isolation. This is partly because he feels he has nothing good to offer them and partly because he feels they have nothing worthwhile to offer him. He sees in them a reflection of his own inner degradation and parasitic existence. Feeling especially vulnerable to exploitation he retires into his shell; absorbed in himself he cannot take an interest in other people. Consequently the anger in him cannot be diffused and builds up to a dangerous pitch.

Last, but not least, I would mention his impatience, his reactive pride, and his desperate need for compensation. We see Raskolnikov spurning working towards ordinary accomplishments. For him it has to be all or nothing, at once or never. He day-dreams of getting rich all at once, longs to do the daring thing, to prove himself extraordinary.

These, then, are aspects of his personality which drive him on in the direction suggested. They drive him towards an act which will, to his thinking, obliterate in one big sweep, and as it were by magic, his passivity, dependency, obligation, guilt and negligibility, and compensate for everything that he has suffered on their account; an act too in which he will be able to express at last all his pent up rage against everything which he feels has kept him down by playing on his guilt and prevented him from becoming himself. This is what I meant earlier when I said that in this extreme action Raskolnikov misguidedly seeks freedom and autonomy. I have already commented on how he finds a suitable object in the pawnbroker to whom he is in debt and how his 'radical' ideas enable him to channel and organize what he seeks and at the same time to sanction it, thus tricking his conscience into consent. Finally, in the first seven chapters of the book Dostoyevsky depicts beautifully the pressures building up on Raskolnikov, increasing his desperation for a magical way out: the weight of his debts, his sense of failure, the way he has dropped out of university, the accusations of his landlady's maid, his mother's letter and her imminent visit, the impending marriage of his sister to Luzhin, his contact with Marmeladov and his family.

It is in this way that Dostoyevsky shows us in one single unusual case, which he himself constructs imaginatively out of his experience, what motivation is like, and gives us a lively awarness of its complexity. More particularly he shows us how a bad conscience and passivity can drive a man to a violent act. If I am right in my reading of Raskolnikov's motive, I think it would be revealing to put Dostoyevsky's depiction of it side by side with the following passage by Melanie Klein which comes from a paper of hers entitled 'The Early Development of Conscience in the Child':

> Since the first *imagos* it (the young child) thus forms are endowed with all the attributes of the intense sadism belonging to this stage of its development, and since they will once more be projected on to objects of the outer world, the small child becomes dominated by the fear of suffering unimaginable cruel attacks, both from its real objects (his parents) and from its super-ego (from those aspects of himself he has modelled on them through identification). Its anxiety (about being attacked by these bad[13] figures, both from within and without) will serve to increase its own sadistic impulses by urging it to destroy those hostile objects (or figures) so as to escape their onslaughts. The vicious circle that is thus set up, in which the child's anxiety impels it to destroy its objects (those figures in relationship with whom he develops or on whom he remains dependent) results in an increase of its own anxiety, and this once again urges it on against its object, and constitutes a psychological mechanism which, in my view, is at the bottom of asocial and criminal tendencies in the individual. Thus, we must assume that it is the excessive severity and overpowering cruelty of the super-ego, not the weakness or want of it, as is usually supposed, which is responsible for the behaviour of asocial and criminal persons.[14]

This is an abstract statement, expressed in semi-technical jargon, of how a person comes to withdraw from other people and develop destructive phantasies which may issue in criminal behaviour. It comes from experience of actual people in the course of psychotherapeutic work. I dissociate myself from the generalization at the end of the passage. It is sufficient that what Melanie Klein describes here should be responsible for the behaviour of *some* asocial and criminal persons. If one is familiar with her work one will understand better what she says in the passage I quoted. But one may read her writings and see little in what she says, in which case a novel like *Crime and Punishment* can shed light on her meaning. So Wisdom says that if one loses grasp of what is being talked about in a passage such as the one I quoted, the remedy is 'to move to and fro from the concrete, presented by the artist, to the general, presented by the scientist'—in this

---

[13] 'Bad' in the sense of hostile, inimical, sadistic.

[14] *Psycho-Analysis Today*, Sándor Lorand (ed.) (Allen and Unwin Ltd, 1948), 67.

case the clinical theorist (op. cit., 261). I am not concerned now with an appreciation of Melanie Klein's or Freud's contribution to an understanding of human beings. What impresses me is how a novelist, like Dostoyevsky, could have come to an understanding which so largely overlaps with that arrived at by such pioneers in clinical psychology.

Obviously Dostoyevsky must have been endowed with a special vulnerability to and receptivity of human emotions and a special understanding of them. In this respect he would not have been different from any gifted clinical psychologist. Presumably a clinical psychologist too is affected by what he meets in his patients, but he is able to master the reverberations which their affective troubles produce in him. He may then subject these to reflection and they may flower, as in the case of Melanie Klein, into theoretical formulations from which it is possible to learn something. In the case of Dostoyevsky, we know from accounts of his life that they were not so controlled. But they were nevertheless transformed imaginatively into works of fiction in which they were clarified and understood. What is of interest to me, philosophically, is the utilization of this knowledge in the composition of works of fiction—I mean the knowledge contained in his responses to the plight of people in psychological and spiritual trouble, in the reverberations which these troubles produced in him.

These reverberations are not out of control in Dostoyevsky's works. On the contrary, they kept him very much on course in what he wrote. With his special talent he was able to harness their energy to produce what are among the deepest novels of their kind in literature. Because of what we learn from these novels we speak of the truth contained in them, the kind of truth about human beings which makes Dostoyevsky a great psychologist. At least this is the aspect of the truth in his novels which interests me in this paper.

II

What, then, does truth mean in this context? And what is the truth about Raskolnikov's motives for the murder? Where does the former truth abide and where the latter, and how are they connected? I shall start with the former question.

In *The Idiot* Dostoyevsky speaks about the way an exaggerated character in a work of literature can light up features in people we know which we had not noticed before: 'Think of the thousands of intelligent people (he says) who, having learnt from Gogol about Podkolyosin, at once discover that scores of their friends and acquaintances are awfully like Podkolyosin. They knew even before Gogol that their friends were like Podkolyosin; what they did not know was that that was their name' (p. 499). Wisdom has shown us well 'what's in a name', and how a new name goes with a new comparison and so reveals a new aspect in the things it names.[15] But, perhaps even more important, is the way what is portrayed in literature can make a more vidid impression on the reader than the real thing. This is partly because of the writer's livelier sensibility and his talent as a writer. He can thus concentrate on what is important for his purposes, alter and adjust the focus of his lens, in one of the many ways at his disposal, so that we can see clearly, without distraction and abstraction, what he depicts. For in real life we may know what we meet only in a second-hand way, we may not be susceptible to its full impact, we may experience it in a muted way.

Conrad tells us that the form of imagined life in a novel can be 'clearer than reality' and it can 'put to shame the pride of documentary history'.[16] Part of the reason for this is to be found in the contrast between the contingency of life and the order of art. In real life events are fragmentary and what we come to know of them is often disjointed. It is *we* who have to make sense of them. A work of literature, on the other hand, whether it be a poem or a novel, is a construction in which the author says or shows something about an aspect of life, or at least attempts to do so. That is the construction or composition is designed to say something, and to this end the author selects or arranges material which he borrows from real life. Dostoyevsky, it seems, was an avid reader of newspapers. In the letter from which I quoted earlier he says : 'In any newspaper one takes up, one comes across reports of wholly authentic facts . . .' This is no doubt is true. But Dostoyevsky does not simply reproduce these. He puts them against a certain background, imagines them surrounded by certain events, weaves them into a story, and he thus gives them an aspect, or several different aspects at once, which they did not have in the newspaper report, or had only in Dostoyevsky's imaginative reading of it.

In this way it is what he imagines that he conveys to us. What he depicts comes to life because, through the artifice of art, he makes available to the reader what he can imagine—I mean the different aspects under which he sees things, things that are of significance to us. By thus shaping what is shapeless in real life he makes us see things in a new light and more vividly. He makes us not only see them thus, but also feel them. What he depicts moves or disturbs us in a way that its counterpart, in reality may not. Freud's case histories do not have this power, nor are they meant to have it. Thus the power of art.

Another reason why what is depicted in a novel can be 'clearer than reality' has to do with the make-believe character of art. We can respond to it without the fear that we might have to follow our responses through.

[15] See, for instance, 'Gods', Wisdom, op. cit.
[16] Quoted from 'A Personal Record' (1912) by Miriam Allott, op. cit., 76.

Yet if the work is an outstanding one, if it depicts some aspect of life without taming or softening it, justly and with compassion, in the response it evokes it will deepen our contact with reality. Paradoxically, the safety we find in the make-believe character of art enables us to see through, if only for a moment, the make-believe of real life. This is a question which Simone Weil discusses in an essay on 'Morality and Literature,[17] and illustrates in her extraordinary discussion of the *Iliad* in 'L'Iliad on le Poème de la Force'.[18] There is a difference between being caught up in something real—war and its brutality, for instance, which is the subject of the *Iliad*—and contemplating its just depiction in a work of literature. Those who are caught up in it, she says, cannot discern the force that impels them and its relation to their particular condition. Those who contemplate it in literature feel this force in the way we feel gravity 'when we look over a precipice if we are safe and not subject to vertigo'.[19] How true this is of the contrast between the perceptive reader of *Crime and Punishment* and Raskolnikov.

Yet, of course, the experience depicted is that of Raskolnikov, the hero of the novel, and not ours. This means, I believe, that it cannot change us in the way it is depicted as changing Raskolnikov, unless it links up with something that exists independently in our own lives. So it is worth remembering that when we say that a book had made a profound impression on us, we do not always imply that what has impressed us has been taken into our lives and made part of it. A profound impression is not the same thing as a profound effect. A profound impression will make a difference to my response to other works and so change my relation to literature without changing me in myself. Although I do not deny that it can do so in time, I am personally impressed by how much would be required for this to happen.

I am not divorcing literature from life. On the contrary, I would argue that escapist literature, sentimental stories, lie about life. They may do so by evoking emotions that are sham, for instance, or by promoting self-indulgence. At an extreme, a person who makes literature a substitute for life will cease to learn from it. No, my point is that although what one finds in literature depends on the relation which literature has to life, so that without such a relation there would be nothing to be found there, there is nevertheless a difference between being accessible to what is in a work of literature and taking it into one's life. When I say that a work of literature can open one's eyes, deepen one's contact with life, I am not denying this difference. Nor yet when I emphasize it am I denying the power which literature has 'to awaken us to the truth'.[20]

[17] *On Science, Necessity and the Love of God*, trans. by Richard Rees (ed.) (Oxford University Press, 1968).
[18] *La Source Grecque* (Gallimard, 1953).
[19] *On Science, Necessity and the Love of God*, 162.
[20] Ibid.

It is this power which makes us speak of the truth in a work of literature. In what sense, then, does *Crime and Punishment* contain truth? And how does this make Dostoyevsky a great psychologist and student of the human soul? When we speak of the novel's truth we mean that what it depicts is true. I said 'what the work depicts'. This could mean two different things. It could mean, first, the fictitious incidents related in the novel, or it could mean, secondly, what the novel conveys about life by means of these incidents. It is the second I have been discussing when I spoke of the power of a work of art to open our eyes, to make us feel what we know only abstractly, to deepen our contact with life. But to say that what the novel depicts, in this sense, is true is to make a double judgment. First it is to make a judgment about what it is that the work depicts. This involves trying to read it correctly and raises questions about what is meant by a 'correct reading' of the work. Secondly, it is to make a judgment about what life is like, and this brings both our values and our experience to bear on the matter. Obviously unless one has some contact or familiarity in one's own life and experience with what the work depicts one will not see it in the work; it will pass one by without making an impression. But one may have some contact or familiarity with it in real life and still know it only abstractly. That is why literature can make us see something new, why it can make us feel what we remain on the outside of in real life.

I said that what the work depicts must be true. It must also be able to make us see it and feel it. Even if the individual reader fails, the work must have this power. Indeed, unless it has it, it does not really depict anything or contain any truth. It either has nothing to say or it falsifies life. We can say of an ordinary description or a documentary record that it is dull but nevertheless true. But we cannot say this of a literary work. Neither can we say: 'It is a very good and vivid description, only what it says is false'. A literary work cannot depict what is false; it can only falsify life. It can, for instance, portray what is sham without recognizing this. But in that case it would not have succeeded in depicting what is sham. For it would not have the power to open our eyes to it, to make us see it for what it is. It can also falsify life by cheapening language in the way that the popular press does. But then again it would not succeed in making us see anything. It would only make clear thinking difficult, deaden sensibility.

If what is described in a work of literature fails to come alive, if the feelings it evokes are sham or sentimental, if it throws no light on what we regard as significant, we would not speak of it as true. Yet these questions are not relevant to the truth of a report or documentary. A report may not have anything to *say* about what it describes fairly and accurately, I mean apart from describing it. Whether or not what a piece of writing describes or a film depicts is fictitious is immaterial to whether it is a piece of literature or a work of art. Thus a documentary film by Eisenstein. Rush Rhees quotes some words by Liam O'Flaherty: 'If you can describe a hen crossing a road you are a real writer'. He comments: 'If he had been giving evidence about a motor accident he could have told the court where the hen was, the direction in which it was moving, etc. But O'Flaherty wanted a description that would make us understand the hen—make us see it as it is.'[21]

Such a description cannot, of course, be reduplicated, and what it says cannot be stated abstractly. If five talented writers produced five different descriptions of the hen of which O'Flaherty would say that they were true, they would still not be equivalent. We would say, perhaps, that they revealed different truths about the hen, or different aspects of it. This is partly connected with the richness which our language gives to the things that are possible objects of our experience. What we can find in them is inexhaustible—something which we would not know if we had no art and no literature. It is also connected with something else, namely that unless the writer speaks for *himself*, is *himself* in what he says, or represents things as *he* sees them, he would have nothing to say, and so could not speak the truth in what he writes in the sense that interests us now. But he can, of course, speak for himself and, at the same time, let what he depicts speak for *itself*. There is no contradiction here.

We must also not forget that the truth we find in a work of literature is bound up not only with what the writer says and how he says it, but also with the attitude he takes towards what he describes. Simone Weil brings this out very well in her discussion of the *Iliad*. In a sensitive essay on *Anna Karenina* Lionel Trilling too touches on this point: 'It is when the novelist really loves his characters (he says) that he can show them in their completeness and contradiction, in their failures as well as in their great moments, in their triviality as well as in their charm'.[22] In this respect he contrasts Tolstoy with Flaubert: 'As the word is used in literary criticism (he writes), Flaubert must be accounted just as objective as Tolstoy. Yet it is clear that Flaubert's objectivity is charged with irritability and Tolstoy's with affection' (ibid.). The point, in one sentence, is that the irritability to which Trilling refers is an expression of personality, a form of intrusion, whereas the kind of love in the medium of which exists every object in the *Iliad* and in *Anna Karenina* is a form of detachment. It is this that makes it possible for the writer to let things speak for themselves. For only then does the self retreat to make place for truth.

I distinguished earlier between an abstract statement and a concrete representation. In his novels Dostoyevsky refrains from the former and so also avoids coming between the reader and what he depicts. In *The Idiot*, for instance, in Pt. IV, §8, there is a scene where the Prince has to choose

[21] 'Art and Philosophy', *Without Answers* (Routledge and Kegan Paul, 1969), 146–147.
[22] Lionel Trilling, op. cit., 69.

between the two women he loves. What happens when he meets them starts a whole chain of events so that it is important to understand it. Dostoyevsky pauses and reflects and he tells the reader what he, himself, finds paradoxical, namely that he has to stick to a bare statement of the facts because he, the author, finds it difficult to explain what took place. He then goes on to explore the events in question by giving the reader the contrasting points of view of different spectators and characters in the novel.

It is very much in this way that Dostoyevsky explores Raskolnikov's motives for the murder; and it is in this way that he is able to convey the richness and complexity of the psychological and spiritual matters he depicts in his novel without falsifying the element of indeterminacy which characterizes them in real life. He gives us, in the guise of fiction, something of the actual feel of these matters which is generally lost in our abstract thinking. He is able to do so because he does not interpose himself between the reader and what he depicts; because he uses his art to let what he depicts speak for itself. The truth in Dostoyevsky's portrayal of Raskolnikov's character and motives lies in just this, and it is this which makes him a great psychologist as well as novelist.

III

I now turn to the second of the two questions I raised earlier. The first concerned the nature of literary truth; the second concerns the truth about Raskolnikov's motives for the murder. My question is not whether the analysis I offered is true, but how the question of its truth is to be settled.

The first thing I would say about it is what should be obvious, namely that it is a critical judgment and not a clinical interpretation. It is my reading of a literary portrayal, not of a real person's motives and character. Yet, as I said before, although one can learn something about real human beings from this portrayal, this possibility presupposes some independent acquaintance with what is depicted. The deeper and livelier this acquaintance the more one can learn from the novel and appreciate what is in it.

Obviously the reader responds to what is in the novel as an individual, with his own experience, values and understanding; his reading of it inevitably draws on his own understanding of himself and his knowledge of human beings. The big difference between coming to know a live human being and understanding a character in a novel is that the reader cannot talk to or question the latter, and that he, in turn, doesn't respond to the reader. A good novel attempts to make an imaginative reader witness to another life, and indeed more than a witness. It attempts to draw him into that life. But this is a conjuring trick, for what one imagines entering into is scripted and what the reader brings to it in his responses, makes no difference to the scenario. He does not engage with the characters of the novel, although he may learn from their engagement with each other as portrayed in the novel.

If the author is successful his characters come alive and assume a 'life' independent of the author. Thus in his notebooks we find Dostoyevsky asking whether or not Aglaya is the 'idiot's' mistress. In other words Dostoyevsky feels that once the writing of the novel is on its way and has got off the ground it is not up to him whether or not Aglaya will be the Prince's mistress. He is asking: Can she be? Would she have him? And is he, 'the poor knight', man enough to have her?[23] Still it remains true that a character in a novel is a construction.

What I have in mind is this. When an author 'constructs' or 'creates' a character he puts him in various situations, makes him the agent of various actions, puts words into his mouth, places him side by side with other characters, depicts him interacting with them and engaging in various activities. If these were snap-shots of a real man we would say that there were lots of gaps between the moments photographed. We would say that there is obviously much more to his life than we find in this series of snap-shots. This is what we cannot say in the case of a character in a novel or play. Here all we have are the snap-shots and what they are meant to suggest. About this there can be much disagreement and debate, but it would be senseless to speculate about what more there is to a character than is to be found in the snap-shots. Professor Dover Wilson puts this point well with reference to Hamlet: 'Apart from the play (he says), apart from his actions, from what he tells us about himself and what other characters tell us about him, there is no Hamlet'. He adds that 'critics who speculate upon what Hamlet was like before the play opens or attribute his conduct to a mother-complex acquired in infancy, are merely cutting the figure out of the canvas and sticking it in a doll's house of their own invention'.[24] He is thinking of Ernest Jones' analysis, in *Hamlet and Oedipus*,[25] of Hamlet's inability to bring himself to kill his uncle and thus avenge his father's death.

I should like to point out, all the same, that the question of what is in a play or novel or character, or what the author has put into it, is not a straightforward one. I said that it would be senseless to speculate about what more there is to a character than is to be found in the snap-shots. I meant to refer to those moments of his 'life' (and I use inverted commas around life) about which the novel is silent. We must not forget, however,

[23] These questions are obviously related to the question Dostoyevsky explored in *The Idiot*, Part IV, secs 8–9.

[24] J. Dover Wilson, 'The New Shakespeare', *Hamlet*, 2nd edn (Cambridge, 1957), xlv-xlvi.

[25] Ernest Jones, *Hamlet and Oedipus* (Victor Gollancz Ltd, 1949).

that the snap-shots are highly selective and that the way they are arranged and juxtaposed makes them revealing in a way that random snap-shots of a live person generally are not. I have already touched on this point earlier. So if one speaks of what is and what is not to be found in the snap-shots one has to bear this in mind. Dover Wilson is absolutely right about the senselessness of putting forward hypotheses about times and aspects of the 'life' of a character in a work of literature about which the work is silent because it helps to make sense of what is problematic about the character. We can do so in real life because the hypothesis is susceptible of independent confirmation.

He is wrong, however, when after having pointed out that Hamlet 'is not a living man or an historical character' but 'a figure in a dramatic composition', he says: 'We can no more analyse his mind than we can dissect his body'.[26] Obviously if the author does not tell us that a character is a hunchback we cannot from the way others in the novel laugh at him conclude that he must be a hunchback. Again if the author does not tell us or in any way hint that a character has some internal organic disease we cannot from the description of his behaviour and the mention of some pains diagnose such a disease. We have to rest in what the author does tell us and try to understand why he has not been more specific in this direction. Equally if the author does not tell us anything about a character's childhood, or his parents, then this delineates the framework in which he wishes to present his character. To try to speculate about this is like trying to see beyond the frame of a painting; and this is what Dover Wilson objects to in Ernest Jones' analysis of Hamlet. On the other hand, an analysis of the mind also involves connecting together the different glimpses an author gives us of a character, trying to discern a pattern there to make sense of what we have been given—provided, of course, that we do not forget that the pattern is part of a larger composition which is the novel. The fact that the author does not spell out the pattern does not make it senseless for us to reflect on what is being suggested. To do so is not to advance hypotheses about what goes beyond the frame of the work; it is to explore the proper way of reading what lies within it.

Put it like this. I spoke of the snap-shots an author weaves together and of what they suggest. The snap-shots are themselves the source of what they acquaint us with in a character. What we thus come to be acquainted with is determined *wholly* by the snap-shots, though often not without much indeterminacy. The point is that there is not an independent way, as in real life, of filling in the gaps in our knowledge. These, in the case of a work of literature, are not really gaps in any case. They do not represent de-

---

[26] J. Dover Wilson, *What Happened in Hamlet?* (Cambridge University Press, 1940), 205.

ficiencies in the reader's knowledge; they are an objective part of the surface of a literary work. True, in a work of literature, as in real life, the snap-shots can be probed, and the aspect under which we see them may change under such probing. Nevertheless it is the snap-shots themselves, the selective glimpses the author chooses to give the reader, which determine the aspect under which they are seen. There is no *other* material, no further snap-shots, on which the reader or critic can draw in his analyses or probings. This is what Dover Wilson emphasizes.

Yet, as I said, the snap-shots can be probed, considered in each other's light and in that of the work as a whole—a work in which the author *may* be concerned to study his main character's mind. Under such probing the snap-shots may change aspect and we may come to see in the author's portrait of a character what we did not see before. Details on which we had not dwelt on our first reading of the work, or which may have puzzled us, may now assume a significance they did not have for us before. In connection with Hamlet this is what Dover Wilson writes: 'Shakespeare never furnishes an explanation of Hamlet's inaction. All he does is to exhibit it to us as a problem, turning it round and round . . .before our eyes so that we may see every side of it, and then in the end having us draw our own conclusions' (ibid., 204). We have seen that this is precisely how Dostoyevsky treats the question of Raskolnikov's motive for the murder. This process of drawing our own conclusions, in the case of *Crime and Punishment,* surely is engaging in an analysis of Raskolnikov's mind—what Dover Wilson does not admit in connection with Hamlet. Of course, the conclusions we draw are not conclusions that can be stated abstractly or have much meaning apart from the novel or play. For what is in question is one's reading of a play or novel and what is depicted in it. It can, therefore, only be in the form of comments on or a discussion of the details of the particular work or of what is depicted in it.

The End of the Road: The Death of Individualism

JACQUELYN KEGLEY

Though John Barth won the National Book Award for his novel, *Giles Goat Boy*, his second novel, *The End of the Road*, proves a more interesting case study for our purposes, namely, to explore the relationship between philosophy and literature. This is so for at least three reasons. First, by the author's own admission, the novel is intended as a refutation of ethical subjectivism, particularly as exposed by Jean Paul Sartre. Secondly, in the novel, Barth, like Virginia Woolf in *To the Lighthouse*, places reason and imagination in contention, suggesting that either faculty in isolation is inadequate in dealing with human experience. Both Barth and Woolf are reflecting and probably criticizing the assumption of a number of contemporary writers and critics, namely, that rational discourse is inadequate to the task of ordering the chaotic, fragmentary world and giving meaning to life and only the poet (novelist) employing his imagination can do this.

E. M. Forster, in an essay 'Art for Art's Sake', expresses this point of view when he writes:

> order in daily life and in history, order in the social and political category is unattainable . . . where is it attainable? . . . the work of art stands up by itself, and nothing else does . . . it is the one orderly product which our muddling race has produced.[1]

Not only is there a separation of reason and the imagination but also an exalting of literary order and the literary world above experience and action. Richard Ohmann, in a book entitled *The Politics of Literature*, summarizes this view as follows: 'The world is complex, discordant, dazzling. We want urgently to know it is unified and meaningful, but action out there in the flux fails to reveal or bring about satisfactory order. The order we need *is* available in literature; therefore literature must be a better guide to truth than experience and action.'[2] Ohmann and others are very concerned with the teaching of literature and seriously consider the question raised by Lionel Trilling in his essay, 'Two Environments', namely 'whether in our

---

[1] *Two Cheers for Democracy* (New York: Harcourt, Brace World; Harvest Books, 1951), 91–92.
[2] Richard Ohmann, 'Teaching and Studying Literature at the End of Ideology', Louis Kampf and Paul Lauter, *The Politics of Literature: Dissenting Essays on the Teaching of English* (New York: Vintage, 1972), 139–140.

culture the study of literature is any longer a suitable means for developing and refining intelligence, particularly as it touches the moral life'.[3] Barth too is very concerned about the state of literature today as is evidenced in his essay, 'The Literature of Exhaustion', in which he discusses the 'used-upness' of certain literary forms.[4]

A third reason Barth's novel *The End of the Road* is worthy of our study is that it examines and allows us to deal with the claim that modern thought and literature has been increasingly dominated by the presupposition that 'each man is locked in the prison of his consciousness'. Finally, Barth is interested in myths and particularly in some of the inadequacy of some of our basic myths. In *The End of the Road* he pokes fun at a basic American myth, that of the rugged, pragmatic, individualist. In fact, he explores in a rather subtle way the nihilistic symptoms of our American society in which existentialism and pragmatism are combined in an irresponsible way.

Before beginning our exploration of the novel, however, it should be pointed out that in one sense one should not take *The End of the Road* seriously as a novel. For example, Barth makes no attempt to delineate characters, or to establish a social or physical setting for the novel. The central characters, in fact, have stock and symbolic names: Jacob Horner, who sat in the corner and mindlessly pulled out plums, and Joe Morgan, whose name probably alludes to J. P. Morgan, the tough, energetic American financer. The novel is narrated by Jake, who constantly reminds us of the possible inadequacy of his story, and, other than Jake's solitary reflections on his states of mind, the book is primarily a debate of ideas. It is clear, in fact, that the novel is intended as a parody: it is so in at least four senses. First, it is a parody in imitating the style of the banal love triangle novel which is part of our trivial culture and which, in turn, parodies love by its very banality. The novel is also a parody in the sense of treating serious ideas of identity, existence, freedom, and right conduct in a ironical manner. The novel may be a parody in the third sense, of a countersong. Rather than being the end of the road, it may be the beginning. Finally, as I have suggested, the novel is a parody of Sartrean existentialism. Both Horner and Morgan are ethical subjectivists, but their reaction to this position and/or expression of it is at opposite poles, and both equally disastrous. Morgan chooses and acts with full consciousness and deadly consistency. Horner acts arbitrarily, inconsistently, and without apparent motive or reason. The novel is, in fact, a duel between chaos and order, between God and the Devil, between, as we have said, imagination and reason. Barth takes seriously Sartre's contention that man desires to be God and that imagination is constitutive of the world as we know it. Barth

[3] Lionel Trilling, 'Two Environments', in *Beyond Culture: Essays on Literature and Learning* (New York: Viking Press; Compass Books, 1968), 209–233.
[4] See John Barth, 'The Literature of Exhaustion', *The Atlantic* **220** (1967), 33.

is also exploring, I believe, Sartre's concept of relations with others as relations of conflict, involving the two poles of sadism and masochism.

The End of the Road for Ethical Subjectivism

In a letter to Gregory Bluestone about the end of his first novel, *The Floating Opera*, Barth writes: 'I deliberately had him (Todd Andrews) end up with that brave ethical subjectivism in order that Jacob Horner might undo that position in #2 and carry all non-mystical value thinking to the end of the road'.[5] The term 'brave' is used by Barth ironically, as we shall see. The phrase 'non-mystical value thinking' is reflective of that degradation of reason and logic so prevalent among literary people today as well as the desperate search for order and meaning referred to by Ohmann.

As already indicated, the two main characters of the novel are both ethical subjectivists in that both accept the propositions that there are no absolute values, that all values are relative, and that ultimately all ethical decision-making is subjective choice. This is also the position of the Doctor, the third main character. Barth seems to be envisaging how the Sartrean notions of freedom and consciousness can be lived out by particular people and he presents us with three possibilities emphasizing different aspects of Sartre's conceptions. Joe Morgan, a history teacher at Wicomico State University reacts to the relativity of all values as a straight-forward Sartrean existentialist. He recognizes that nothing can ultimately be rationally defended, that it must be his own personal responsibility, that there are no excuses, and that every act has a motive. In fact, the whole action of the novel centres on the assertion 'it is impossible to act without a motive'. Morgan tells Horner 'In my ethics the most a man can do is to be right from his point of view'.[6] Again, he says, 'the only demonstrable index to a man's desires is his acts, when you're speaking of past time: what a man did is what he wanted to do'.[7]

Joe Morgan is a complete man of decision. Jake says of Joe, '. . . Indecision was apparently foreign to him; he was always sure of his ground; he acted quickly, explained his actions lucidly, if questioned, and would have regarded apologies for missteps as superfluous'.[8] Again, Jake observes, 'Joe Morgan was the sort who heads directly for his destination, implying by his example that paths should be laid where people walk, instead of

[5] Gregory Bluestone, 'John Walh and John Barth: The Angry and the Accurate', *The Massachusetts Review* **I** (Fall 1959–Summer 1960), 586.
[6] John Barth, *The End of the Road* (New York: Doubleday Company Inc.; Bantam Books, 1967 and subsequent), 46.
[7] Ibid., 49.
[8] Ibid., 33.

walking where the paths happen to be laid'.[9] Morgan is both an existentialist and a rugged American individualist. He says to Jake, 'when you
say good-bye to objective values, you really have to flex your muscles and
keep your eyes open, because you're on your own. It takes *energy*, not just
personal energy, but cultural energy, or you're lost. Energy is what makes
the difference between American pragmatism and French existentialism—
where the hell else but in America could you have a cheerful nihilism for
God's sake?'[10]

It turns out that Joe Morgan is anything but cheerful. He takes everything seriously, including his walking. Joe is proud that he takes his wife,
Rennie, seriously. In a marriage relationship, he tells Jake, 'the parties
involved must be able to take each other seriously'.[11] The irony is that he
doesn't take Rennie seriously at all or perhaps takes her too seriously, as
we shall see. The point is he takes himself and his philosophy too seriously.
When Rennie, who has adopted Joe's philosophical position, though we
should say, has had it imposed on her, apologizes for their lack of furniture,
Joe hits her. Jake ironically observes:

> I was interested in the story of Rennie's first encounter with the Morgan
> philosophy, and the irresistible rhetoric Joe had employed to open her
> eyes to the truth. It demonstrated clearly that philosophy was no game
> to Mr Morgan.[12]

What then about Jake Horner? He too believes in the relativity of all
values, but he is Joe Morgan's opposite. He is the complete man of
indecision. Jake suffers from paralysis of will. He tells us that 'when faced
with a multitude of choices, no one choice seems satisfactory for very
long by comparison with the aggregate desirability of all the rest, though
compared to any one of the others it would not be found inferior'.[13] All
possibilities seem equally plausible to Jake so that he is 'held static like the
rope maker in a tug-of-war where the opposing teams are perfectly
matched'.[14] This metaphor of the tug-of-war applies to the whole novel.
Barth creates another symbol of this kind of equal contest and that is the
statue of Laöcoon which Jakes keeps on his mantle. Laöcoon is immobilized
by two serpents, later identified as Knowledge and Imagination. Jake
takes cues from the statue for his moods and when he refers to certain
paradoxes he speaks, ironically I presume, of Laöcoon's smile.

Unlike Morgan who believes there is a motive for every act, Jake does

9 Ibid., 20.
10 Ibid., 47.
11 Ibid., 45.
12 Ibid., 48.
13 Ibid., 3.
14 Ibid., 5.

things for no particular reason. He has no persistent feelings, no personal continuity. Sometimes he rocks on his heels intoning 'Pepsi Cola hits the spot' tunelessly to make sure he exists. At other times he is weatherless, without any moods, rocking in his rocking chair. He even has a dream about the prediction of a weatherless day. Thus, Jake Horner is anything but the self-conscious clear-headed existentialist with a project. In fact, the novel opens with the theme of his fluidity and non-identity. 'In a sense I am Jacob Horner.'[15]

Not only is Jake incapable of deciding, he ends up in a state of complete immobility on his twenty-eighth birthday in Penn Station in Baltimore, unable to decide where to go and with no reason to do anything. He tells us that he is suffering from *cosmopsis*, the cosmic view of all possibility. He is rescued from this situation by the Doctor, a mysterious, elderly Negro who runs an extra-legal Remobilization Farm. The Doctor is an important figure in the novel and for several reasons. First, he, like Joe Morgan, responded to nihilism by combining existentialism and pragmatism, but in a contrasting way. Joe takes existentialist premises seriously and tries to apply them in a rational, consistent way. The Doctor doesn't take existentialism seriously, rather he uses its premises as a ground for the application of arbitrary therapies and rules. Second, it is the Doctor who opposes knowledge to freedom, and who believes in arbitrary order as opposed to the order opposed by external reality. Thirdly, Barth intends a clear parallelism between the doctor–patient relationship of the Doctor and Jake and the relationship of Joe and Rennie. The furnishings of the Morgan house, like those of the Doctor's office, are functional and the walls are white. Jake once says to Joe about Rennie, 'you speak of her as if she is your patient'.[16] And both Joe and the Doctor are called, at points in the book, 'God' or 'Lord'. Finally, it is the Doctor who is instrumental in bringing about crucial events: Joe's applying for a position at Wimcomico and Rennie's fatal abortion.

The Doctor's combination of existentialism and pragmatism is readily evident in the book. He is described by Jake as 'some combination of quack and prophet . . . a kind of superpragmatist'. He has a wide variety of therapies all tailored to fit the patient—Conversational Therapy, Sexual Therapy, Devotional Therapy, Occupational Therapy and Preoccupational Therapy, Philosophical Therapy, Scriptotherapy and many others. The Doctor tells Jake, 'you must always be *conscious* of motion'.[17] He suggests Jake read Sartre and become an Existentialist, though only to keep him moving until something more suitable is found. He puts forth what are clearly Sartrean theses when he says to Jake, 'Choosing is existence; to the

[15] Ibid., 1.
[16] Ibid., 44.
[17] Ibid., 84.

extent that you don't choose, you don't exist. Now, everything we do must be oriented toward choice and action'.[18]

Though the Doctor sees existentialism as a merely useful tool he uses it to ground the main therapy which he prescribes for Jake, which is mytho-therapy. It is based on two assumptions:

> that human existence precedes human essence, if either of these terms really signifies anything; and that man is free to choose his own essence but change it at will. Those are both existentialist premises, and whether they're true or false is of no concern to us—they're *useful* in your case.[19]

The emphasis is on usefulness. Jake is to orchestrate scenes which are to help him stay mobile. Jake should see life as a drama, in which the individual, like the dramatist, assigns roles to oneself and to others. The Ego, points out the Doctor, is a mask, nothing more.[20] (Here one is reminded of Sartre's claim in the *Transcendence of Ego* that consciousness creates the 'mask' of an Ego.) However, the Doctor goes on to say, contrary to Sartre's notion of Bad Faith, 'masks cannot be *insincere*—impossible word!—it only means they are incompatible'.[21] In fact, the juxtaposition of sincerity and insincerity are also part of the theme of the novel. Jake and the Doctor do not take things seriously; Joe and Rennie take them too seriously. The Doctor tells Jake that myth creating is not a serious project; it is rather a fanciful, wild, promiscuous playing with life, using whatever myth 'works' for the moment. It is a completely arbitrary and subjective project.

> Everyone is necessarily the hero of his own life story. *Hamlet* could be told from Polonius' point of view, and called *The Tragedy of Polonius, Lord Chamberlain*—not only are we the heroes of our own life stories—we're the ones who conceive the story, and give other people the essences of minor characters. But since no man's life story as a rule is ever one story with a coherent plot, we always reconceiving just the sort of hero we are and consequently just the sort of minor roles that other people are supposed to play.[22]

In addition to combining existentialism and pragmatism, the Doctor is the one who put forth the notion of Knowledge and Truth as immobilizing choice, thus opposing freedom and knowledge and imagination and reason.

[18] Ibid., 83.
[19] Ibid., 88.
[20] Ibid., 90.
[21] Ibid., 90.
[22] Ibid., 89.

In a conversation with Jake about the seating capacity of the Cleveland Stadium he says:

> The *world is everything that is the case*, and what is the case is not a matter of logic. If you don't simply *know* how many people can sit in the Cleveland Municipal Stadium, you have no real reason for choosing one number over another . . . But if you have some Knowledge of the World you may be able to say, 'Seventy-seven thousand seven hundred' just like that. No choice is involved.[23]

Also, the order provided by imagination and human will is contrasted to the order imposed by reality and embodied in scientific knowledge. Further in the name of freedom, order is rigidly imposed. The Doctor ironically *chooses* Jake's 'calling' and tells him there must be rigid discipline in order for his occupation to be 'therapeutic'. 'There must be a body of laws. You will teach prescriptive grammar. No description at all. No optional situations. Teach the rules. Teach the *Truth* about grammar.'[24]

He advises Jake to read the Almanac, and to take walks to predetermined places. He also advises Jake to act impulsively, not getting stuck too long between alternatives. He prescribes as follows:

> If the alternatives are side by side, choose the one on the left, if they are consecutive in time, choose the earlier. If neither of these applies, choose the alternative whose name begins with the earlier letter of the alphabet. These are the principles of Sinistrality, Antecedence, and Alphabetical Priority—there are others, and they're arbitrary, but useful.[25]

Such methodology as practised by the Doctor is, of course, a parody, a *reductio ad absurdum* of all systematic therapy. The Doctor's practice is illegal, arbitrary and, in fact, malpractice.

It is significant that Horner easily falls prey to such fakes as the Doctor and turns to him for help in desperation. This is a sign that in our society knowledge is no longer trusted, it does not have the cultural standing it once had. Barth is trying to take into account the general attack on objectivity, on science, on confidence in reason. The Doctor may stand for something one might call the 'California Syndrome', namely the endless and ephemeral cropping up of wacky therapies and devices to get more out of experience in far-out, 'imaginative', half-baked and often risky ways. It's the victory of volatility over stability. In Horner's case his therapy will end in disaster.

At first the mythotherapy prescribed by the Doctor comes easy to Jake for he is a natural mimic and can easily create many personae. In his job

[23] Ibid., 81–82.
[24] Ibid., 5.
[25] Ibid., 85.

interview he plays brilliant improvisations on the role of the profoundly committed idealistic young teacher. He picks up Peggy Rankin, an old-maid school teacher and at first kiss starts unzipping her bathing suit, humiliating her, and yet she submits. During this sordid sex scene, Horner observes it all in terms of drama, a game spoiled by Peggy's not playing the role he had assigned to her. It is interesting, as well as evidence for my claim that Barth is parodying Sartre's existentialism, that Jake looks upon Peggy as a 'masochist', one of the possibilities Sartre poses for sexual relations, and she continually says 'God damn your eyes'. (A reference to Sartre's notion of The Look.) Jake exits (notice he can exit) from this scene quickly, observing that he had 'stayed out of a characteristic disinclination to walk out of any show, no matter how poor or painful, once I'd seen the first act'.[26] Two points are important here. First, mythotherapy works on the assumption that others will play the role assigned; it is based on domination and humiliation of others. Second, it assumes the world itself can be arranged like so many props.

Joe Morgan's ethical subjectivism also involves these assumptions. Thus he is a Pygmalion to his wife, Rennie. Pygmalion, you recall, hated women but fell in love with a statue he himself had made. Joe tries to make Rennie into his image of her as a rational, self-sufficient, and private person. Rennie married Joe to have him remake her in his image. Before her marriage, she had been a 'big blob of sleep'. She says, 'I threw out every opinion I owned because I couldn't defend them. I think I completely erased myself so I could start over.' Joe is convinced he has made Rennie into a independent, self-sufficient person and thus when he confronts Jake he is determined both to test Rennie and to make Jake a self-sufficient existentialist.

This is Morgan's project, the ironic one of an existentialist seeking justification, of a man who denies objective values yet who plays God. Joe deliberately badgers Jake into going along with Rennie on long horse-back rides. Jake takes on the role of 'examiner' (note the medical metaphor) seeking to convince Rennie that there could be nothing sillier than Joe's idea of choosing and living coherently. He realizes Rennie is uncertain and observes that though Rennie claims that she has chosen to be moulded by Joe, 'she chose it as I chose my position in the Progress and Advice Room'. In the course of their long conversation Joe is continually referred to as an Eagle Scout and God and Jake as a devil's advocate. Rennie sees him as just like Joe, a first-rate mind, and yet as nothing, a non-existent. Meanwhile Horner and Morgan carry on an endless debate with Jake characteristically advocating first one view than another. Rennie finally tells Jake that she dreamed that Joe was playing tennis with the devil to test his strength. She says:

[26] Ibid., 30.

I thought Joe had invited the Devil to test me too . . . But this Devil scared me because I wasn't that strong yet, and what was a game for Joe was a terrible fight for me . . . Then when Joe saw how it was, he told me that he had conjured up the Devil out of his own strength just as God might do. Then he made me pregnant again so I'd know *he* was the one who was real . . . so I'd grow to be just as strong as he is, and stronger than somebody who isn't even real![27]

Rennie tells Jake that Joe is genuine because 'he is the same man today as he was yesterday'. Jake then persuades Rennie to spy on Joe, a very unSartrean thing to do! Rennie protests, '*Real* people aren't any different when they're alone. No masks. What you see of them is authentic.'[28] They discover Joe parading naked in front of the mirror, uttering nonsense, and then he picks his nose and masturbates at the same time.

It is at this point that Jake starts acting like Joe with the Doctor and Peggy. He tells Peggy they are to have a completely honest relationship and hits her to prove it, a parody of Joe's action with Rennie. The Doctor also hits Jake at one point because he won't take a stand. Soon the inevitable adultery with Rennie occurs. Jake notes that to him it was without significance, a matter of a few inarticulated sentiments. It was unpremeditated and entirely unreflective.[29] But when called by Rennie to discuss what to do about the adultery, he is struck with 'a sudden marvellous sensation of guilt'.[30] This is followed by fear and sympathy. For once he notes he is not self-conscious or playing a role. But 'Self-consciousness soon returns along with curiosity'.[31] It is curiosity to find out what the outcome will be—escape or confrontation.

Morgan does confront him and the real contest begins. Joe demands to know why Jake did it, and, of course, Jake has no reasons. Morgan is determined to have a motive for the action, for this is pivotal to his philosophy: action cannot occur without a motive. Joe even forces a re-enactment of the adultery so motives can be discovered. And he tells Jake that he has bought a Colt 45 and some bullets in case any one wanted to use it. This gun becomes an overwhelming image for Jake. He writes:

Even in my room it makes itself terrifically present as the concrete embodiment of an alternative: the fact of its existence put the game in a different ball park, as it were; it flavoured all my reflections on the subject with an immediacy . . . which my isolation, if nothing else had kept me

---

27 Ibid., 68.
28 Ibid., 70.
29 Ibid., 101.
30 Ibid., 103.
31 Ibid., 106.

from feeling. It was its finality that gave the idea of the Colt its persistence. It was with me all the time.[32]

The gun becomes a nightmarish reality when the Morgans bring it with them to Jake's room to confront him with the fact of Rennie's pregnancy. Jake observes 'we formed most embarrassingly a perfect equilateral triangle with the gun in the centre'.[33] Joe characteristically demands that Jake take a position on what to do about the pregnancy. Jake, characteristically, cannot take one. Rennie poses a black-and-white set of choices: abortion or suicide. Joe tells her she can't pose those alternatives because abortion is not permitted in Wicomico. At that point Rennie moves toward the gun and Jake finally carries out an act by grabbing the gun so that the suicide is prevented. It is all melodramatic and yet all deadly serious. Morgan tells Horner '. . . if there's one thing I'd kill you for, Horner, its for screwing up the issues so that we have to act before we've thought, or, taking something as important as this out of the realm of choice'.[34] Horner observes, 'It is a demoralizing thing to deal with a man who will see, face up to, and un-hesitantly act upon the extremest limits of his ideas'.[35]

Jake is suddenly awake to the reality of the situation. It is no mere game or drama he can stage. Yet he acts in the only way he knows how to act, through drama. He stages an elaborate drama playing both a distraught husband and psychiatrist to try to persuade a local doctor to perform a legal abortion only to have Rennie refuse to lie and play the role he set up. He tries to get Peggy Rankin, the old maid, to help him by pretending he will marry her only to find she has tricked him. Finally, he turns to the last resort, the Doctor. The Doctor tells him that if he had practised his therapy this would not have happened. However, on the condition that Jake will give him all his money and come with him to a new location of the Remobilization Farm, he agrees to the abortion. A bizarre and horrifying scene then occurs—during the abortion Rennie chokes on her own vomit and dies. Joe takes all responsibility for the events and loses his job, though Jake tells us that he craved responsibility. In the last scenes of the novel, Jake feels a terrific incompleteness. He cannot even decide what to feel. He writes:

. . . my limbs were bound like Laöcoon's by the serpent's Knowledge and Imagination, which grown great in the fullness of time no longer tempt, but annihilate.[36]

[32] Ibid., 147.
[33] Ibid., 148.
[34] Ibid., 154.
[35] Ibid., 155.
[36] Ibid., 196.

He speaks to his statue, 'Who can live any longer in the world?'[37] There was no reply. Joe calls him on the phone:

> 'Well, what's on your mind, Jake? What do you think about things.'
> (Tears run down Jake's face as he stands naked in the dark.)
> *I said I don't know what to do.*
> Oh.
> Another pause, a long one; then he hung up and I was left with a dead instrument in the dark.[38]

The next day, weatherless Jake abandons his Laöcoon, climbs into a cab, and utters to the driver the last word of the novel, 'Terminal'.

What is Brought to an End in The End of the Road?

Having described the novel in some detail it is now time to argue some of our main theses. First, I believe it is evident that Barth is taking some central assertions of Jean Paul Sartre's ethical subjectivism and by exaggeration reduces them to absurdity. The main Sartrean ideas used by Barth in the novel are: (1) Consciousness is a no-thing, in a sense it is a *nothing*. (2) Consciousness is dynamic—it is spontaneous, indeterminate, ceaseless creativity—'Thus, each instant of our conscious life reveals to us a creation *ex nihilo*', spontaneity opens up a 'vertigo of possibility' beyond one's confident control. Seeing itself as perpetually unsettled, desirous of escaping from threatening indeterminancy, consciousness creates the 'mask' of an ego, 'as if to make the ego its guardian and its law' from which to hide itself from itself'.[39] (3) Consciousness is imagination that constitutes the given to be a world. (4) Being-itself is a brute giveness; the world given to consciousness stands powerless before consciousness, making no demands and claiming no obligations. (5) Being-with-others is conflict. In trying to achieve love, the for-it-self only attains sadism or masochism. Sexual desire tries to grasp the consciousness of the other through the body. But all one gets is the other's body and then one only possesses 'a dispouille' (cast-off) and in doing so one has deprived the other of his or her freedom. (6) *Pour-soi's* most fervent project is to become God, a project which will be defeated by the density of an absurd and incomprehensible reality. (7) All action is conscious act in the sense that it involves a motive.

Jake's problem is his endless creativity. In order to be a self, which the

[37] Ibid., 197.
[38] Ibid., 197.
[39] Jean Paul Sartre, *The Transcendence of Ego*, trans. Forest Williams and Robert Kilpatrick (New York: Farrar, Straus & Girous-Noonday, 1957), 99-100.

Doctor asserts is to be a *person*, a mask, he must create endless drama in which he is the controller of the situation. He is imagination constituting his world; creating *ex nihilo* each role and situation. Likewise, Joe, because he believes resolute choice and tough-minded action is the only way to deal with the relativity of everything, must control every situation. He must be fully and consciously in charge of each event; he must know clearly the motive or reason for each action. He is a sort of Nietzschean who seeing a cultural and spiritual vacuum believes true values are created by wilfully manipulating oneself and other people.

In order to maintain their positions, both Morgan and Horner must have Sartre's Cartesian world, namely, an inert physical world, manipulable by their wills. Thus, there is very little of the physical world in the novel, very little furniture and props and it is all functional. Further, the human environment must be likewise inert and/or manipulable to their wills. Thus Rennie erases herself so that Joe can remake her into his own image. Peggy likewise is malleable to Jake's manipulation. Both women are defined by their animality and their lack of discipline. Jake notes that Rennie was inadequate at both action and articulation. Rennie was seen by him as a clumsy animal except when engaged in strenous physical activity. Several times in the novel Jake strokes Rennie's hair, 'speaking softly in her ear the wordless, grammarless language she's taught me to calm horses with'.[40]

What is implied here is that Rennie and Peggy represent feminine, passive, formless matter, waiting to be formed by the active male with his reason and language. We need to ask, of course, if this is Barth's sexism or Sartre's. In order for Morgan and Horner to successfully deal with the world in their way they must subjugate and dominate. This is consistent with Sartre's version of the sexual relation—either masochism or sadism. Joe and Jake fight over Rennie's soul by trying to possess her body and when it is uncertain whose creation she carries in her body, the alternatives are abortion or suicide. Relations with others is definitely a conflict situation. The version of freedom that is operative in the novel is put forth by a character in another Barth novel: 'Tis philosophic liberty: a man must impose his version on the world if he is to avoid the world imposing its scheme on him'.[41]

Also, in order for the projects of Jake and Joe to succeed, they must maintain a position of complete non-involvement with the world—an irony for a philosophy of engagement. There must be complete control, complete consciousness of what role one is playing and what one is doing and for what reason. Joe is the completely cold rationalist, thinking everything out before he acts. He is terrifyingly clear-headed. He insists on endless discussion of a situation and on complete verbal honesty. He tries

[40] *The End of the Road*, 71.
[41] John Barth, *The Sot-Weed Factor*.

to resolve the adultery situation by bringing about a replay of the scene with each player analysing his feelings while playing it. It becomes a grotesque situation, leading to Rennie's pregnancy and death. To Socrates' famous dictum 'the unexamined life is not worth living' Barth once retorted, 'Oedipus and I aren't so sure'.[42] Barth seems to be saying that such self-consciousness, such continual re-examination of life is inhuman and leads to tragedy.

Further, relative to Barth's second theme of the juxtaposition of Knowledge (Reason) and Imagination, the reason put forth by the Doctor is lack of imagination. Notice that Rennie poses only two alternatives to the pregnancy: suicide or abortion. The Doctor tells Jake:

> If any one displays almost the same character day in and day out, all day long, it's either because he has no imagination or because he has an imagination so comprehensive that he sees each particular situation of his life as an episode in some grand overall plot and can so distort the situations that the same type of hero can deal with them all. But this is most unusual.[43]

Mythotherapy fails, as the Doctor notes, because those who practise it either end up getting caught without a script or with the wrong script in a given situation. This happens to Jake and he becomes Jake in a corner. The action does not proceed as Jake desires. The Colt 45 and the pregnancy are things which cannot be manipulated by Jake. Reality impinges on his fiction. Rennie and Peggy refuse to play the role assigned them. One cannot ignore others and the environment; they are not completely malleable to one's will. Jake himself notes the inadequacy of mythotherapy:

> Mythotherapy, in short, becomes increasingly harder to apply, because one is compelled to recognize the inadequacy of any role one assigns. Existence not only precedes essence; in the case of human beings it rather defies essence . . . The trouble, I suppose, is that the more one knows a given person, the more difficult it becomes to assign a character to him, that will allow one to deal with him effectively in an emotional situation.[44]

This theme of the particularity of things defying all attempts to systematize and order them appears throughout the novel. Jake reflects on Rennie's inability to say what she felt about Jake:

> The apparent ambivalence of Rennie's feelings about me, I'm afraid, like the simultaneous contradictory opinions that I often amused

[42] Quoted by Harold Farwell in *John Barth's Tenuous Affirmation: 'The Absurd, Unending Possibility of Love'*, *The Georgia Review*, xxviii (1979) p. 303.
[43] *The End of the Road*, 89.
[44] Ibid., 128.

myself by maintaining, was only a pseudo-ambivalence whose source was in the language not in the concepts symbolized by the language. I'm sure, as a matter of fact, that what Rennie felt was actually neither ambivalent nor even complex; it was both single and simple, like all feelings, but like all feelings it was also completely particular and individual, and so the trouble started only when she attempted to label it with a common noun such as *love* or *abhorrence*. Things can be signified by, nouns only if one ignores the differences between them; but it is precisely these differences, when deeply felt, that make the nouns inadequate . . . Assigning names to things is like assigning roles to people; it is necessarily a distortion, but it is a necessary distortion if one would get on with the plot, . . .[45]

Language, conceptualization, literature, cannot adequately deal with human reality, yet one must persist in trying:

To turn experience into speech—that is, to classify, categorize, to conceptualize, to grammarize, to syntactify it—is always a betrayal of experience, a falsification of it, but only so betrayed can it be dealt with at all, and only in so dealing with it did I ever feel a man, alive and kicking.[46]

Jake and Joe don't believe in rules or absolutes. Further, they don't communicate; they debate, argue, impose. Jake tells his grammar class:

You're free to break the rules, but not if you're after intelligibility, . . . then the only way to get 'free' of the rules is to master them so thoroughly that they're second nature to you.

But once a set of rules for etiquette or grammar is established and generally accepted . . . then one's free to break them only if he's willing to be regarded as a savage or an illiterate.[47]

Though the rules of language are arbitrary they are necessary for intelligibility, for communication, for civilization. Though language, conceptualization, logic can never capture the complexities of life, they are necessary for normal human functioning.

This brings us to a very important point. Horner says 'articulation is his absolute', but it is also evident that he is sensitive to the limits of articulation. What is crucial is not determining what Barth believes about language and its limits. Rather, the focus should be the reason why Horner is worried about the difficulties with articulation. It is because he wants to be attentive to the personal reactions of people, and such, more intimate communication, is advised to be aware of linguistic distortions. Horner has a sensitivity

[45] Ibid., 141–142.
[46] Ibid., 119.
[47] Ibid., 136–135.

to people, a moral sensitivity. The Doctor tells Jake that he failed because he allowed himself to become involved. He forgot he was playing a role. He became a 'penitent villain'. He allowed himself to be drawn into human contact and emotion. He actually felt guilt, fear, and sympathy. He lost his self-consciousness, giving lie to Sartre's belief that even feeling and emotion must be self-conscious and involve a motive. Jake began to care about Joe's treatment of Rennie as a manipulable object. He does act, though ineffectually. He takes the gun away from Rennie and he tries to get the abortion she wants.

Barth is faulting Sartrean existentialism on at least two crucial grounds. First, in emphasizing absolute freedom and consciousness as nothingness, he is led to describe all human relations in terms of conflict of alien freedoms. Being-with-others is founded on being-for-others which involves the look, the objectification of self which produces shame and fear for one's freedom. Thus, Sartre writes:

> . . . Shame . . . is shame of self; it is the *recognition* of the fact that I am indeed that object which the Other is looking at and judging. I can be ashamed only as my freedom escapes me in order to become a *given* object (BN 350).[48]

Sartre's arch-individualism doesn't allow him to take into account a basic fact of reality, namely, the fundamentally social nature of human beings. And, as we shall argue shortly, his phenomenological analysis of human experience fails because he doesn't realize that a person's first experiences with others is not one of conflict, but of at-one-with.

Secondly, Barth's novel dramatically shows us that ultimately Sartrean existentialism has no room for ethics. Sartre, in an interview in 1964 said 'From the period when I wrote *La Nausée* I wanted to create morality. My evolution consists in no longer dreaming of doing so.'[49]

Mary Warnock in her chapter on Sartre in her *Existentialist Ethics* writes:

> For them, (the Existentialists), if freedom and its exercise are the highest good, the problem of the distribution of freedom, the reconciling of my freedom with yours, must, one might argue, present the greatest problem of all. Their systems of ethics should consist largely in its solution.
>
> But here we come upon a paradox. For though it seems obvious that some solution to this problem must be the beginning of any ethical theory for the Existentialists, in fact they are curiously silent on the subject.[50]

[48] Jean Paul Sartre, *Being and Nothingness*, 350.
[49] Quoted in Konstantin Kolenda, *Philosophy's Journey*.
[50] Mary Warnock, *Existentialist Ethics*, 38.

In talking about Heidegger's concern with the authentic facing of death by each man, Warnock also notes: "There is a sort of heroism in this attitude, but very little humanity'.[51]

Morgan, Horner, and the Doctor are concerned only with their own freedom and in different ways. In trying to be free they treat other as objects and without respect. Joe Morgan, as we have observed, is a Nietzschean terror who manipulates self and others with cold calculation. He says he wants to have Rennie make her own choices. In fact he terrorizes her . . . he strikes her, and he introduces the threat of a gun, either as a means of murder or suicide. These are terrorist tactics. Morgan's glorification of choice is a fraud. The most gripping scene in the novel is the abortion scene. It is so, not only because of the physically horrifying elements in the scene, but even more because of the moral horror of it all. Rennie dies a horrible death while Morgan calmly works on his dissertation on energy and innocence in American history. The Doctor performs the abortion ineptly and without seeking the knowledge that Rennie has just eaten. As a result he kills her. Horner watches it all deeply sickened at the consequences of his irresponsible freewheeling. All three men indulgingly demand their freedom and display a complete lack of concern for others. There is no concern with reconciling their freedom with that of others. And, as Warnock points out, without this concern, without a sense of humanity, their philosophies become ethically empty.

Further, our world is a social one. In order to live in society one must learn to limit one's freedom, creatively (not arbitrarily) reconciling it with the freedom of others. George Lukas, the influential Marxist critic, has argued that what is wrong with modern literature is its ontology. Man is social by nature, says Lukas, but 'the ontological view governing the image of man in the work of leading modernist writers is the exact opposite of this. Man, for these writers is by nature solitary, asocial, unable to enter into relationship with other human beings.'[52] This is Sartre's ontology.

There is, of course, some truth in Sartre's analysis concerning the potentiality for conflict in human relations. This potentiality is grounded at minimum in the inevitable disparity between finite perspectives. Each of us conceives or interprets the world from his own point of view, which is influenced by history, culture, language, gender, education, experience and so on. But the question to be asked is: is the conflict tantamount to the eternal damnation so vividly described by Sartre in his play *No Exit*? Does not Sartre ignore what others have argued, namely, it is really 'being-with-others that is the primordial experience, not being-for-others,

[51] Ibid.
[52] George Lukas, 'The Ideology of Modernism', in John Oliver Perry, *Backgrounds to Modern Literature* (San Francisco: Chandler, 1968), 248.

or for myself. Thus Merleau-Ponty contends that cogito and distinction from others is a late experience in life:

> The child lives in a world which he unhesitantly believes accessible to all around him. He has no awareness of himself or others as private subjectivities, nor does he suspect that all of us, himself included, are limited to one certain point of view of the world (p. 335).[53]

It is only at age 12 or so, argues Merleau-Ponty.

> At this state (12) . . . he discovers himself both as a point of view on the world and also as called upon to transcend that point of view, and to construct an objectivity at the level of judgment.[54]

Josiah Royce, the American philosopher, makes a similar point.

> Nobody amongst us men comes to self-consciousness, so far as I know, except under the persistent influence of his social fellows. A child in the earlier stages of his social development . . . shows you, as you observe him, a process of development of self-consciousness in which, at every stage, the Self of the child grows and forms itself through Imitation, and through functions that cluster about the Imitation of others, and that are secondary thereto . . . and his self-consciousness, as it grows, feeds upon social models, so that at every stage of his awakening life his consciousness of the Alter is a step in the advance of his consciousness. His playmates, his nurse, or mother, or the workmen whose occupations he sees, and whose power fascinates him, appeal to his imitativeness and set him copies for his activities. He learns his little arts, and as he does so, he contrasts his own deeds with those of his models, and of other children. Now contrast is, in our conscious *life, the mother of clearness. What the child does instinctively, and without comparison with the deeds of others, may never come to his clear consciousness as his own deeds at all.* What he learns imitatively, and then reproduces, perhaps in joyous obstinacy, as an act that enables him to display himself over against others—this constitutes the beginning of his self-conscious life.[55]

Royce and Merleau-Ponty make another point which tells against Sartre's analysis of relations with others and which has to do with Horner's concern with language and civilization. The very conflict of perspectives Sartre talks about presupposes the prior experience of community. When my perspective is called into question I seek to substantiate it or modify it

---

[53] Maurice Merleau-Ponty, *Phenomenology of Perception*, trans. C. Smith (London: Routledge and Kegan Paul, 1966), 355.

[54] Ibid.

[55] Josiah Royce, *The World and The Individual* (New York: Second Series, Dover Publications, 1959), 261–262, italics are Royce's.

by recourse to the ideal of objective truth. What does this appeal to objectivity reveal? Merleau-Ponty tells us:

> My awareness of constructing an objective truth would never provide me with anything more than an objective truth for me, and my greatest attempt at impartiality would never enable me to prevail over my subjectivity . . . if I had not, underlying my judgments, the primordial certainty of being in contact with being itself, if, before any voluntary *adoption of a position*, I were not already *situated* in an intersubjective world . . . with the cogito begins that between consciousness . . . For the struggle ever to begin, for each consciousness to be capable of suspecting the alien presences which it negates, all must necessarily have some common ground and be mindful of their peaceful co-existence in the world of childhood (p. 355).[56]

In other words, the original communality, the common and public world of perceptual and linguistic experience provides the model of objectivity and truth. Lacking this as reference conflict between perspectives would not emerge; the other's world, like his dreams, would be his private affair and would have no bearing on my life. Only where our perspectives intersect does agreement or dispute become relevant or possible, and these merge into each other says Merleau-Ponty, (where) 'we coexist through a common world'.[57]

Josiah Royce makes an even more telling point when he argues that the individualism so highly prized by Sartre and by Joe Morgan can only come to fruition in a communal context. In his *The Problem of Christianity*, Royce provides a careful analysis of how highly cultivated societies train their members both in individualism and collectivism. He points out that the individual gains self-consciousness by opposition to the social will, while the social will inflames self-will. The socially trained individual is taught not only to value his own will by opposition to the collective will, but also to respect the collective will. Royce writes, '*Individualism and collectivism are tendencies each of which, as our social order grows, intensifies the other*'.[58]

Indeed, Royce would suggest that the arch-individualism of Sartre which sees the self as a self-contained, independent existence leads to collectivism. If relations with other selves constitute no essential part of the self that is related, all forms of togetherness of selves becomes accidental and external. All forms of community become mere collectivisms (Sartre-

---

[56] Merleau-Ponty, op. cit., 355.

[57] Ibid., 354.

[58] Josiah Royce, *The Problem of Christianity*, I (Chicago: Henry Regnery Company, 1981), 152.

Marxism). Further, Royce recognizes and describes very well how such individualism leads to ethical emptiness. He writes:

> the Self seems to stand within its own realm, as a sort of absolute authority, over against any external will or knowledge that pretends to determine its own nature, or its precise limits, or its meaning . . . It is thus a separate entity, in its essence unapproachable . . . possessing perhaps its own unalienable rights, the unit of all ethical order, the centre of its own universe . . . the principal problem for any such realistic Individualism, always becomes the question of how this Self, whose interests are essentially its own, can rationally come to recognize any responsibility to other Selves or to God, or to any Absolute Ought beyond its own caprice.[59]

The answer to the dangers of collectivism about which the existentialists were concerned is not to argue for absolute individual freedom, but rather, it is the building of community through interpretation and dialogue. Royce describes this process extensively in *The Problem of Christianity* but that is beyond the scope of this paper. One can, however, make two points: it is the case that being-with-others can be threatening and lead to conflict, but it is also the case that being-with-others can bring more freedom, more self-development, common meaning and purpose. Others can help as well as hinder our ethical self-projects. Royce writes:

> Our fellows are known to be real and have their own inner life, because they are for each of us the endless treasury of *more ideas*. They answer our questions; they tell us news; they make comments, they pass judgments; they express novel combinations of feelings; they relate to us stories, they argue with us, and take counsel with us . . . *Our fellows furnish us the constantly needed supplement to our own fragmentary meanings*.[60]

We need each other to broaden our vision and lives. Likewise reason needs imagination for it can too easily lead to the narrow-mindeness, reductionism and dogmatism of Joe Morgan. And imagination needs reason or it will lead to the crass opportunism of the Doctor or the irresponsibly freewheeling of Jake Horner. And philosophy needs literature to dramatize ideas as Barth has so skilfully done so that one can see the horrors one's ideas might lead to if taken seriously. And, as Lukas notes, literature needs philosophy to give it an ontology to play out and test. Indeed, one might ask, does the presentation of Sartrean ideas in a literary work make the arguments against Sartre more 'compelling' either logically or psychologically? In answering this question I would make three points. First,

[59] Josiah Royce, *The World and the Individual*, 282–283.
[60] Ibid., 171–172, italics are Royce's.

Barth began with a philosophical ontology that was ready at hand. Secondly, the analysis of Barth's work provided in this paper has been informed by a philosophical perspective and that perspective has, it is admitted, received more attention than the literary aspects of Barth's novel. Perhaps one might want to claim that some of the literary aspects of Barth's novel suffer because of its heavy philosophical emphasis. Thirdly, however, the literary dramatization of Sartrean ideas reawakens our interest in them and ask us to look at them in a new light.

Finally, I can't think of any better ethical task for the future for both literature and philosophy than the one put forth by Royce in *The Problem of Christianity*. It is this:

> however you can, and whenever you can, so act as to help towards making mankind one loving brotherhood, whose love is not a mere affection for morally detached individuals, but a love of the unity of its own life upon its own divine level, and a love of individuals in so far as they can be raised to communion with this spiritual community itself.[61]

[61] Royce, *The Problem of Christianity*, I, 356–357.

The Noble

JOHN CASEY

We can try to imagine a people who in circumstances of hardship and danger—in hunting and warfare, for instance—show endurance, persistence, indifference to pain, and an unflinching readiness to accept death. Yet it may be that these qualities do not have any important place in their picture of themselves. Their courage is simply something they take for granted and it does not go with any practice of praise and blame. They are not proud of themselves when they act bravely, nor ashamed of themselves if they fail to do so. This would be a courage that would be independent of the social practices of praise and blame, admiration and contempt, pride and shame. It would be a courage that did not fit into a scheme of values. This raises the question whether it could properly be regarded as an ethical quality, as a virtue.

This sort of courage perhaps corresponds to what Aristotle called the 'natural' analogue of the true virtue of courage—a natural disposition that can exist without education and moral training, and without other virtues such as practical wisdom and justice.

Another sort of courage different from the moral virtue of courage would be a specialized skill—like the well-based confidence of lion tamers, or even of professional soldiers. The admiration we might have for such a specialized skill might stop short of our respecting someone 'as a man' because of it—which is another way of saying that we do not regard it as a moral virtue.

Aristotle and Hume have offered an account of courage that firmly links it to a whole set of human qualities that we can respect and admire, and which make it a matter of shame and honour within a social practice. For Aristotle courage must involve deliberate choice, and the right motive; most like true courage is the behaviour of citizen soldiers facing death in battle under orders, and acting out of fear of disgrace and desire for honour. Hume says: 'The utility of courage, both to the public and to the person possessed of it, is an obvious foundation of merit. But to anyone who duly considers of the matter, it will appear that this quality has a peculiar lustre, which it derives wholly from itself, and from that noble elevation inseparable from it. Its figure, drawn by painters and poets, displays in each feature a sublimity and daring confidence, and diffuses, by sympathy, a like sublimity of sentiment over every spectator.[1]' And his

---

[1] *Enquiry Concerning the Principles of Morals*, sect. VII.

discussion is in the context of 'greatness of mind' which he relates to 'a certain degree of generous pride or self-value' which he holds is so 'requisite' that its absence displeases 'after the same manner as the want of a nose or an eye, or any of the most material feature of the face or member of the body'.[2] This greatness of mind he connects with the sublime, quoting Longinus who says that the sublime is often nothing but the echo or image of magnanimity. In the *Treatise* Hume says that although courage has 'some foundation in nature' it 'derives its merit in a great measure from artifice'.[3]

This points to a way of thinking about one virtue—courage—which insists that it be connected with a certain sort of deliberate choice, with a certain sort of motive, and with a certain satisfaction or self-valuing: pride. It also sees it as commanding admiration and a respect that seems to go beyond the respect that Kant thinks we are constrained to feel towards the morally good man. For Hume courage is not an object purely of a moral attitude, but also calls forth sentiments that we might want to call 'aesthetic'. The sublime is, after all, primarily a notion in aesthetic theory, even though both Longinus and Hume connect it with magnanimity (*megalopsychia*). Furthermore, courage understood in this way is not a virtue that can be thought of purely in terms of good intentions, or the good will, since it also includes success in acting upon the world, a particular sort of appearance in the eyes of others, perhaps even a mode of comportment. It seems to imply a public role and a social practice.

On this picture the brave man wishes to have a certain sense of himself. Aquinas[4] says that the brave man's 'immediate end' is 'to express the reflection of his quality in his acts'. It is not simply that he wants certain good ends which his courage can bring about. Nor is it simply that he derives from his courage the confidence that he can do certain things. It also involves his seeing himself as the sort of person who can claim certain attitudes and reactions from others. Courage on this view intrinsically involves self-value and a corresponding claim to be valued by others. People in whom courage was entirely 'natural' and unconscious would not in the same way think of themselves as brave. And they would not think of courage as part of moral goodness. The conception of courage that we find in both Hume and Aristotle connects it with demands for recognition and respect, and with such practices as paying honour. The honour to which courage lays claim, in both the ancient and Renaissance tradition, could probably not be offered simply by an inner assent of the mind independent of any customs of recognition, of honouring. And for Aristotle the end of courage is the *noble*.

[2] Ibid.
[3] Bk III, Part II, sect. XII.
[4] *Summa Theologica*, 2a2ae.123,8.

I. The Concept of the Noble

Do we need the concept of the noble? Can it play an important role in ethics? Many people would answer 'No' and would argue that the notion of nobility, supposing it to be intelligible at all, is at best marginal in helping us to understand human moral goodness. And we should concede straightaway that there is at least one tradition of thought about moral goodness—the Kantian—which on the face of it excludes most of the qualities that enter into a traditional idea of the noble from contributing to moral merit. The traditional concept of the noble seems to run together the ethical and the aesthetic, morality and manners, the individual and the social, that which it is in the power of every man to will and that which is in their power only contingently. It blurs (as Hume would have wished to blur) any sharp distinction between moral and non-moral qualities.

The true problem in any attempt to describe, or to resuscitate, a notion of the noble does not lie in the qualities of character that should come under it. A generosity of spirit, a disdain of the petty, a tempering of egoism that is not poor-spiritedness but rather a *contemptus mundi* that arises from the contemplation of 'whatsoever is grave and constant in human sufferings'[5]—all these qualities can be adduced that correspond roughly with the ancient and Renaissance idea of the noble. They can still be understood, whether or not they seem relevant to the conditions of our own lives. The problem lies precisely at that point where certain morally good qualities—such as goodness of will—pass over into something else. The ancient and Renaissance conception of the noble certainly does not coincide with the Kantian picture of the man of good will. It does not place all its weight upon intentions, since it also takes account of success in acting upon the world. It assumes that certain admirable personal qualities may depend for their realization upon contingency. Certainly Aristotle seems to have assumed that the man who above all pursued noble ends was most unlikely to be a slave. (It is also worth remembering that the Homeric hero who was enslaved actually lost much of his *arete* by that very fact.) And it is notorious that in his picture of the man of 'greatness of mind' Aristotle includes qualities that seem purely accidental: he moves slowly and has a deep voice.[6]

And the traditional connection between courage and nobility perhaps adds to the difficulty. For the importance of courage as a moral virtue seems to derive from its being capable of great achievement. Courage aims actively at the highest, greatest things in practical life; for instance

---

[5] C.f. Joyce, *A Portrait of the Artist as a Young Man*, p. 209.

[6] However, cf. Aquinas's defence of the magnanimous man (*Summa*, 2a2ae. 129,3). Aquinas argues that the magnanimous man's slow step and deep voice proceed from his concentration upon great matters.

it faces death in battle on behalf of one's city. If a virtue is defined as 'the highest manifestation of a power'[7] then it will be natural to understand any particular virtue through an objective assessment of the ends which it achieves. If courage is to be valued partly on account of the greatness of its end, then it will follow (as Aristotle thought it followed) that courage with a lesser end—the courage, for instance, of enduring sickness patiently—will be a lesser thing, even though it require as great a subjective endurance by the sufferer. And this is connected with the pride which is characteristic of the courageous man in both Hume and Aristotle. This pride, which is a demand for honour, values one's own character and actions not simply because of a purity of intention, but also because of actual or possible greatness of achievement. (It is worth remembering that Nietzsche thought that it is precisely a stress on successful action, rather than on good intentions, which chiefly distinguishes the 'noble ethic' from the 'slave ethic'.)

So a central problem for us about the noble, if it is understood in anything like its traditional form, is that it does seem to be partly an ethical quality, to involve dispositions which perhaps every human being necessarily has reason for cultivating, while at the same time it seems to characterize a superior human specimen—the 'highest manifestation of a power'—who possesses qualities and advantages which cannot express a universal human obligation, and which are probably impossible for many—or, as Aristotle would say, for 'the many'.

We should notice in passing another difficulty—primary and derivative uses of words. We can talk of a noble action and a noble character. We can also talk of a noble piece of music (cf. Elgar's regular direction *nobilmente*) and a noble building. Indeed as an aesthetic term 'noble' is probably most commonly used of architecture. (We might say that Lutyens tried to see how a noble expressive tradition could be continued with a considerable modification of the inherited classical vocabulary of architectural nobility.) We can also talk of a noble face. Furthermore—and this is significant—we can think of the human body itself as noble; and yet we may think that this is a matter of how one can imagine it, or even of a tradition of representing it in art. The nobility of the human body may be an artistic discovery.

The simple solution would be to say that there are two (or even three) uses of 'noble' denoting three different concepts. There is noble character and action, which is the primary concept. Then there is the noble face, and finally, aesthetic nobility proper, these being derivative concepts. This would be analogous to Croce's argument[8] that 'sincerity' as a term in aesthetics has a quite different sense from—and is only punningly

[7] Aristotle, *De Čaelo*.
[8] *Aesthetic*, Ch.VI.

related to—its *primary* use in ethics. For present purposes I shall simply say that I shall treat these various uses of 'noble' as expressing the same concept, so that the word is not being used in two or three different senses.[9] This simplicity certainly begs the main question, since I have already indicated that I am concerned with a quality that includes both a man's intentions, and other qualities for which he values himself and is valued by others, that for want of a better term we might call 'aesthetic'.

So let me now make another assertion. Nobility is something that can be presented directly to the eye. It can appear (to use Hegel's words) 'in concrete form'. The seated statues of Lorenzo and Giuliano Medici in the Tomb at San Lorenzo visually express two aspects of the noble. One is the noble as active; the other the noble as contemplative. In neither case do we infer a quality of mind or character from outward signs. The statues do not symbolize nobility, or make us think of nobility. The nobility of the two figures is something that we can actually see, and not something we infer, any more than we infer certain expressive qualities in a piece of writing, or the sadness or gaiety in a piece of music. It is worth remembering some illuminating things that Hegel says in his lectures on aesthetics about 'symbolic' art. For Hegel 'symbolic art' is a particular style or phase of art, distinct from and probably inferior to full representation. Standing behind what Hegel says is this sort of common phenomenon: I recognize an old friend whom I have not seen for many years. At first the face is unfamiliar, but then it suddenly becomes familiar. In Wittgenstein's words 'I see the old face in the altered one'. What is this phenomenon of recognition? It is not just that the face before me brings the thought of my old friend to mind. For I may be thinking of him precisely at the moment when I am looking at him, and still not recognize him. Rather I must somehow incarnate him in the face before me; I must see the old face in the altered one. Analogously, if through the gestures of a mimic I see 'Maurice Chevalier' (to use an example of Sartre's)[10] I must see him, incarnate him in the gestures—not simply notice resemblances between the mimic's gestures or dress and his, or simply think of him.

The act of recognition is immediate and not some sort of inference from an experience to an idea. The 'idea' of my friend is present in the act of recognition. This immediacy is, for Hegel, present in all our experience of art. In the case of the mimic we do not make an inference from the present experience to the absent man. We see Chevalier in or through the face and gestures of the mimic. We can describe what we see only by referring to the subject of the mimicry, and our recognition

---

[9] For further discussion of this point in relation to 'sincerity' the reader is referred to my '*The Autonomy of Art*', *Institute of Philosophy Lectures* **6** (1971/2).
[10] *The Psychology of Imagination*, 28.

of him is immediate. For Hegel this would be a paradigm of art. All art involves the presentation of ideas in sensuous form. In understanding a work of art we do not make an inference from what we see to the ideas that are being conveyed. When a figure is designed (as Hegel thought Egyptian figures were designed) merely in order to stand as a symbol of the human mind, reminding the spectator of things that are in no way intrinsic to his perception of the figure itself, then we do not have true art. In Greek sculpture by contrast, we find an 'appearance' that is alive with the idea of the human mind. The spectator sees in the sculpted figure qualities of mind and soul that are distinctively Greek. The sculpture is not a mere step in a process of inference, but a concrete embodiment of ideas; and our perception of the sculpture cannot be described without some reference to these ideas.

Our admiration of the Michaelangelo statues will not, on this view, be simply a response to certain abstract ideas that the statues symbolize. We will somehow see the noble in the form, the pose, the appearance of the statues. The appearance of the sculpted bodies is a noble appearance. But if this is so—if such an idea is intelligible—then our response to these statues will also be a response to whatever it is that allows the noble to appear visually in persons. In the Medici statues there is expressed Hume's 'greatness of mind' (i.e. *megalopsychia*) which at the same time suggests what I can only call a peculiar consonance between these men and the world. That is to say, their nobility includes not only something inner or spiritual, but also comportment, a sense of how they are to be looked at, how they are to appear. Qualities of mind and spirit have objectified themselves, turned themselves into objects for the gaze of others. The serenity of mind that we see in these statues seems to imply a sense of unity with the world, a sense of their having a secure, recognized and pre-eminent existence in the world. A public world is for them somehow the fulfilment and condition of their sense of themselves. Honour, and indeed glory, is what is demanded by their deepest sense of what they are. And this vision is something that we can see, and which enters into our aesthetic appreciation of these sculptures.

At this point it may well be suggested that we are really seeing the noble as a matter of *style*—and indeed of a style that may be possible only at certain periods in history. I do not think that that is a problem for the line of thought that I am trying to develop. Indeed it is something for which I shall be arguing. I think that it is possible to hold, on the one hand, that the human body can be seen, is to be seen, as noble, and yet also to think (as perhaps Hegel thought) that the noble aspect of the human form was a stylistic and spiritual discovery of the Greeks and their sculptors; that it is difficult to have a sense of the body as noble outside such a tradition; that the human form in pre-classical art—even in Egyptian art—is not 'noble'.

The idea towards which we are moving is that the noble involves not only a certain disposition of mind or spirit but also certain expectations of social and material conditions. That is to say, it is a concept (to use Sartrian language) of 'being-in-the-world'. The serenity that Hegel finds (influenced by Winckleman and not—if one may so put it—by Nietzsche) in the sculpted figures of Greek gods is not simply a state of mind outwardly symbolized by a physical pose. The statues are of the nobly human, an idea that is captured in the vision of the human body that they express. If there is a particular philosophy or religion that envisages man as noble, then these sculptures are not propaganda for it but concrete expressions of it.

A central difficulty for modern men in thinking about the noble arises from the picture of the self that it seems to presuppose. Philosophers in the empiricist tradition have tended to understand the self in atomic terms. One's true self is precisely that which can be brought under descriptions which uniquely identify it without bringing in social, political or cultural concepts. There has been an important shift of criteria from Renaissance to modern times as to what is to be included within the notion of a man's self, a shift which it would not be unreasonable to suppose reflects social and political change. The ancient Greeks included as part of a man's self not only his social rôle, but even his fate. 'His early death is *part* of Achilles, as much constitutive of his identity as his great prowess and invulnerability.'[11] One way in which people may express their identity with a social world is in looking for honour from their city—as Aristotle says brave citizen soldiers do. Men can find that their real self is the self that finds pride in, looks for honour from something that transcends the individual—a group, city or state. On this view one finally knows what people are only when one sets them within a social world. The 'truth' of man is his social reality. This way of thinking allows for an identification with the public realm that gives rise to feelings that are as intense and as real as those of private life. Notoriously patriotism can express the most intense human attachments, and this can include attachment to language and culture as much as to place. ('Thus, love of a country/ Begins as attachment to our own field of action'.)[12] So grief for the misfortunes of one's country can be no less real in revealing what one is than private grief. This might be related to the distinction that many feel exists between tragedy and pathos, with the idea that tragic suffering is somehow more representative.

So the idea of the noble that I have been trying to capture, and which relates it to some thoughts of Aristotle and Hume, is an idea of being-in-the-world, of one's self being fulfilled in a social rôle or function,

[11] Charles Taylor, *Hegel*, 502.
[12] T. S. Eliot, 'Little Gidding'.

and of an identification of oneself with a public world, an identification that is expressed in feeling and action.

What I am saying perhaps sounds like the insinuation of an unreconstructed Renaissance ethic into the modern world. In fact it is intended as a rational reconstruction of, or at least a rough approximation to, the best account of the noble that exists—that given by Hegel in *The Phenomenology of Mind*.[13] The noble consciousness is, for Hegel, one which identifies itself with the state, and with state wealth and power. The noble consciousness finds the state, in its universality, to be the reality of itself; it finds itself in the state. This means that it finds itself in a service to the state that will go as far as the most complete self-sacrifice —in death. Hegel calls this 'the heroism of service'. Hegel also suggests that the noble consciousness, in thus identifying itself with what I have been calling (weakly) a public realm, but which he calls 'state power', 'acquires reverence for itself, and gets reverence from others' (p. 527). What Hegel seems to be saying is that we have here a picture of the self that achieves its reality, its realization, through the state; and at the same time *ipso facto* the state becomes 'real' for the self. Power, and indeed wealth, become 'essential' to the noble consciousness.

I shall not dwell on the details of Hegel's fascinating account of the noble consciousness. Instead I shall go straight on to a very fine account of the same topic that draws explicitly upon Hegel, and in particular upon Hegel's treatment of Diderot's *Rameau's Nephew*—that given by Lionel Trilling in *Sincerity and Authenticity*.[14] Trilling points out (recapitulating Nietzsche without mentioning him) that the term 'noble' is not traditionally used as part of a polarity of 'good and evil', but so that the polar opposite of the noble is the 'base'. The values that have historically gone with the noble—such as the Aristocratic and martial virtues— are essentially self-regarding: 'The noble self is not shaped by its beneficent intentions towards others; its intention is wholly towards itself, and such moral virtue as may be attributed to it follows incidentally from its expressing the privilege and function of its social status in mien and deportment'. Trilling goes on to associate the noble consciousness depicted by Hegel with the vision given supreme expression in the late plays of Shakespeare: '. . . the norm of life which they propose is one of order, peace, honour and beauty, these qualities being realized in, and dependent upon, certain material conditions. The hope that animates this normative vision of the plays is the almost shockingly elementary one which Ferdinand utters in *The Tempest*—the hope of "quiet days, fair issue, and long life". It is reiterated by Juno in Prospero's pageant: "Honour, riches, marriage,

---

[13] Ref. pp 522ff. Ch. VI 'Spirit in Self-Estrangement; Culture and its Realm of Reality'. trans Baillie.
[14] Ch 11.

blessing,/Long continuance and increasing". It has to do with good harvests, full barns and the qualities of affluent decorum that Ben Jonson celebrated in Penshurst and Marvell in "Appleton House", and that Yeats prayed for in his daughter's domestic arrangements.'[15]

II. The Noble in Shakespeare

Shakespeare is indeed of central importance in our understanding of the noble. This is, first, because Shakespeare's plays—and unlike Trilling I would concentrate upon the tragedies rather than the late plays— certainly express the ethic of the noble. Since our appreciation of these plays is not simply 'aesthetic' but involves an imaginative and sym- pathetic entering into the experience they convey, it would seem that the noble is a value that can, at least on occasion, have a profound and lively meaning for us. Secondly, in the tragedies the noble is characteristically a contested concept, probed and questioned as much as affirmed. The difficulties that beset the modern mind in trying to take it seriously have nearly all been anticipated by Shakespeare.

One reason why the noble is a contested concept is this: I have per- haps over-simply contrasted the man who pursues a noble end with the Kantian man of good will. An objection frequently brought against the Kantian good man is that if we take it as a fundamental requirement for moral merit that one act 'from principle' rather than from 'human feeling' —from natural benevolence, for instance—then morality and its supreme importance in and authority over human life becomes mysterious. Yet what of the noble man? Does it not begin to look as though he himself acts from motives that are in the end equally obscure? Does it not begin to look as though he acts for the value of 'nobility' rather than out of his fullest sense of being human? Does it not look as though he does the noble from the motive of nobility—i.e. from a desire to have a certain picture of himself, and for others also to have a picture of him as appearing in a certain light? It begins to look, in fact, as though the noble essentially becomes a matter of style, a certain performance. And the Aristotelian insistence that the motives for the truest courage are shame and the desire for honour—so that the desire to be courageous will include the wish to be seen as being a certain sort of person—would seem to lead to just such a conclusion.

This is the point at which a strategy of the anti-noble may be developed, which holds either that the noble, being essentially a matter of style,

---

[15] The relevance of this passage, and of Trilling's argument in general, was drawn to my attention by Christopher Edwards.

John Casey

can give rise only to values of style and performance; or in Juvenal's words (echoed by Johnson and Jonson) 'nobilitas sola est atque unica virtus' (Satire viii, 20).

The Shakespearian play which most pressingly raises for us the question of nobility is *Othello*, with its hero 'the noble Moor'. Some twentieth-century critics—notably T. S. Eliot and F. R. Leavis—have wanted to say either that Othello is not truly noble, or that his insistence upon his own nobility—the spectacle of it—means that he is not truly good. T. S. Eliot wrote that in his last speech Othello is 'cheering himself up'. That is to say, he is 'endeavouring to escape reality, he has ceased to think about Desdemona, and he is thinking about himself . . . (He) is dramatizing himself against his environment'. Eliot thought that this self-dramatizing was a characteristic feature of Renaissance heroes— a wish above all to see oneself in a certain light, to see oneself as noble, this nobility involving above all the playing of a role. The critical case against Othello has gone so far as to accuse him of failing to see the human reality just because he is more concerned with holding fast to a picture of himself as noble.

For Othello, his rôle in the world is part of what he is, so that in losing that he loses what is essential to himself. Othello's sense that he has lost Desdemona expresses itself as a farewell to his 'occupation' as a soldier:

I had been happy if the general camp,
Pioneers and all, had tasted her sweet body,
So I had nothing known. O, now for ever
Farewell the tranquil mind! Farewell content!
Farewell the plumed troops, and the big wars
That makes ambition virtue! O, farewell!
Farewell the neighing steed and the shrill trump,
The spirit-stirring drum, th' ear piercing fife,
The royal banner and all quality,
Pride, pomp, and circumstance of glorious war!
And O ye mortal engines whose rude throats
Th' immortal Jove's dread clamours counterfeit,
Farewell! Othello's occupation's gone.

(III. iii)

Othello is moved by the sadness of his own fate, by 'the pity of it'. It is not simply self-pity: the war, its glory, is bound up with his love for Desdemona, and hers for him. Othello *is* a warrior, and in losing that 'occupation' he loses himself. Similarly in *Antony and Cleopatra*, Cleopatra's love for Antony cannot be separated from her sense of his greatness, his glory. Antony's magnificence—in the sense of the Aristotelian *virtue* of magnificence, which includes greatness of mind, imagination in display, and bounty—is as much an object of her love and loyalty as anything else.

However, the play of Shakespeare's that most repays our study as an example of a sustained exploration of the noble is *Coriolanus*. Shakespeare's Coriolanus is a man who has a conception of what is noble, of what is courageous. He too identifies himself with 'state wealth and power' and in the play we see such a self-identification branch out into a consciousness of even the body itself as expressing an impersonal ideal, becoming thing-like, an adamantine instrument, an 'engine', related to a state that has also become a palpable thing, a juggernaut. Coriolanus as an engine—. . . when he walks, he moves like an engine, and the ground shrinks before his treading: he is able to pierce a corslet with his eye; he talks like a knell, and his hum is a battery' (V. iv)—goes well with the juggernaut state:

> . . . . you may as well
> Strike at the heaven with your staves as lift them
> Against the Roman state, whose course will on
> The way it takes; cracking ten thousand curbs
> Of more strong link asunder than can ever
> Appear in your impediment.
> (I. i)

Coleridge writes of Coriolanus that he 'pursues honour as an end in itself'. Coriolanus's exclusive attachment to honour means that he divides Rome into the honoured and honourable patricians, and the plebeians who are scabs, curs, rats, who do not belong to 'the fundamental part of the state'. And Coriolanus's honour is undoubtedly an identification with Rome whose perfect instrument he is to be, an identification with a perfect fighting role that in its rejection of all human weakness becomes something like an attempt to cut free from all human relations—an attempt which must fail at the very moment when he most explicitly commits himself to it: 'I'll never/Be such a gosling to obey instinct, but stand/As if a man were author of himself/And knew no other kin'—spoken just before he will surrender to the importunities of his mother. Coriolanus's attachment to honour 'as an end in itself' inevitably becomes pride and egotism, a pride that the tribunes seriously or hypocritically see as inhuman:

> You speak o' the people
> As if you were a god to punish, not
> A man of their infirmity.
> (III. i)

Coriolanus's attachment to honour is indeed expressed in the strangely insistent physicality of the play. And not only is his honour deeply involved in physicality, but his sense of courage is a sense of the body which becomes either a thing or an emblem of the state. His body is identified with the state in becoming its sword—his very body is to be made a sword by the soldiers, an apt expression of his proud dedication to the honour of the warrior: 'They all shout, and wave their swords; take him up in their arms, and cast up their caps': 'O me, alone, make you a sword of me?' And his mother sees him as Rome's instrument, her weapon killing men, in the disturbing lines:

> Death, that dark spirit, in's nervy arm doth lie,
> Which, being advanc'd, declines, and then men die.
> (II. i)

His sense of his own honour is a sense of his masculinity and manliness. When he agrees to humble his pride and abase his honour by speaking gently to the plebeians, he sees his putting aside of his *natural* disposition, his pride, as an abnegation of his manliness:

> ... Well, I must do 't.
> Away my disposition, and possess me
> Some harlot's spirit! My throat of war be turned
> Which choired with my drum, into a pipe
> Small as an eunuch or the virgin voice
> That babies lulls asleep.
> (III. ii)

The flesh in Coriolanus is never seen *as* flesh, except when he is suddenly overcome by it, as when he kisses his wife, Virgilia. His pride in what he understands as the highest value—*pietas* towards the state—calls for a transformation of ordinary human feeling, of the ordinary weakness of the body into something rigid, unfleshly, adamantine. It is to become a thing, an object, an emblem, something that incarnates all that '*virtus* or valiancy' which Plutarch (in North's translation) says was honoured in Rome above all other virtues, and which can be finally understood only as service to and identification with the state. Aufidius, the rival of Coriolanus, also sees his body as something of superhuman hardness:

> Let me twine
> Mine arms about that body, where against
> My grained ash an hundred times hath broke
> And scarr'd the moon with splinters.
> (IV.v)

And he inspires in Aufidius that 'sublimity of sentiment' that Hume says the actual representation or figure of courage inspires 'by sympathy':

> Know thou first
> I loved the maid I married; never man
> Sighed truer breath; but that I see thee here,

Thou noble thing, more dances my rapt heart
Than when I first my wedded mistress saw
Bestride my threshold.
(IV. v)

Volumnia sees her son as destined to exist and exert himself in the public realm:

> ... when youth with comeliness plucked all gaze his way ... I considering how honour would become such a person—that it was no better than picture-not-like to hang it on the wall, if renown made it not stir—was pleased to let him seek danger where he was like to find fame. To a cruel war I sent him, from whence he returned his brows bound with oak. I tell thee, daughter, I sprang not more in joy at first bearing a man-child than now in first seeing he had proved himself a man.

This public realm can be understood only as a denial of something else—the ignoble, scurrying world of the plebeians. Hence for both Coriolanus and his mother genuine virtue is inseparable from genuine pride.[16] His love of Rome must involve pride because it has become something self-contained and complete in itself, an attachment to a certain image, which includes an image of himself and his own role. This goes naturally with a series of oppositions between man as a creature of flesh and blood and man as embodying the Roman state which will keep its course

> cracking ten thousand curbs
> Of more strong link asunder than can ever
> Appear in your impediment.

We might notice, incidentally, the part played in all this by images of blood. As the body itself becomes simply an instrument of Rome, so the *wounded* body is turned into an emblem: as part of the instrumentality of the body Coriolanus's blood is seen by his mother as sharing in the beauty of courage:

> Vol.   His bloody brow
> With his mailed hand then wiping, forth he goes,
> Like to a harvest-man that's tasked to mow
> Or all or lose his hire.
> Virg. His bloody brow? Jupiter, no blood!
> Vol. Away you fool! It more becomes a man
> Than gilt his trophy. The breasts of Hecuba,
> When she did suckle Hector, looked not lovelier
> Than Hector's forehead, when it spit forth blood

---

[16] Cf. Wilson Knight, *The Imperial Theme.*

At Grecian sword, contemning.
(I. ii)

Speaking to his soldiers before Corioli, Marcius himself exults in his blood:

>   If any such be here—
> Which it were sin to doubt—that love this painting
> Wherein you see me smeared; if any fear
> Lesser his person than an ill report;
> If any think brave death outweighs bad life,
> And that his country's dearer than himself . . .
>   (I. vi)

Blood in *Coriolanus* is an image of all that is *overcome* in courageous action. The wound itself means nothing: it is only where blood can be taken as the accompaniment of and the counterpoint to the sacrificial action that it has meaning. The images of honour and glory in *Coriolanus* set the warrior apart from the weaknesses of the flesh: blood shed in battle is a symbol of all that is passive in man being overcome in the exercise of martial courage; it is all that spontaneous life that is controlled or transcended in the sacrifice of the warrior. It is only the 'honourable wound' that is seen in this way. We do thus not see menstrual blood, or blood from internal bleeding, nor even the wound of Amfortas in *Parsifal*, which expresses private, unaccepted suffering rather than noble sacrifice. In the same way *Coriolanus* takes into account that ancient and medieval sense of the wholeness of courage as something both mental and physical, a natural fact and a value. The body thus attains its *significance* in a public world, a world of allegiance, sacrifice, honour.

I have not adduced Shakespeare *simply* as an example of a writer who is seriously concerned with the noble ethic. But I suggest that in his tragedies the idea of the noble is assumed but questioned, asserted and denied in a way that makes it possible for us to see how it is not simply an historical idea, a survival of the aristocratic ethic of the Renaissance, but a way of probing human values. In *Othello, Antony and Cleopatra* and *Coriolanus*, Shakespeare presents the noble as intimately involved in the most profound and general choices men may make of their values. Ethical choice never fossilizes into a matter simply of comportment, of style. This is true even of *Antony and Cleopatra* where Cleopatra, talking of her death, says '. . . what's brave, what's noble,/Let's do it after the high Roman fashion./And make death proud to take us . . .' Her sense of a style in dying, here as elsewhere, has led some critics to find an element of the insincere, even of the frivolous, in her attitude to death, and hence in her love for Antony. Her nobility seems mere glamour. But if her death is 'noble' this is not because it has those qualities which a *Roman* (such as Caesar) would recognize as noble—Cleopatra's choosing to die rather than to live as a slave of Caesar—but because it is a death recognizing an ideal that the world (i.e. the Romans and Caesar) could not recognize. Cleopatra recognizes an ideal greater than Caesar's—in Antony s life, in his having lived more freely and fully than anything Caesar and his world could even imagine. Her nobility has a genuineness and power, even though it is not represented by Shakespeare as cancelling out the nobility of Caesar and the Roman world.

When Cleopatra, after her great description of the Antony whose joys were dolphin-like ('they showed their back above/The element they lived in') asks Dolabella whether such a man as this she dreamt of could ever have existed, and he replies 'Gentle Madam, no', this suggests that the play *imagines* the noble, enacts dramatically the possibility of conceiving a nobility that as well as looking for greatness in the world can also define itself in opposition to the world in defeat: the 'nobility of failure'. In defeat Antony himself finds a dignity in death by a form of interiorization—finding a victory in his defeat:

> Peace!
> Not Caesar's valour hath o'erthrown Antony,
> But Antony's hath triumph'd on itself.

And where Plutarch has the dying Antony say that he is a Roman vanquished by another Roman, Shakespeare by the omission of one word, turns it into a noble victory over himself:

> The miserable change now at my end
> Lament nor sorrow at: but please your thoughts
> By feeding them with those my former fortunes
> Wherein I lived: the greatest prince o' the world,
> The noblest; and do not now basely die,
> Not cowardly put off my helmet to
> My countryman: a Roman, by a Roman
> Valiantly vanquished.
> (IV. xiv)

The characters in Shakespeare's Roman plays do not dress themselves up in borrowed robes—as do the characters of Dryden's *All for Love*; or as did the rulers of revolutionary France when they played at being Roman republicans. And the existence in Shakespeare of such profound probing of the concept of nobility, with the sense that an ideal that involves a conception of one's appearance to others is always in danger of allowing a conception of one's role to take the place of a pursuit of the truly good (so replacing proper pride with vanity) does not mean that the idea of the noble is found intrinsically wanting. The opposed values of Cleopatra and Caesar, of Falstaff and Hotspur, are not to be reduced to an emphasis on personal authenticity quite opposed to all those ways in which personal values may seek to find themselves reflected in the public world. Cleopatra's valuing of Antony reaches out into all sorts of excellences that suggest a place in the world; his joys are dolphin-like; realms and islands are as plates dropped from his pocket.

Antony: The nobleness of life is to do thus. (*embracing*)

To value certain things in the way we do, to have a system of preferences which might be summed up under (for instance) the word 'culture' *is* to place a value on 'nobleness'—even if we are reluctant to use the *word* or to admit that we value it. Such reluctance may of course reflect serious reservations about the implications of the idea of nobility. It may reflect also a 'democratic' servility: *was uns alle bandigt—das gemeine.* In this context even Aristotle's account of the magnanimous man's deportment—his manner of walking and speaking—is intelligible: they may reflect a sense of values that go beyond conscious decision, and which reflect a man's 'being in the world'. Questions about what place 'moral' reasons for action should have in human life; what are the best forms of life; what pleasures are satisfying—all these are intelligible questions, and indeed relate to the question whether 'the nobleness of life is to do thus'. In other words the *content* of such ideals extends across the whole range of life—and in *its* terms we have to conceive of people rather differently from the way in which a morality of action-guiding principles, a morality of the will—what we might call a 'conduct morality'—conceives of them only as 'rational agents'.[17]

III.   The Noble in the Novel

The noble man is representative of the ordering principles of society, of institutions. It is because of this that it is natural to introduce the notion of *appearance*. Let us take, for instance, the character of Mr Knightly in Jane Austen's *Emma*. Mr Knightly's slim and upright figure, his downright and authoritative manner suit his station and his wealth, and represent the role of his class, which is a role of ordering society in a way that is accepted as *natural* by all. We might say that the very fact of its being possible for Mr Knightly's self to be fully expressed in a code of *manners*—a code that involves judgment, an active candour, and which finds its ultimate justification in promoting a detailed and wise concern for the feelings of others—is part of what constitutes a sense of this social order as *natural*. For what Hegel called 'state power and wealth' thus to come

[17] I am greatly indebted at this point to criticisms and suggestions made by S. L. Goldberg, and to his article 'Morality and Literature', *The Critical Review* (1980).

to be expressed in a code of manners, an ease of converse among the classes that still insists upon due respect and honour, is for social institutions to be taken as essentially beneficent—as they *are* taken in Jane Austen. For it to seem natural and necessary that this directing class *appear*, that it exist through a code of manners, of speech, *is* for the social order that it represents to be taken as beneficent and hence virtuous. It is the point also at which the *noble* passes over into the *gentleman*. The morality of the gentleman is a subject in itself, and one that has been deeply explored in the English Novel.[18] Suffice it to say now that although the gentleman accepts the world as he finds it, its institutions, religion and morality, nevertheless his acceptance of them is mediated through a peculiar individuality, sometimes eccentricity, that allows him to be much more of a 'personality' with hobby-horses and quirks than the noble man of Hegel, or the noble hero of Shakespeare. The novel is peculiarly apt for the depiction of the gentleman; and already with Fielding's Parson Adams and Squire Weston, and Sterne's Uncle Toby, we see how that is so. Mr Knightly can rebuke Emma with authority, referring to Miss Bates's 'age, character and situation'; and it is Emma's acceptance of this authoritative rebuke that sets in train her final coming to maturity, with the realization that 'Mr Knightly should marry no one but herself'. Emma too finds her true self in an identification with the social world, but, as always in Jane Austen, this identification is expressed in the institution of *marriage*.

IV. Conclusion

I began by asking the question: do we need a concept of the noble in ethics? I cannot claim to have given a conclusive answer to it. And I end not by attempting some conclusive answer, but with some suggestions. The greater part of human life is not, on the one hand, a life of instinct, nor yet one of purely free, private choice. Nor is it one of membership of large aggregates, institutions, which seem alien to us, and which cannot be the 'truth' of ourselves. Rather it is the life of custom—of customary practices, traditions, manners, modes of address, with the different customs of each sex. We can perhaps as easily define what people are by their customary life as by anything else. This is, after all, the first step towards defining them by their culture. And customary life will very naturally see the world in terms of certain symbolic gestures. So Bloom, in *Ulysses*, shows his real attachment to the public world by remembering with pride how he had handed Parnell's hat to him after it

[18] For an excellent discussion of this topic, cf. Shirley Letwin, *The Morality of the Gentleman*.

had been knocked off his head in a brawl—for which Parnell thanked him. This gesture of civility is for Bloom an expression of his striving towards the public world. Molly, by contrast, exists purely in the instinctive and private. She despises Bloom's sense of the larger world, the world of honour, and is destructive towards it.

We might say that the noble seeks to enact itself. It seeks to embody itself in forms and institutions, and in appearances. The noble will aim to appear as *natural*, and to make the society in which it exists appear as natural. It is the very fact that it assumes that the ordering principles, the power and wealth of society can *appear*—can be embodied in representative figures, in a code of manners, as it were in a social ceremony, is precisely what it is to present itself as part of the natural order of things. Its appearing in this way, its being open to inspection as a system of forms, is what it is for it to regard itself and be regarded by those it contains, as *beneficent*.

If we think about the noble we have also, of course, to take seriously the concept of *honour*. 'For the love of honour alone is untouched by age, and when one comes to the ineffectual period of life it is not gain as some say that gives the greater satisfaction, but honour'—as Pericles says in his funeral oration (Thucidides, ii, XLIV). But for Thucidides the realm of honour is not just any public realm, but what it was also for Aristotle and also for most other philosophers until very recent times—the realm of politics. Yet if the political realm is what completes the individual, the political realm itself will not be seen essentially as the means to certain substantive ends. For Aristotle the civil condition will denote a mode of association amongst people—broadly, the political mode, distinguished from family, marriage and friendship (although the last is a moral and as it were proto-political relationship). It is a realm in which people 'appear' to each other in a particular way—'the forward youth that would appear', as Marvell writes.

This conception of politics will centrally employ ethical ideas, and ideas of form and of ceremony. It will also centrally affirm a conception of *politics* that Burke is opposing to the French revolutionaries when he dilates upon the sufferings of Marie Antoinette, and laments that chivalry has been ousted by a collection of sophisters and calculators. And when Paine said that Burke 'pities the plumage but forgets the dying bird' he was missing, or evading, the point.

So the upshot of this paper is that *if* there is a concept of the noble, then it is a concept which is not simply ethical, although it starts from and includes the ethical; and it is a concept that necessarily involves the connection of the individual consciousness with the larger human world. I suppose that if one is to think in these terms at all there will be a sort of natural progression towards thinking in political terms. And if the noble is a style in aesthetics, then it is also a style in politics. It is, as I suggested, a style that sees the state and its social arrangements as natural, part of a natural order of things, and perhaps sees the political realm as importantly one of forms, honour, appearance, representative individuals. This presumably means that there are certain sorts of society or polity in which the noble cannot exist: for instance, in essentially competitive or 'open' societies such as liberal democracies. (It also cannot exist under Communism and Fascism.) I think that to take the 'noble' seriously is to accept, not a political position, but a particular language of politics. If we assume that it is the destiny of the individual to find himself in a world of already existing institutions, customs, policies and modes of feeling, then we may consider that these practices are the chief, the only means by which he realizes himself. There might be no way of explaining human conduct that stands quite outside such practices (or traditions); and consequently men cannot picture to themselves their own activities outside of that network of institutions, customs and loyalties that constitute in the broadest sense the political realm. (This would be a sort of conservative analogue to the Marxist emphasis on the 'species life' of man.) But this assumption, that there is no way of describing human conduct that radically departs from established customs and institutions, so that there cannot, as it were, be any external critique of such institutions, is to treat them as, in effect, natural, rather than the creation of human beings for particular purposes. In other words, to take the concept of the noble seriously might be seen to have certain implications. It could be considered, indeed, as an exercise in remystification.[19]

[19] I am indebted to Christopher Edwards, James Hopkins and, especially, to S. L. Goldberg for suggestions and criticisms.

When Do Empirical Methods Bypass 'The Problems Which Trouble Us'?

FRANK CIOFFI

His discussion of aesthetics was mingled in a curious way with criticism of assumptions which he said were made by Frazer in *The Golden Bough* and also with criticisms of Freud (G. E. Moore, *'Wittgenstein's Lectures, 1930–33)'*.

Every explanation is an hypothesis ... But for someone worried by love, an explanatory hypothesis will not help much. It will not bring peace ... The crush of thoughts that do not get out because they all press forward and are wedged in the door ('Remarks on Frazer's *Golden Bough*').

For us, the concept of a perspicuous presentation is fundamental ... This perspicuous presentation makes possible that understanding which consists in seeing the connections ('Remarks on Frazer's *Golden Bough*').

An entirely new account of correct explanation. Not one agreeing with experience, but one accepted. You have to give the explanation which is accepted. This is the whole point of the explanation (*Lectures and Conversations in Aesthetics*).

I

Wittgenstein thinks it was wrong of Frazer to respond to the fire festivals by launching an investigation into their origins, and of Freud to respond to dreams by looking for causal relations between them and other aspects of our lives. What kind of mistake is this? Is it the same mistake? Is it really a mistake?

Wittgenstein's criticisms of Freud and Frazer have an interest which extends beyond Wittgensteinian exegesis because they raise a much broader problem, which one might formulate as follows:

There are questions which present themselves as empirical, i.e. such that they require further information for their resolution, but with respect to which we are told, or come to feel obscurely ourselves, that this is an illusion, that the consummation we are seeking is not to be found in more empirical knowledge, or via scientific explanation, but elsewhere and otherwise. What is the character of this 'elsewhere and otherwise'? Is it such that we may, nevertheless, speak of knowledge and understanding, of ignorance relieved by further reflection? And if the error is not to be characterized in these terms, that is in terms of mistaking one kind of epistemic need for another, how is it to be characterized?

Wittgenstein implies that his criticisms of Freud and Frazer are of a piece with his objections to a scientific or experimental aesthetics. This sets us the exegetic puzzle, which Moore expresses in his phrase 'mingled in a curious way', of finding the common element in these criticisms.

I will say straightaway, dogmatically, without any attempt at exegetical justification, what common feature it was that Wittgenstein was recording, or thought he was recording, using Wittgenstein's own idioms. They (Freud, Frazer and also I. A. Richards and Frank Ramsey in their dealings with aesthetic questions) all confounded formal, internal relations with external, causal ones; hypotheses with similes and 'further descriptions'; the notion of truth with that of truthfulness; explaining with 'explaining' or making clear; directed with non-directed feelings or states of mind; scientific speculation with the provision of synoptic views.

There are two possible constructions to be placed on the confusion of which Wittgenstein speaks. Both have exegetical warrant. Both presuppose that there are certain phenomena which induce in us a desire for a clearer grasp of the relation in which we stand to them, or, to use Wittgenstein's own expression, a sorting out of our 'crush of thoughts' with respect to them. (Some other expressions he uses in this connection are 'being intrigued and wanting to describe', 'the sort of explanation one longs for', the thought 'at the back of one's mind', the impression—particularly with music—that an experience seems to be 'saying something, and it is as if one had to discover what it was saying'.)

The first of the two confusions I referred to is to think of the situations described above as requiring empirical investigation for their resolution; of thinking that when I ask why I am impressed, I am asking the same kind of question as when I ask why I am bilious, only about my mind instead of my body; of failing to see the difference between 'What is it that I am feeling?' and 'What is it that I am sitting on?'

There is reason to think that Freud does sometimes make this mistake, particularly in his joke book. I don't think that Frazer does, or that Freud invariably does. The alternative construction that can be placed on 'confusion' raises issues that are both more profound and more intractable. The confusion consists not in employing an empirical method on problems for which it is inappropriate, but in ignoring the problems for which it is not appropriate for problems for which it is. On this view, Frazer's mistake was not that having raised the question 'Why do the Beltane fires impress us?' he then foolishly (and incomprehensibly) began investigating their origins in hopes of an answer, but that having come to hear of fire festivals he pursued empirical investigations with respect to them instead of reflecting on his own response to them and what gave this response the character that it had.

There is a discussion of an analogous error in a book which we know had a profound influence on Wittgenstein, Heinrich Hertz's *Principles of Mechanics* (I have abridged the passage):

> ... One hears with a wearisome frequency that the nature of force is still a mystery, that one of the chief problems of physics is the investigation of the nature of force, and so on. ... Now, why is it that people never in this way ask what is the nature of gold. ... Is the nature of gold better known than that of force? ... I fancy the difference must lie in this. With the term ... 'gold' we connect a large number of relations to other terms; and between all those relations we find no *contradiction which offends us*. We are therefore satisfied and ask *no further questions*. But we have accumulated around the term 'force' ... more relations than can be completely reconciled amongst themselves. We have an obscure feeling of this, and want to have things cleared up. Our confused wish finds expression in the confused question as *to the nature* of force ... But the answer we want is not really an answer to this question. It is not by finding out more and fresh relations and connections that it can be answered; but by removing the contradictions existing between those already known, and thus perhaps by reducing their number. When these painful contradictions are removed, the question as to the nature of the force will not have been answered; but our minds, no longer vexed, will cease to ask illegitimate questions.[1]

There is a difference between Hertz's philosopher of nature and the man who comes to feel that what he wants regarding a phenomenon is a perspicuous view of his crush of thoughts with respect to it rather than 'more and fresh relations', such as its developmental history, its historical circumstances, its remote origins, etc. For in the case of Hertz's physicist there may well be a conceptual incongruity about conjoining the notion of force with a demand for an account of its nature, such as we have in the case of gold. There is no such incongruity in the case of ritual sacrifice or dreams. So the mistake that someone might come to feel that he had made with respect to these phenomena must be of a different order. That is, in the case of the nature of force there seems no alternative direction in which to go but that of conceptual clarification of the concept of force; but in the case of phenomena investigated by Freud and Frazer there are no such conceptual obstacles to empirical enquiry.

Let us first ask what the character of this discourse is which does not depend for its successful prosecution on the gathering of more information

[1] Heinrich Hertz, *The Principles of Mechanics* (Macmillan, 1899), 8.

than we already have at our disposal. A good way to begin to answer this question is by adapting what Wittgenstein says about Freud's analysis of jokes:

> All we can say is that if it is presented to you, you say 'Yes, that's what happened' . . . Freud transforms the joke into a different form which is recognized by us as an expression of the chain of ideas which led us from one end of the joke to the other.[2]

If we substitute a more generic term, like 'impression', for 'joke', we get:

> (The analysis) transforms (the impression) into a different form which is recognized by us as an expression of the chain of ideas which led us from one end to another of (the impression). (Or where the experience has no marked sequential structure, we can say 'which is recognized by us as an expression of the crush of thoughts which comprised the experience').

Wittgenstein's objection to Frazer, Freud and the practitioners of scientific aesthetics can then be restated: they either raise questions for which the only mode of validation is 'Yes, that's what happened', and fail to realize this, or fail to raise (or, having raised, fail to confine themselves to) questions for which the mode of validation is 'Yes, that's what happened'. What grounds have we for saying that Frazer committed either of these errors?

Moore tells us that one of the chief points on which Wittgenstein 'seemed to wish to insist' was 'that it was a mistake to suppose that why, e.g., the account of the Beltane Festival impresses us so much is because it has "developed from a festival in which a real man was burnt"'. He accused Frazer of thinking that this was the reason.'[3] It is incredible that anyone should think that the impression made by a ceremony in which an effigy is burned could be explained by the fact that it is the lineal descendant of a ceremony in which a man was burned, though someone might mistakenly think that his *belief* that a man was once burned explains the impressiveness of a ritual in which an effigy is burned. Frazer's error may have been to confound the idea of the ritual burning of a man as a 'formal' term, related to the impression of the fire festival in making it the impression that it was, with its external relation to the fire festival as its original or causal antecedent.

But this is not the conceptual confusion Frazer is being accused of, which involves the unlikely assumption that someone should spend years

---

[2] Ludwig Wittgenstein, *Lectures and Conversations* (Oxford 1966), 18.
[3] G. E. Moore, *Philosophical Papers* (New York, 1962), 308–309. For further reflections on this issue see 'Wittgenstein and the Fire-festivals', in *Perspectives on the Philosophy of Wittgenstein*, Irving Block (ed.) (Oxford: Blackwell, 1982).

amassing empirical evidence about a phenomenon (the Nemi priesthood say, which Frazer tells us initiated his researches) if what he explicitly wanted to know was why he felt about it as he did. Frazer's recognition of his error, unlike that of Hertz's natural philosopher, would not consist in his seeing that the amassing of all this material was a quite unsuitable way of determining 'why the Beltane Festival impresses us', or 'what makes human sacrifice sinister', but in coming to realize that it was these questions to which he really wanted an answer, and not the speculative pre-history ones which he had raised. But did Frazer even commit this error? It being the kind of error it is, Frazer alone could tell us.

There is one qualification to be made of the lest remark; but it is one whose weight it is difficult to assess. Someone might produce the impression that though explicitly raising empirical questions, these were not the questions he really wished to raise, because his discourse was marked by preoccupations of a kind not to be served by advances in empirical knowledge. His discourse would manifest what I shall call 'expressive incongruity'. I will illustrate this notion from an essay on the holocaust.

George Steiner's essay 'Post-script to a Tragedy' is a review of two books about the holocaust—Chaim Kaplan's *Warsaw Diary* and J-F. Steiner's *Treblinka*. Steiner begins his essay with two horrific anecdotes. Immediately after he has a paragraph which evokes potently the state we are left in by facts such as he has just related:

> One of the things I cannot grasp, though I have often written about them, trying to get them in some kind of bearable perspective, is the time relation ... Precisely at the same hour in which Mehring or Langner were being done to death, the overwhelming plurality of human beings, ten miles away on the Polish farms, five thousand miles away in New York, were sleeping or eating or going to a film, making love or worrying about the dentist. This is where my imagination balks. The two orders of simultaneous existence are so different ... their existence is so hideous a paradox.[4]

In the 'hideous paradox' to which Steiner refers we can recognize a familiar ingredient in our response to facts such as he recounts, as to tragedy generally. There are moments when it is found especially troubling that 'while the mourner is burying his friend the reveller is hasting to his wine'. 'The roar on the other side of silence' was George Eliot's phrase for this paradox, and she stressed the necessity for cultivating a degree of deafness to this roar. But when Steiner goes on to raise the question of the failure of the RAF and US Airforce to bomb the gas ovens and/or rail lines leading to the death camps he has ceased to address the problems raised in his account of the state of mind induced in us by his anecdotes. The question

[4] George Steiner, 'Postscript to a Tragedy', *Encounter* **28** (February 1967), 33.

of at how early a stage the Allies realized what was going on in the camps, and whether they might not have made more vigorous efforts at intervention, raise issues of an entirely different order from that of 'the hideous paradox', issues which require a great deal of information and assessment of evidence for their solution; whereas our recognition that Steiner in invoking 'the hideous paradox' of the collateral contemporaneity of the demonic and the quotidian had hit on a prominent component of the impression made on us by the idea of the holocaust, one of the 'crush of thoughts' this idea provokes, requires no such information or assessment. The possible culpability of the Allies in not taking preventive action, however deplorable, does not constitute a hideous paradox, and seems oddly out of place in a discussion of it. We feel we could justifiably chide Steiner in Wittgenstein's words: 'Every explanation is an hypothesis. But for someone who is troubled an explanation will not help much. It will not bring peace.' If the question is 'Did Heaven look on and would not take their part?', can the answer be 'Anyway, it seems the Allied Air Forces did'?

But an appeal to expressive incongruity can hardly be conclusive. Not only because the judgment on which it is based is an imponderable one, but because the defence could be made that the discourse was not confusing two incommensurable issues, but merely raising both.

To make a conceptual error in attempting questions like 'What makes human sacrifice deep and sinister?', 'Why does the Beltane Fire Festival impress us?', 'Why is there something especially terrible in the fact that in choosing the sacrificial victim by lots they use a cake?' would be to go in search of more information than we already have.

There is no reason to think that in these particular cases anyone has made that conceptual mistake. If the search for further information in such cases is a mistake, then it is both a more interesting and a more contentious one. It is to neglect these questions for others, for the solution of which more information is requisite. For example, how did they come to use *a cake* for casting lots?

It is one thing to object that Frazer's developmental speculations cannot untrouble us (whatever force we give to 'untrouble' (beruhigen); either, sort out our crush of thoughts with respect to a phenomenon, or, reconcile us to the incipient realizations which composed it), and quite another to object that, like Freud and the practitioner of a scientific aesthetics, Frazer first posed a question which required only that we bethink ourselves, and then went in search of irrelevant empirical data.

There is no reason to believe that Frazer thought either that discovering the origins of the fire festivals was the way to answer the question why they seem sinister, nor that determining why they seem sinister would settle the question of their origins. Frazer's methods did not pass his problems by; they passed *our* problems by, if, like Wittgenstein, we wish to know, 'What makes human sacrifice so sinister anyway?'

That Wittgenstein's objections to Freud's practice of dream interpretation are as much an objection to Freud's raising causal questions at all as
to his proffering conceptually inappropriate answers to non-causal questions
is suggested by his discussion of Freud's treatment of a dream which I will
refer to as the flowery dream. (This is indexed under 'the language of
flowers' in the appendix to *The Interpretation of Dreams*.) On one occasion
Wittgenstein complained of this dream interpretation of Freud's that in
giving a causal account of the elements of the dream Freud was doing
something 'tremendously wrong' and that he was 'cheating' the patient.[5]
The dream in question is used by Freud as an example of a biographical
dream, uncommon outside analysis, he says, which expressed the dreamer's
joy at having passed through life 'immaculately'. The element in the
dream about Freud's treatment of which Wittgenstein particularly com-
plains involved the patient floating down from a height while carrying a
flowering branch in her hand, the blossoms of which looked like red camellias, and some of which had faded at the conclusion of her descent. Freud
subjects this to his standard treatment; but at this point it doesn't seem to
be Freud's tendentiousness of which Wittgenstein is complaining, but of
his assumption that his interpretation had a content over and above the
patient's endorsement of it, and so was independent of this endorsement,
i.e. was a matter of truth and not merely of truthfulness. During this
dream episode the dreamer felt herself exalted. The branch she carried she
later likened to the lily spray carried by the Angel in pictures of the Annun-
ciation, and the situation in general to 'the girls in white robes walking in
the Corpus Christi processions when the streets were decorated with green
branches'. The dream 'expressed her joy at having passed immaculately
through life', i.e. without sinning against purity. Thus far we have 'further
descriptions', characterizations of the dream which makes it the dream
that it was, characterizations which are not matters of inference. Freud
then produces his interpretation of the dream in which these characterizations are contradicted. The branch is a phallic symbol, the red camellias
are an allusion to *La Dame aux Camellias* whose favourite flower they were,
and who wore them white for most of the month and red when she was
menstruating, and (presumably) since she was a courtesan, the dreamer is
alluding wistfully to a life richer in sexual gratification.

But in this instance Freud was not making the mistake, which there is
some reason for saying he made in his comments on jokes, of failing to see
that 'the correct explanation is the one accepted'. This can't be the nature
of Freud's error in the case of the Flowery Dreamer, because there is a
blatant discrepancy between her own view of the dream and that of Freud,
and since Freud does not on that account think he is mistaken, he has given
the strongest possible reasons for concluding that he does not see himself

---

[5] Ludwig Wittgenstein, *Lectures and Conversations* (Oxford, 1966), 23–24.

as trafficking in further descriptions, or in the elaboration of the ideas with which the dream seemed pregnant. This must be obvious to Wittgenstein, so what is the ground of his objection? It must lie in the feeling of the irrelevance of causal questions, rather than in the incongruity of causal answers to intentionalist questions. And this would be perfectly acceptable, or at least arguable, but for the fact that the dreamer was also a patient.

The judgment in which we are involved in these discussions is not narrowly conceptual, but is rather like this (an entry for 1948 from Wittgenstein's 'Miscellaneous Remarks'):[6] 'What is intriguing about a dream is not its causal connection with events in my life, etc., but rather the impression it gives of being a fragment of a story'. The criticism of Freud, then, would be that he addresses himself to the first of these questions, that of discovering the causal connection between the dream and events in the dreamer's life rather than attempting to fill out the story of which it seems to be a fragment. So that this is a case of the thinker rather than the method bypassing the problem, and of whether he is justified in doing so.

There are reasons for saying Freud was so justified. For why should the inferences that the dream suggests or permits as to the shameful thoughts of the dreamer be eligible as interpretations of the dream only if they coincide with, or are continuous with, the nimbus of significance that a dream sometimes trails behind it? Psychoanalytic dream interpretation may well be one of the intellectual impositions of our time, but this is not *a priori* true, and there is no objection to be made in principle to the causal explanation of a dream, whether on Freudian lines or any others.

If the causal relations into which a phenomenon enters, it is a matter of urgency to elicit, as in psychopathology, then, however intrigued by the reverberations of the experience, we would eschew 'further descriptions' and 'similes' and 'words that sum it up' and pursue empirical investigations.

When we turn from dreams to symptoms, in spite of their miscellaneous-ness, in neither construal of the error does it seem one to fail to confine ourselves to 'further descriptions'; neither because they are the only conceptually appropriate response, given the nature of the question, nor because the questions to which they are answers are the ones to raise, given the nature of the occasion. Not the first, since there is no conceptual impropriety about asking for a causal explanation (in the very wide sense of 'the one agreeing with experience' as opposed to 'the one accepted'). Whether a patient felt the harsh reproof of a husband as 'like a slap in the face' is a question of whether this is 'a good simile', and this she can tell us, but the question of whether this simile played a role in the production of a trigeminal neuralgia (conversion hysteria) is something she cannot tell us. In this case the conceptual impropriety would consist rather in treating

6 Ludwig Wittgenstein, *Culture and Value* (Oxford, 1980), 68–69.

such problems as ones in which we had to give the explanation that is accepted.

A 'dream story' may well have 'a charm of its own', as Wittgenstein puts it. And causally connecting this story with fragments of the dreamer's past may well dissipate this charm, and we might justifiably find this gratuitous; but do symptoms have a charm? A delusion might have something akin to charm, it may strike us as 'an idea pregnant with possible developments', but would we not have misgivings about pursuing these (unless in the service of a diagnostic or therapeutic aim)? Neither would we think it sensible to pursue the experience of an attack of trigeminal neuralgia in the direction of 'excellent similes'.

Of course Freud has signally failed in the case of the flowery dreamer to provide 'the sort of explanation one longs for' when one wakes from a dream pregnant with significance, just as would a neurologist who responded to a patient's account of the aura of imminent revelation that preceded his epileptic fits with talk of epileptic foci and neuronal discharges. On the other hand, it seems right and proper that we should go from the rapture and the sense of imminent revelation which sometimes signals the onset of epileptic seizures, to a discussion of epileptic foci in the brain rather than in search of 'the sort of explanation one longs for' in connection with aesthetic impressions. The point is, what may be a mistake with respect to our impression of a dream (or of human sacrifice), need not be a mistake with respect to our afflictions where it is a causal investigation, either into their historical antecedents, or the neurophysiological substrate which is called for.

Though an hypothesis is an inappropriate response to a request for a further description, a request for a further description may be an inappropriate request. When we are dealing with psychopathological phenomena, the questions we want answered cannot be settled by reflection, and the questions which can be settled by reflection we ought not to be raising. If the patient complained she felt deprived because our hypotheses lacked the charm of her own elaborations of the meaning of her experience of illness, we should reconcile ourselves to this rather than capitulate to it.

But there are reservations we may need to make about this thesis. Let us first ask what it is we can be made to acknowledge we want and only then whether we ought to cease to want it.

II

One case in which it is sometimes felt that problems and method have passed one another by is that of disenchantment with biographical knowledge: the realization that there are questions, or at any rate yearnings, provoked by our encounters with others ('the other who assaults our being' as Sartre puts it), that no amount of information about them can assuage.

Our wonder at others seems naturally to take the form of empirical speculation, of which, when pressed, we can often give no determinate account with which the wonder is commensurate. Tolstoi, on several occasions, displays his characters in this posture of wonder.

Kitty Scherbatsky wonders at her friend Varenka:

> What is it in her? What gives her this power to disregard everything, to be so quietly independent of everything? How I should like to know it, and learn it from her!

Later, Kitty tells Varenka of her humiliation at being rejected by Vronsky:

> 'There isn't a girl who hasn't experienced the same thing. And it is all so unimportant.'
>
> 'Then what is so important?' asked Kitty . . .
>
> 'Oh, there is so much that is important', said Varenka smiling.
>
> 'What?'
>
> 'Oh there's so much that's more important', replied Varenka, not knowing what to say. Kitty held her by the hand, and with passionate curiosity and entreaty questioned Varenka with her eyes: 'What is it— what is it that is so important? What gives you such tranquillity? You know, tell me!'
>
> But Varenka did not even understand what Kitty's eyes were asking her . . . Kissing Kitty once more, without having told her what was important, she stepped out into the twilight of the summer night, bearing away her secret of what was important, and what gave her her enviable calm and dignity.

The tendency to see the problem presented us by our wonder at the lives of others as that of a secret to be penetrated is illustrated again in a later passage where it is Levin who 'feels a longing, dissatisfied as he was with his own life, to get at the secret which gave Svisahky such clarity, definite- ness and courage in life'.

Alexie Karenin, too, when 'with a sense of shame and regret he reviewed his past', asks himself:

> 'How have I been to blame? . . .' and as usual the question set him wondering whether all those other men—the Vronskys and Oblonskys and those gentlemen of the bed-chamber with their fine calves—felt differently, did their loving and their marrying differently. And there rose before his mind's eye a whole row of those vigorous, dashing, self-confident men who always, and everywhere, drew his inquisitive attention in spite of himself.

Suppose those gentlemen of the bed-chamber with their fine calves were disposed to indulge Karenin's inquisitiveness (as Oblonsky certainly would), what could they have told him? At most what Freud said of Goethe, and hinted of himself, that they had been 'the undisputed darlings of their mothers'. But would this have relieved Karenin's inquisitiveness?

In a biographical piece on General Marshall I read: 'Without doubt much of his command power derived from his remarkable presence which radiated superiority. It seemed never to be calculated reserve but rather the natural attitude of the full man under perfect control. We who witnessed it ever wondered how he got that way; it was a secret to be coveted.'

If the writer so impressed with Marshall's 'presence' later discovered that the General practised transcendental meditation, would this have satisfied him? Or would his curiosity have then been directed to this further nexus? I don't mean this question to be rhetorical. I only want to suggest that there are occasions on which questions of this kind would be sufficient to produce in someone the feeling that he had misunderstood himself, and that his desire for further knowledge had been a mechanical response, due perhaps to the fact that it had on other occasions proved pertinent and successful.

For there are problems presented to us by the abilities and propensities of others which the revelation of what is hidden from us does sometimes illuminate. Basil Willey tells us in his autobiography how he would attempt to overcome his dread of an interview or lecture or party by reminding himself of his ordeal in the trenches of the Western Front: 'Come on now, you fool: suppose you were going over the top tomorrow, what would you think of all these trifles then?' He says it never worked. But let us suppose that it did. We would then have a determinate answer to the question 'What is the secret of Willey's calm?'

But there are cases where our interest is directed to what might be called 'a quality of being', and these don't lend themselves to the sort of resolution achievable in the Willey case. Napoleon kept the returns of his army under his pillow at night to refer to in case he was sleepless and would set himself problems at the Opera while the overture was playing: 'I have ten thousand men at Strasbourg; fifteen thousand at Magdeburg; twenty thousand at Wurzburg. By what stages must they march so as to arrive at Ratisbon on three successive days?' This explains something but not why he was Napoleonic. Is there some secret which stands to the Napoleon who 'assaulted the being' of so many generations of Frenchmen as the practice cited stands to his logistic prowess?

Sartre objected to Paul Bourget's biography of Flaubert that due to its reductionist method 'the being whom we seek . . . Flaubert, the man whom we can love or hate, blame or praise, who represents for us the *other* who assaults our being, vanishes in a dust of phenomena bound together by external connections'. In place of Bourget's 'external connections', Sartre proposes a search for 'something like a radical decision which, without ceasing to be contingent, would be the veritably psychic irreducible . . . which, when established, would produce in us an accompanying feeling of satisfaction'. No doubt it is possible through biographical enquiry and psychological speculation to resolve enigmas, plug up narrative gaps, in the case of Flaubert as in that of any other man.

But even if it were reasonable to believe that there were a set of conditions, or 'radical decisions', which when found would confer intelligibility not only on Flaubert's reclusiveness, his anti-populism, his antiquarianism, but on *Madam Bovary*; even if there were not reasons intrinsic to such a programme likely to render it futile, how would its successful consummation explain Flaubert's capacity to 'assault our being'? Among those who consider this question some may come to feel that their search for further empirical data had been misplaced, and that they stood to the quality of being which prompted this search not as Hertz's physicist stood to gold but as he stood to force. For why should Sartre's programme, any more than Bourget's, illuminate for us the Flaubert 'who is the other who assaults our being'? Would not an enquiry into the assaultability of our being by Flaubert be more pertinent? Sartre speaks of 'the being whom we seek', but how can a being whom we have not as yet found assault us, or be the object of our 'love or hate, blame or praise'?

Consider the case of someone who, impressed by the following passage, finds himself recurring to it in an attempt to fathom its expressiveness, to understand what draws him to it and others like it.

> In the fifty-second year of my age, after the completion of an arduous and successful work, I now propose to employ some moments of my leisure in reviewing the simple transactions of a private and literary life . . .
>
> I am endowed with a cheerful temper, a moderate sensibility, and a natural disposition to repose rather than activity; some mischievous appetites and habits have perhaps been corrected by philosophy or time. The love of study, a passion which derives fresh vigour from enjoyment, supplies each day, each hour, with a perpetual source of independent and rational pleasure, and I am not sensible of any decay of the mental faculties. The original soil has been highly improved by cultivation; but it may be questioned whether some flowers of fancy, some grateful errors, have not been eradicated with the weeds of prejudice (Edward Gibbon, *Memoir of My Life and Writings*).

It is easy to imagine how an informational account of this passage might run. It would speak to us of Gibbon's temperament, and of whether the passages quoted fairly represent it; also of the development of English prose, and where Gibbon's style stands in this development; and perhaps of the influence of Gibbon's latinity on his English. But another kind of comment is possible, one whose adequacy we are competent to assess without scholarship, e.g.:

'What strikes us in Gibbon's retrospect of his life is generated by our sense of the unavailability to us, those of us it does strike, for whom it wears a special aspect—of a distinctive register and cadence—a mode of self-reference which we couldn't employ without a sense of strain and affectation. The orderliness of Gibbon's progression through life (or at least his ordered sense of that progression) intensifies by contrast the phantasmagoric character of our own reminiscences, which normally yield nothing more determinate than the sense of having lurched from one exigency to another.'

What this comment does is to divert our attention from the external relations of the phenomenon which impresses us to the features of our situation which confer on it the aspect which makes it the phenomenon it is—which account for our being struck.

Another instance in which the wonder provoked by another proves to be intransitive with respect to biographical knowledge is that of the diary of Samuel Pepys, the occasion of what one critic has called 'the most delightful euphoria in literature'. It is this euphoria to which our wonder is directed. Sometimes this wonder takes more determinate form as a confused desire to experience directly this quality of being ('What was it like to be Pepys?'); at others to explain it ('How did Pepys become Pepys?'). We tend to think of this quality of being, of which we crave a more intimate knowledge, as an experiential content between which and ourselves a barrier is interposed, as if there were some species of ostension to be enjoyed, as if we could pass from description to acquaintance. Sartre speaks of 'the taste which a man necessarily has for himself, the savour of his existence'. Gerard Manley Hopkins uses the same analogy; and it is a very natural one. But it is difficult to spell out the notion of ourselves feeling those states which, when evinced in speech, writing, music, painting or gesture, arrest or delight us in so distinctive a way.

Perhaps what we want with respect to Pepys and other assaults on our being, we already have, if we could look at them in the right way. Was Pepys really better placed than we to know what it was like to be Pepysian? Did Blake's tiger know that it brightly burned? 'What did Macbeth feel when he said, "Duncan is in his grave"?'[7] What did Pepys feel when he wrote, 'Mighty merry'? Isn't knowing what they said knowing what they felt? 'Is what is linguistic not experience?' (*Philosophical Investigations*). Perhaps Pepys' diary makes us Pepysian in the way that 'a walnut makes us round' (La Fontaine).

---

[7] *Lectures and Conversations* (Oxford, 1966), 33. This question, from the fourth lecture on Aesthetics, is followed by the remark, 'Can I describe his feelings better than by describing how he said it?'

What we might call 'the Pepys music' owes its effect in part to his extraordinary power of absorbing himself in his circumstances. This has the effect of intensifying our own sense of what Sartre calls 'non-immediacy', our sense of 'that solid world these hands can never reach', of being what Heidegger calls 'a creature of distances'. Whether this is so or not, we have in the remark that it is, a specimen of the kind of assertion whose appraisal does not require more knowledge than we already possess and, in fact, precludes the use of such knowledge, since it can have played no role in determining our relation to the being at whom we wonder.

It sometimes happens that the intensity of our interest in the lives of those figures whose quality of being compels our 'inquisitive attention' is parasitic on a craving for a perspicuous view of the characterological aspirations and reforms round which our own hopes, efforts and self-reproaches centred. And it then takes only for this possibility to be mentioned for us to realize that it is so. (Dilthey makes a pertinent remark in this connection. 'It is only in comparing myself to others that I come to experience what is individual in myself.')

Another reason for feeling that 'the being whom we seek' is not to be found through biographical investigation is that there is an ingredient in my wonder at such beings which it shares with my wonder at creatures who never had a being of their own, and therefore whom, of necessity, I cannot seek. It is not only Gibbon, Pepys and Flaubert who assault my being, but Odysseus, Sir Galahad, Falstaff, Don Juan, Figaro, Captain MacWhirr, Jeeves, Bugs Bunny and Sergeant Bilko. And here it is clear that this assault consists of an internal relationship between these figures and what Ortega calls 'the programmatic personage who has to be realized'.

There are also occasions when what we want with respect to another's quality of being is less ambitious or profound, and is more akin to what Wittgenstein called 'the sort of explanation one longs for when one talks of an aesthetic impression', and which may find satisfaction if we 'find a verbal form of expression ... the word that seems to sum it up'. John Cowper Powys, wishing to evince in communicable terms the tranquillizing effect of the personality of a pious friend, invoked the Collect for the Twenty-first Sunday after Trinity, which contains the phrase 'pardon and peace'. Sartre's Roquentin may have been more astute than his creator when he satisfied his craving to know more of the life of the composer of 'Some of These Days' by inventing a presence and a milieu for him.

III

There is another area in which we tend mistakenly to think that what we require to dissipate our perplexity is a knowledge of causal relations, that of the influence of our remote past on our personal development, where we tend to confuse the role of past episodes as causal influences with their status as intentional objects of reminiscence and rumination.

In an essay on the poet John Berryman, I came across the following:

> Much of Berryman's energy in later years was given over to self-analysis, a thoroughgoing process whereby he attempted to discover whether his father's suicide—which occurred when he himself was eleven years of age—did have the crippling effect on his psychological development that he thought . . . or whether he was rationalizing his subsequent neurotic conflicts, and imputing them to that cause.

There is something wrong with this. It makes Berryman's predicament in regard to his father's suicide too much like Pepys wondering why he peed so much one winter's night, and whether it was due to the unusual cold or to the oysters he had eaten. But would a straightforward answer to Berryman's question, construed as a simple counterfactual, have satisfied him? Suppose we had a highly determinate index of the neural effect of traumas, something as measurable as the piece of ass's hide in Balzac's *La Peau de Chagrin* which shrank with every wish, and we were in a position to convey this information to Berryman: his depression threshold had dropped so many notches as a consequence of his father's death: would he have seen in this the understanding for which he was seeking?

Now, of course, I can imagine a context in which the causal question was all-important, and the synoptic one frivolous: if we were conducting an epidemiological investigation of childhood traumas in the hope of devising prophylactic child-rearing regimens. But was this the basis of Berryman's interest? And, of course, the question 'Would Berryman have committed suicide had his father not committed suicide?' is perfectly licit, and of course it demands an empirical method. But it does not follow that Berryman's own question was, or was entirely, without residue, of this kind. The predicament of someone 'bewildered at the sort of person he has turned out to be', as Rush Rhees puts it, calls for a something other, or at least more, than the display of causal relations between his past and his present.

It might be asked why Berryman should desert his causal question for the more explicitly intentionalist one, 'What is it about my father's suicide which so troubles me?' Only because if that question occurred to him, or were brought to his attention, he might be willing to see in it, rather than in the causal one, the proper heir to his anguish over the manner of his father's death. This can be generalized to suggest that an entire class of questions as to the influence of our personal past on our current lives may be usurpers. If Berryman had a clearer conception of what an answer to his causal question really came to, would he have spent as much time and energy wondering about it as he did? What could a successful issue to Berryman's enquiries when construed causally have given him? At most an otiose demonstration that 'if some things were different other things would be otherwise' (as the griffin remarked to the minor canon). On the other hand, suppose Berryman's attempts at self-consolation had time and again been undermined by the reflection, 'how in a world in which such things can happen can I go on living?' And that among 'such things', lost among the crush of thoughts, and only brought to prominence by after-reflection, was the idea of his father's suicide. Might he not be willing to count this, though free of causal implication, a gain in knowledge of the significance of his father's suicide? Another example of this distinctive kind of knowledge would be Berryman's coming to an explicit realization that a prominent theme of his rumination about his father's suicide was speculation as to whether the torments which drove him to it were like Berryman's own. What Berryman may have really wanted, which took the misleading form of a causal question, was a synoptic view of the countless reveries into which the thought of his father's suicide entered, a clearer view of what he really felt about it, of what he ought to feel about it, of what he felt he ought to feel about it.

In some other place I came across these sentences from the correspondence of Diderot: 'The more I examine myself, the more I am convinced that in our youth there comes a moment which is decisive for our character. A little girl, as pretty as a heart, bit me on the hand. When I complained to her father, he pulled up her dress before me, and that little rump stayed in my mind and will stay there as long as I live. Who knows the influence on my morals?' Is not there something to be said about this little rump without entering into causal questions, something which reflection is privileged to uncover? One wants to ask 'What is so special about that little rump?' And 'What have little rumps to do with morality?' But we know, or could make a good guess; and so it seems likely that Diderot was capable of coming to understand quite a bit about his relation to that rump without entering into difficult counter-factual questions. Having sorted out the crush of thoughts occasioned by his memory of the rump, he might have come to feel that it was not strictly causal knowledge for which he was asking. For suppose the answer was, 'No. The little rump had no influence whatever on your morals', would Diderot have straightaway lost interest in it?

Our reflections on such matters don't always find their natural consummation in the discovery of causal relations. Consider Medea's lament for Jason.

Why lyked me thy yellow hair to see
More than the bondes of mine honestie?

Would it have been to the point to tell her she had been imprinted? Isn't this kind of case one where, as Wittgenstein says, 'an explanatory hypothesis will not help much'?

In accounting for the development of his vocation Constable invoked 'the sound of water escaping from mill dams, willows, old rotten planks, posts and brick work. I love all such things. These scenes made me a painter, and I am grateful.' Perhaps what Berryman wanted was to stand to the theme of his father's suicide as did Constable to the source of his impulse to paint. And if this is causal knowledge, it is so only in the sense in which Constable was manifesting causal knowledge.

Though the synoptic array may encompass factors which also stand in a causal relation to the life of the subject, they are not relations which raise evidential questions in any acute way, since they not only influence thoughts, feelings, fantasies, but participate in them.

What we want with respect to certain phenomena are not their causes, but their bearings. The lack of closure, the sense of unfinished business that we experience with respect to them is not always a matter of factual ignorance, to be relieved by the discovery of causal relations.[8]

In *Tractatus* 6.4312, Wittgenstein says of the assumption that survival after death is 'a solution to the riddle of life' that since 'this eternal life is as enigmatic as our present one this assumption will not do for us what we have always tried to make it do'. And this is what we are sometimes inclined to say of advances in knowledge, not that they are without interest or value in themselves, any more than immortality is, but that 'they will not do for us what we have always tried to make them do'. There are those for whom the argument that we sometimes ask for further knowledge when what we need are perspicuous views of what was hidden in the crush of thoughts will have no force whatever. They are never struck; they are never intrigued; they are never impressed; nothing ever seems to be saying anything; they experience no crush of thoughts. And that's that. And so it is.

But there is another objection to the preoccupation with the source of our impressions which is more worrying because less total. Though quite familiar with the experience of being intrigued and wanting to describe, of a crush of thoughts that all try to push forward and cannot get out, of phenomena that seem to be telling them something, etc., etc., those who make it do not see why these experiences should not be ignored in favour of the task of enlarging our knowledge of the phenomena which produce them. There is nothing to object to in this, once recognition has been extended to the fact that there is, nevertheless, a mode of transaction with the phenomena of our lives other than the empirical—a desire for other than a knowledge of their causes and conditions. There may be no question of convicting someone who does not acknowledge a failure of fit between his problems and his methods of error independent of his own concurrence. This thesis with regard to him may have the same character as the prob-

[8] There is an illuminating discussion of this issue in Christopher Cherry's 'Explanation and Explanation by Hypothesis', *Synthese* 33 (1976).

lems to whose distinctiveness his attention is being directed. All that can be done is to reformulate the problems which trouble him, bringing out the irrelevance of further knowledge to their solution; and either he then says 'That's what I really wanted' or he doesn't.

But in neither case is there any compulsion to acknowledge that this attempt to arrive at a clear view of the feelings and thoughts, which by virtue of their relation to certain impressions confers on them their distinctive aspect, results in a special kind of knowledge, one which is generally slighted or misunderstood. And we know that many will not say this, but will prefer to say instead that, except for a narrow range of conceptual problems whose solution is ministerial to the advance of science, when we have turned away from the search for 'more and fresh relations' we have abandoned thinking for brooding.

Devant la loi

JACQUES DERRIDA

. . . : ainsi faict la science (et nostre droict mesme a, dict-on, des fictions légitimes sur lesquelles il fonde la vérité de sa justice); (. . .) (Montaigne, Essais II, f. XII).

Un titre résonne parfois comme la citation d'un autre titre. Mais dès lors qu'il nommerait autre chose, il ne citerait plus simplement, il détournerait l'autre titre à la faveur d'un homonyme. Tout cela n'irait jamais sans quelque préjudice ou usurpation.

A ces possibilités je donnerai droit en commençant par lire, et lire ici revient à citer, le récit de Kafka intitulé *Vor dem Gesetz*, en français *Devant la loi*. Je le lis naturellement dans sa traduction anglaise. La traduction du titre, *Before the Law*, pourra paraître problématique. En trois mots elle concentre d'avance et formalise tous nos enjeux. [. . .]

Permettez-moi maintenant de souligner un peu lourdement quelques trivialités axiomatiques. Sur chacune d'elles, j'ai tout lieu de le supposer, un accord initial serait facile entre nous, même si mon intention reste de fragiliser ensuite les conditions d'un tel consensus. Pour en appeler à cet accord entre nous, je me réfère peut-être imprudemment à notre communauté de sujets participant dans l'ensemble à la même culture et souscrivant, dans un contexte donné, au même système de conventions. Lesquelles? Je vais essayer de le préciser un peu.

Première croyance d'allure axiomatique : au texte que je viens de lire nous reconnaissons une identité à soi, une singularité et une unité. Nous les considérons comme intouchables, si énigmatiques que demeurent en définitive les conditions de cette identité à soi, de cette singularité et de cette unité. Il y a un commencement et une fin à ce récit dont les bordures ou les limites nous paraissent garanties par un certain nombre de critères établis, entendez établis par des lois et des conventions positives. Ce texte, que nous tenons pour unique et identique à lui-même, nous croyons savoir qu'il existe dans sa version originale, faisant corps en son lieu de naissance avec la langue allemande. Selon la croyance la plus répandue dans nos régions, telle version dite originale constitue l'ultime référence quant à ce qu'on pourrait appeler la personnalité juridique du texte, son identité, son unicité, ses droits, etc. Tout cela est aujourd'hui garanti par la loi, par un faisceau de lois qui ont toute une histoire même si le discours qui les justifie prétend le plus souvent les enraciner dans des lois naturelles.

Deuxième élément de consensus axiomatique, essentiellement inséparable du premier: ce texte a un auteur. L'existence de son signataire n'est pas fictive, à la différence des personnages du récit. Et c'est encore la loi qui exige et garantit la différence entre la réalité présumée de l'auteur, porteur du nom de Franz Kafka, enregistré par l'état civil sous l'autorité de l'Etat, et d'autre part la fiction des personnages à l'intérieur du récit. Cette différence implique un système de lois et de conventions sans lesquelles le consensus auquel je me réfère présentement, dans un contexte qui nous est jusqu'à un certain point commun, n'aurait aucune chance d'apparaître, qu'il soit ou non fondé. Or ce système de lois, nous en pouvons en connaître au moins l'histoire apparente, les événements juridiques qui en ont scandé le devenir sous la forme du doit positif. Cette histoire est très récente et tout ce qu'elle garantit reste essentiellement labile, aussi fragile qu'un artifice. Comme vous le savez, des oeuvres nous sont léguées dont l'unité, l'identité et la complétude restent problématiques parce que rien ne permet de décider en toute certitude si l'inachèvement du corpus est un accident réel ou une feinte, le simulacre délibérément calculé d'un ou de plusieurs auteurs, contemporains ou non. Il y a et il y a eu des oeuvres dans lesquelles l'auteur ou une multiplicité d'auteurs sont mis en scène comme des personnages sans nous laisser des signes ou des critères rigoureux pour décider entre les deux fonctions ou les deux valeurs. Le Conte du Graal, par exemple, pose encore aujourd'hui de tesl problèmes (achèvement ou inachèvement, inachèvement réel ou feint, inscription des auteurs dans le récit, pseudonymie et propriété littéraire, etc.). Mais sans vouloir annuler les différences et les mutations historiques à cet égard, on peut être sûr que, selon des modalités chaque fois originales, ces problèmes se posent de tout temps et pour toute oeuvre.

Troisième axiome: il y a du récit dans ce texte intitulé *Devant la loi* et ce récit appartient à ce que nous appelons la littérature. Il y a du récit ou de la forme narrative dans ce texte; narration entraîne tout à sa suite, elle détermine chaque atome due texte même si tout n'y apparaît pas immédiatement sous l'espèce de la narration. Sans m'intéresser ici à la question de savoir si cette narrativité est le genre, le mode ou le type du texte, je noterai modestement et de façon toute préliminaire que cette narrativité, dans ce cas précis, appartient selon nous à la littérature; pour cela j'en appelle encore au même consensus entre nous. Sans toucher encore aux présuppositions contextuelles de notre consensus, je retiens que pour nous il semble s'agir d'un récit littéraire (le mot 'récit' pose aussi des problèmes de traduction que je laisse en réserve). Est-ce que cela reste trop évident et trivial pour mériter d'être remarqué? Je ne le crois pas. Certains récits n'appartiennent pas à la littérature, par exemple les chroniques historiques ou les relations dont nous avons l'expérience quotidienne: je puis vous dire ainsi que j'ai comparu devant la loi après avoir été photographié au volant de ma voiture, la nuit, conduisant près de chez moi à une vitesse excessive. Ce n'est donc pas en tant que narration que *Devant la loi* se définit pour nous comme un phénomène littéraire. Ce n'est pas davantage en tant que narration fictive, ni même allégorique, mythique, symbolique, parabolique, etc. Il y a des fictions, des allégories, des mythes, des symboles ou des paraboles qui n'ont rien de proprement littéraire. Qu'est-ce qui décide alors de l'appartenance de *Devant la loi* à ce que nous croyons entendre sous le nom de littérature? Et qui en décide? Pour aiguiser ces deux questions (quoi et qui), je précise que je ne privilégie aucune des deux et qu'elles portent sur la littérature plutôt que sur les belles-lettres, la poésie ou l'art discursif en général, bien que toutes ces distinctions restent fort problématiques.

La double question serait donc la suivante: 'Qui décide, et selon quelles déterminations, de l'appartenance de ce récit à la littérature'?

Pour ne pas ruser avec l'économie de temps dont je dois tenir compte, je dirai aussitôt sans détour que je n'apporte et ne détiens aucune réponse à une telle question. Peut-être penserez-vous que je veux vous conduire vers une conclusion purement aporétique ou en tous cas vers une surenchère problématique: on dirait ainsi que la question était mal formée, qu'on ne peut raisonner en termes d'appartenance à un champ ou à une classe lorsqu'il y va de la littérature, qu'il n'y a pas d'essence de la littérature, pas de lire et comprendre le texte intitulé *Devant la loi*, il le lirait comme un récit et le classerait conventionnellement dans le domaine de la littérature. Il croirait savoir ce qu'est la littérature et se demanderait seulement, si bien armé: qu'est-ce qui m'autorise à considérer ce récit comme un phénomène littéraire?

Il s'agirait donc de faire comparaître cette question, le sujet de la question et son système d'axiomes ou de conventions 'Devant la loi', devant 'Devant la loi'. Qu'est-ce que cela veut dire?

Nous ne pouvons réduire ici la singularité de l'idiome. Comparaître devant la loi, dans l'idiome français ou allemand, signifie venir ou être amené devant les juges, les représentants ou les gardiens de la loi, au cours d'un procès, pour y témoigner ou y être jugé. Le procès, le jugement (*Urteil*), voilà le lieu, le site, la situation, voilà ce qu'il faut pour qu'ait lieu un tel événement, 'comparaître devant la loi'.

Ici, '*Devant la loi*', expression que je mentionne entre guillemets, c'est le titre d'un récit. Voilà la quatrième, de nos présuppositions axiomatiques. Je dois l'ajouter à notre liste. Nous croyons savoir ce qu'est un titre, notamment le titre d'une oeuvre. Il est situé en un certain lieu très déterminé et prescrit par des lois conventionnelles: avant et au-dessus, à une distance réglée du corps même du texte, devant lui en tous cas. Le titre est en général choisi par l'auteur ou par ses représentants éditoriaux dont il est la propriété. Il nomme et garantit l'identité, l'unité et les limites de l'oeuvre originale qu'il intitule. Comme il va de soi, les pouvoirs et la valeur d'un titre ont un rapport essentiel avec quelque chose comme la loi, qu'il s'agisse de titre en général ou du titre d'une oeuvre, littéraire ou non.

Une sorte d'intrigue s'annonce déjà dans un titre qui nomme la loi (*Devant la loi*), un peu comme si la loi s'intitulait elle-même ou comme si le mot 'titre' s'introduisait insidieusement dans le titre. Laissons attendre cette intrigue.

Insistons sur la topologie. Autre aspect intriguant: le sens du titre figure une indication topologique, *devant la loi*. Et le même éconcé, le même domaine proprement littéraire et rigoureusement identifiable en tant que tel, et qu'enfin ce nom de littérature étant peut-être destiné à rester impropre, sans concept et sans référence assurée, la 'littérature' aurait quelque chose à faire avec ce drame du nom, avec la loi du nom et le nom de la loi? Vous n'auriez sans doute pas tort. Mais la généralité de ces lois et de ces conclusions problématiques m'intéresse moins que la singularité d'un procès qui, au cours d'un drame unique, les fait comparaître devant un corpus irremplaçable, devant ce texte-ci, devant 'Devant la loi'.

Il y a une singularité du rapport à la loi, une loi de singularité qui doit se mettre en rapport sans jamais pouvoir le faire avec l'essence générale ou universelle de la loi. Or ce texte-ci, ce texte singulier, vous l'aurez déjà remarqué, nomme ou relate à sa manière ce conflit sans rencontre de la loi et de la singularité, ce paradoxe ou cette *énigme* de l'être-devant-la loi; et l'*ainigma* c'est souvent, en grec, une relation, un récit, la parole obscure d'un apologue: 'L'homme de la campagne ne s'attendait pas à de telles difficultés; la loi ne doit-elle pas être accessible à tous et toujours ...'. Et la réponse, si on peut encore dire, vient à la fin du récit, qui marque aussi la fin de l'homme: 'Le gardien de la porte, sentant venir la fin de l'homme, lui rugit à l'oreille pour mieux atteindre son tympan presque inerte: "Ici nul autre que toi ne pouvait pénétrer, car cette entrée n'était faite que pour toi. Maintenant, je m'en vais et je ferme la porte".'

Ma seule ambition serait donc, sans y apporter de réponse, d'aiguiser, au risque de la déformer, la double question (qui décide, et à quel titre, de l'appartenance à la littérature?) et surtout de faire comparaître devant la loi l'énoncé même de cette double question, voire, comme on dit facilement en France aujourd'hui, le sujet de son énonciation. Un tel sujet prétendrait nom, car le titre est un nom, le même groupe de mots en tous cas n'aurait pas valeur de titre s'ils apparaissaient ailleurs, en des lieux non prescrits par la convention. Ils n'auraient pas valeur de titre s'ils apparaissaient dans un autre contexte ou à une autre place dans le même contexte. Par exemple ici même, l'expression '*Vor dem Gesetz*' se présente une première fois ou, si vous préférez, une deuxième fois, comme l'incipit du récit. C'est sa première phrase: '*Vor dem Gesetz steht ein Türhüter*', 'Devant la loi se tient (ou se dresse) un gardien de la porte un portier'. Bien qu'on puisse leur supposer le même sens, ce sont plutôt des homonymes que des synonymes car les deux occurences de la même expression ne nomment pas la même chose; elles n'ont ni la même référence ni la même valeur. De part et d'autre du trait invisible qui sépare le titre du texte, l'un nomme l'ensemble du texte dont il est en somme le nom propre et le titre, l'autre désigne une situation, le site du personnage localisé dans la géographie intérieure du récit. L'un, le titre, se trouve *devant* le texte et il reste extérieur sinon à la function, du moins au contenu de la narration fictive. L'autre se trouve aussi en tête du texte, devant lui, mais aussi en lui; c'est un premier élément intérieur au contenu fictif de la narration. Et pourtant, bien qu'il soit extérieur à la narration fictive, à l'histoire que le récit raconte, le titre (*Devant la loi*) demeure une fiction signée elle aussi par l'auteur ou son tenant-lieu. Le titre appartient à la littérature, dirions-nous, même si son appartenance n'a pas la structure ni le status que ce qu'il intitule et à quoi il reste essentiellement hétérogène. L'appartenance du titre à la littérature ne l'empêche pas d'avoir une autorité légale. Par exemple, le titre d'un livre permet la classification en bibliothèque, l'attribution des droits d'auteur et de proprieté, etc. Toutefois cette fonction n'opère pas comme le titre d'une oeuvre non-littéraire, d'un traité de physique ou de droit par exemple.

La lecture que je tenterai maintenant de *Devant la loi* sera soumise à deux contraintes ou, si vous préférez, à deux programmes. Tout d'abord à la série de conférences que vous avez intitulée 'Philosophie et Littérature'. Honoré d'une invitation par The Royal Institute of Philosophy, je devais orienter mon propos pour aller à la recontre de vos anticipations. Je devais interroger *Devant la loi*, oeuvre dite littéraire mais visiblement riche en teneur philosophique, en ce point où la différence entre philosophie et littérature paraît à la fois la plus assurée et la moins claire. S'agissant de la scène présente, je crois devoir rappeler que mon propre discours n'a pas pu ne pas être marqué par de profonds effets de traduction: effets de traduction au sens couramment linguistique puisque traitant d'un texte allemand, j'ai écrit en français un essai dont je savais que je ne le lirai pas dans sa forme dite 'originale'. Et dans ce triangle linguistique, nous voyons se multiplier les drames, les séductions et les apories de la traduction, à commencer par celle du titre. Cette situation n'a pas pu être sans conséquence sur la préparation de cette conférence, son écriture et son énonciation. Effets de traduction encore, en un sens plus ouvert: j'ai senti que plus ou moins volontairement je pliai d'avance le style de mes questions et de ma présentation à ce que, à tort ou à raison, plus ou moins confusément, j'interprétais comme la normativité dominant le discours philosophique anglais. Je ne pense pas aux normes d'une doctrine ou d'une position philosophique mais aux codes rhétoriques, stylistiques, problématiques, aux contrats implicites, aux conventions et à la loi commune qui rendent une discussion possible dans un milieu donné, à tout ce consensus sans lequel l'expression même d'un désaccord serait impraticable. Non que je me sois d'avance assujetti à ce code et à cette loi — d'ailleurs je les connais trop mal pour cela — mais enfin une négociation subtile a dû s'engager en moi, comme la chimie à peine consciente d'obscurs échanges diplomatiques dont je vous laisse juges. Bref moi aussi, homme de la campagne continentale, je me trouve ici devant une loi à laquelle je n'aurai sans doute jamais accès.

Un certain programme aura marqué cette lecture. Il s'agit d'un Séminaire de l'Ecole Normale Supérieure au cours duquel, l'an dernier, j'ai dû harceler ce récit de Kafka. En vérité c'est lui qui harcela le discours que j'essayais sur la loi morale et le respect de la loi dans la doctrine kantienne de la raison pratique, sur les pensées de Heidegger et de Freud dans leur rapport à la loi morale et au respect (au sens kantien). Je ne peux ici reconstituer les modes et les trajets de ce harcèlement. Pour en désigner les titres et les *topoi* principaux, disons qu'il s'agissait d'abord du statut étrange de l'exemple, du symbole et du type dans la doctrine kantienne. Comme vous savez, Kant parle d'une *typique* et non d'un schématisme de la raison pratique; d'une présentation *symbolique* du bien moral (le beau comme symbole de la moralité, au §59 de la *Critique de la Faculté de Juger*; enfin d'un respect qui, s'il ne s'adresse jamais aux choses, ne s'adresse néanmoins aux personnes qu'en tant qu'elles donnent l'*exemple* de la loi morale: le respect n'est dû qu'à la loi morale, qui en est la seule cause bien qu'elle ne se présente jamais ell-même. Il s'agissait aussi du 'comme si' (*als ob*) dans la deuxième formulation de l'impératif catégorique: 'Agis comme si la maxime de ton action devait devenir par ta volonté loi universelle de la nature'. Ce 'comme si' permet d'accorder la raison pratique avec une téléologie historique et la possibilité d'un progrès à l'infini. J'avais essayé de montrer comment il introduisait virtuellement narrativité et fiction au coeur même de la pensée de la loi, à l'instant où celle-ci se met à parler et à interpeller le sujet moral. Alors même que l'instance de la loi semble exclure toute historicité et toute narrativité empirique, au moment où sa rationalité paraît étrangère à toute fiction et à toute imagination, fût-elle transcendantale, elle semble encore offrir *a priori* son hospitalité à ces parasites. Deux autres motifs m'avaient retenu, parmi ceux qui font signe vers le récit de Kafka: le motif de la hauteur et du sublime qui y joue un rôle essentiel, enfin celui de la garde et du gardien. Je ne peux pas m'y étendre, je dessine seulement à gros traits le contexte dans lequel j'ai lu *Devant la loi*. Il s'agit d'un espace où il est difficile de dire si le récit de Kafka propose une puissante ellipse philosophique ou si la raison pure pratique garde en elle quelque chose de la phantastique ou de la fiction narrative. Et si la loi, sans être elle-même transie de littérature, partageait ses conditions de possibilité avec la chose littéraire? Telle pouvait être l'une de ces questions.

Pour lui donner ici, aujourd'hui, sa formulation la plus économique, je parlerai d'une *comparution* du récit et de la loi, qui comparaissent, paraissent ensemble et se voient convoqués devant l'autre: le récit, à savoir un certain type de *relation* se rapporte à la loi qu'il relate, il comparaît ce faisant devant elle qui comparaît devant lui. Et pourtant, nous allons de lire, rien ne se présente vraiment en cette comparution; et que cela nous soit donné à lire ne signifie pas que nous en aurons la preuve ou l'expérience.

Apparremment, la loi ne devrait jamais donner lieu, en tant que telle, à aucun récit. Pour être investie de son autorité catégorique, la loi doit être sans histoire, sans genèse, sans dérivation possible. Telle serait la loi de la loi. La moralité pure n'a pas d'histoire, voilà ce que semble d'abord nous rappeler Kant, pas d'histoire intrinsèque. Et quand on raconte des histoires à son sujet, elles ne peuvent concerner que des circonstances, des événements extérieurs à la loi, tout au plus les modes de sa révélation. Comme l'homme de la campagne dans le récit de Kafka, des relations narratives tenteraient d'approcher la loi, de la rendre présente, d'entrer en relation avec elle, voire d'entrer en elle, de lui devenir *intrinsèques* rien n'y fait. Le récit de ces manoeuvres ne serait que le récit de ce qui échappe au récit et lui reste finalement inaccessible. Mais l'inaccessible provoque depuis son retranchement. On ne peut pas avoir affaire à la loi, à la loi des lois, de près ou de loin, sans(se)demander où elle a proprement lieu et d'où elle vient. Je dis 'la loi des lois' parce que, dans le récit de Kafka, on ne sait pas de quelle espèce de loi il s'agit, celle de la morale, du droit ou de la politique, etc. Ce qui reste invisible et caché en chaque loi, on peut donc supposer que c'est la loi elle-même, ce qui fait que ces lois sont des lois, l'être-loi de ces lois. Inéluctables sont la question et la quête, autrement dit l'itinéraire en vue du lieu et de l'origine de la loi. Celle-ci se donne en se refusant, sans dire sa provenance et son site. Ce silence et cette discontinuité constituent le phénomène de la loi. Entrer en relation avec la loi, à celle qui dit 'tu dois' et 'tu ne dois pas', c'est à la fois faire comme si elle n'avait pas d'histoire ou en tous cas ne dépendait plus de sa présentation historique, et du même coup se laisser fasciner, provoquer, interpeller par l'histoire de cette non-histoire. C'est se laisser tenter par l'impossible: une théorie de l'origine de la loi, et donc de sa non-origine, par exemple de la loi morale. [. . .]

Patientons aussi. N'allez pas croire que j'insiste sur ce récit pour vous égarer ou pour vous faire attendre, dans l'antichambre de la littérature ou de la fiction, un traitement proprement philosophique de la question de la loi, du respect devant la loi ou de l'impératif catégorique. Ce qui nous tient en arrêt devant la loi, comme l'homme de la campagne, n'est-ce pas aussi ce qui nous paralyse et nous retient devant un récit, sa possibilité et son impossibilité, sa lisibilité et son illisibilité, sa nécessité et son interdiction, celles aussi de la relation, de la répétition, de l'histoire?

Cela semble tenir, au premier abord, au caractère essentiellement inaccessible de la loi, au fait, d'abord, qu'un 'premier abord' en soit toujours refusé, comme le donnerait à entendre déjà le doublet du titre et de l'incipit. D'une certaine manière, *Vor dem Gesetz* est le récit de cette inaccessibilité, de cette inaccessibilité au récit, l'histoire de cette histoire impossible, la carte de ce trajet interdit: pas d'itinéraire, pas de méthode, pas de chemin pour accéder à la loi, à ce qui en elle aurait lieu, au topos de son événement. Telle inaccessibilité étonne l'homme de la campagne au moment du regard, à l'instant où il observe le gardien qui est lui-même l'observateur, le surveillant, la sentinelle, la figure même de la vigilance, on pourrait dire la conscience. La question de l'homme de la campagne, c'est bien celle du chemin d'accès: est-ce que la loi ne se définit pas justement par son accessibilité? N'est-elle, ne *doit*-elle pas être accessible 'toujours et pour chacun'? Ici pourrait se déployer le problème de l'exemplarité, par exemple dans la pensée kantienne du 'respect': celui-ci n'est que l'*effet* de la loi, souligne Kaut, il n'est dû qu'à la loi et ne comparaît en droit que *devant la loi*, il ne s'adresse aux personnes qu'en tant qu'elles donnent l'exemple de ce qu'une loi peut être respectée. On n'accède donc jamais *directement* ni à la loi ni aux personnes, on n'est jamais *immédiatement* devant aucune de ces instances—et le détour peut être infini. L'universalité même de la loi déborde toute finité et fait donc courir ce risque.

Mais laissons cela qui nous détournerait aussi de notre récit. La loi, pense l'homme de la campagne, devrait être accessible toujours et à chacun. Elle devrait être universelle. Réciproquement, on dit en français que 'nul n'est censé ignorer la loi', dans ce cas la loi positive. Nul n'est censé l'ignorer, à la condition de ne pas être analphabète, de pouvoir en lire le texte ou déléguer la lecture et la compétence à un avocat, à la représentation d'un homme de loi. A moins que savoir lire ne rende la loi encore plus inaccessible. La lecture peut en effet révéler qu'un texte est intouchable, proprement intangible, *parce que lisible*, et du même coup illisible dans la mesure où la présence en lui d'un sens perceptible, saisissable, reste aussi dérobée que son origine. L'illisibilité ne s'oppose plus alors à la lisibilité. Et peut-être l'homme est-il homme de la campagne en tant qu'il ne sait pas lire ou que, sachant lire, il a encore affaire à de l'illisibilité dans cela même qui semble se donner à lire. Il veut voir ou toucher la loi, il veut s'approcher d'elle, 'entrer' en elle parce qu'il ne sait peut-être pas que la loi n'est pas à voir ou à toucher mais à déchiffrer. C'est peut-être le premier signe de son inaccessibilité ou du retard qu'elle impose à l'homme de la campagne. La porte n'est pas fermée, elle est 'ouverte' comme toujours (dit le texte) mais la loi reste inaccessible et si cela interdit, barre la porte de l'histoire généalogique, c'est aussi ce qui tient en haleine un désir de l'origine, une pulsion généalogique; celui-ci s'essouffle aussi bien devant le processus d'engendrement de la loi que devant la génération parentale. La recherche historique conduit la *relation* vers l'exhibition impossible d'un site et d'un événement, d'un avoir-lieu où s'origine la loi comme interdit. [. . .]

Si la loi est fantastique, si son site originel et son avoir-lieu ont vertu de fable, on comprend que 'das Gesetz' demeure essentiellement inaccessible alors même qu'elle se présente ou se promet. D'une quête pour parvenir jusqu'à elle, pour se tenir devant elle, face à face et respectueusement, ou pour s'introduire à elle et en elle, le récit devient le récit impossible de l'impossible. Le recit de l'interdit est un récit interdit.

L'homme de la campagne voulait-il entrer en elle ou seulement dans le lieu où elle se tient gardée? Ce n'est pas clair et l'alternative est peut-être fausse dès lors que la loi est-elle même une sorte de lieu, un topos et un avoir-lieu. En tous cas, l'homme de la campagne, qui est aussi un homme d'*avant la loi*, comme la campagne avant la ville, ne veut pas rester devant la loi, dans la situation du gardien. Celui-ci aussi se tient *devant la loi*. Cela peut vouloir dire qu'il la respecte: se tenir devant la loi, comparaître devant elle, c'est s'y assujettir, la respecter, d'autant plus que le respect tient à distance, maintient en face et interdit le contact ou la pénétration. Mais cela peut vouloir dire que, debout devant la loi, le gardien la fait respecter. Il monte alors la garde *devant elle* en lui tournant le dos, sans lui faire face, sans être 'in front of it', sentinelle qui surveille les entrées de l'edifice et tient en respect les visiteurs qui se présentent devant le château. L'inscription 'devant la loi' se divise donc une fois de plus. Elle était déjà double selon de lieu textuel en quelque sorte, titre ou incipit. Elle se dédouble aussi dans ce qu'elle dit ou décrit: un partage du territoire et une opposition absolue dans la scène, au regard de la loi. Les deux personnages du récit, le gardien et l'homme de la campagne sont bien devant la loi mais comme ils se font face pour se parler, leur position 'devant la loi' est une opposition. L'un des deux, le gardien, tourne le dos à la loi devant laquelle néanmoins il se trouve ('*Vor dem Gesetz steht ein Türhüter*'). L'homme de la campagne, en revanche, se trouve aussi devant la loi mais dans une position contraire puisqu'on peut supposer que, prêt à y entrer, il lui fait face. Les deux protagonistes sont également devant la loi mais ils s'opposent l'un à l'autre de part et d'autre d'une ligne d'inversion dont la marque n'est autre, dans le texte, que la séparation du titre et du corps narratif. Double inscription de 'vor dem Gesetz' autour d'une ligne invisible qui divise, sépare et d'elle-même rend divisible une unique expression. Elle en dédouble le trait.

Cela n'est possible qu'avec le surgissement de l'instance intitulante, dans sa fonction topique et juridique. C'est pourquoi je me suis intéressé à ce récit ainsi intitulé plutôt qu'à tel passage du *Procès* qui raconte à peu près la même histoire sans comporter, bien évidemment, aucun titre. En allemand commeen français 'Devant la loi' s'entend couramment dans le sens de la comparution respectueuse et assujettie d'un sujet qui se présente devant les représentants ou les gardiens de la loi. Il se présente devant des représentants: la loi en personne, si on peut dire, n'est jamais présente, bien que devant la loi semble signifier 'en présence de la loi'. L'homme alors est en face de la loi sans jamais lui faire face. Il peut être *in front of it*, il ne l'affronte jamais. Les premiers mots de l'incipit, happés par une phrase dont il n'est pas sûr qu'elle soit simplement à l'état d'interruption dans le titre ('*Vor dem Gesetz*', '*Vor dem Gesetz steht ein Türhüter*') se mettent à signifier tout autre chose, et peut-être même le contraire du titre qui les reproduit pourtant comme souvent certains poèmes reçoivent pour titre le début d'un premier vers. La structure et la fonction des deux occurences, des deux événements de la même marque sont certes hétérogènes, je le répète, mais comme ces deux événements différents et identiques ne s'enchaînent pas dans une séquence narrative ou one conséquence logique, il est impossible de dire que l'un *précède* l'autre selon quelque ordre que ce soit. Ils sont tous deux premiers dans leur ordre et aucun des deux homonymes, voire synonymes, ne cite l'autre. L'événement intitulant donne au texte sa loi et son nom. Or c'est un coup de force. Par exemple au regard du *Procès* auquel il arrache ce récit pour en faire une autre institution. Sans engager encore dans la séquence narrative, il ouvre une scène, il donne lieu à un système topographique de la loi prescrivant les deux positions inverses et adverses, l'antagonisme de deux personnages également intéressés à elle. La phrase inaugurale décrit celui qui tourne le dos à la loi (tourner le dos, c'est aussi ignorer, négliger, voire transgresser) non pas pour que la loi se présente ou qu'on lui soit présenté mais au contraire pour interdire toute présentation. Celui qui fait face ne voit pas plus que celui qui tourne le dos. Aucun des deux n'est en présence de la loi. Les deux seuls personnages du récit sont aveugles et séparés, séparés l'un de l'autre et séparés de la loi. Telle est la modalité de ce rapport, de cette relation, de ce récit: aveuglement et séparation une sorte de sans-rapport. Car ne l'oublions pas, le gardien est aussi séparé de la loi, par d'autres gardiens, dit-il, 'l'un plus puissant que l'autre' (*einer mächtiger als der andere*): 'Je suis puissant. Et je ne suis que le dernier des gardiens [dans la hiérarchie, *der unterste*]. Mais devant chaque salle il y a des gardiens, l'un plus puissant que l'autre. Je ne peux même pas supporter l'aspect (*den Anblick . . . ertragen*) du troisième après moi.' Le dernier des gardiens est le premier à voir l'homme de la campagne. Le premier dans l'ordre du récit est le dernier dans l'ordre de la loi et dans la hiérarchie de ses représentants. Et ce premier-dernier gardien ne voit jamais la loi, il ne supporte même pas la vue des gardiens qui sont *devant* lui (avant et au-dessus de lui). C'est inscrit dans son titre de gardien de la porte. Et il est, lui, bien en vue, observé même par l'homme qui, *à sa vue*, décide de ne rien décider. Je dis 'l'homme' pour l'homme de la campagne, comme par fois dans le récit qui laisse ainsi penser que le gardien, lui, n'est peut-être plus simplement un homme, et que cet homme, lui, c'est l'homme aussi bien que n'importe qui, le sujet anonyme de la loi. Celui-ci se résout donc à 'préférer attendre' à l'instant où son attention est attirée par les pilosités et le nez pointu du gardien. Sa résolution de non-résolution fait être et durer le récit. La permission, avais-je rappelé, ne lui avait pourtant jamais été refusée. On l'avait seulement retardée, ajournée, différée. Tout est question de temps, et c'est le temps du récit, mais le temps lui-même n'apparaît que depuis cet ajournement de la présentation, depuis la loi du retard ou l'avance de la loi, depuis cette anachronie de la relation.

L'interdiction présente de la loi n'est pas une interdiction, au sens de la contrainte impérative, c'est une différance. Car après lui avoir dit 'plus tard', le gardien précise: 'Si cela t'attire tellement, dit-il, essaie donc d'entrer malgré ma défense'. Auparavant il lui avait seulement dit 'mais pas maintenant'. Puis il s'efface sur le côté et laisse l'homme se baisser pour regarder par la porte à l'intérieur. La porte, est-il précisé, reste toujours ouverte. Elle marque la limite sans être elle-même un obstacle ou une clôture. Elle marque mais n'est rien de consistant, d'opaque, d'infranchissable. Elle laisse voir à l'intérieur (*in das Innere*), non pas la loi elle-même, sans doute, mais le dedans de lieux apparement vides et provisoirement interdits. La porte est physiquement ouverte, le gardien ne s'interpose pas par la force. C'est son discours qui opère, non pour interdire directement, mais pour interrompre et différer le passage, ou le laisser-passer. L'homme dispose de la liberté naturelle ou physique de pénétrer dans les lieux, sinon dans la loi. Il doit donc, et il le faut bien, il faut bien le constater, s'interdire lui-même d'entrer. Il doit s'obliger lui même, se donner l'ordre non pas d'obéir à la loi mais de ne pas accéder à la loi qui en somme lui fait dire ou lui laisse savoir: ne viens pas à moi, je t'ordonne de ne pas venir encore jusqu'à moi. C'est là et en cela que je suis la loi et que tu accéderas à ma demande. Sans accéder à moi.

Car la loi est l'interdit. Tel serait le terrifiant *double-bind* de son avoir-lieu propre. Elle est l'interdit: cela ne signifie pas qu'elle interdit mais qu'elle est elle-même interdite, un lieu interdit. Elle s'interdit et se contredit en mettant l'homme dans sa propre contradiction: on ne peut arriver jusqu'à elle et pour avoir *rapport* avec elle selon le respect, *il faut ne pas, il ne faut pas* avoir rapport à elle, *il faut interrompre la relation*. Il faut *n'entrer en relation* qu'avec ses représentants, ses exemples, ses gardiens. Et ce sont des interrupteurs autant que des messagers. Il faut ne pas savoir qui elle est, ce qu'elle est, où elle est, où et comment elle se présente, d'où elle vient et d'où elle parle. Voilà ce qu'*il faut* au *il faut* de la loi. *Ci falt*, comme on écrivait au Moyen Age à la conclusion d'un récit.

Voilà le procès, le jugement, processus et *Urteil*, la division originaire de la loi. La loi est interdite. Mais cette auto-interdiction contradictoire laisse l'homme s'auto-déterminer 'librement', bien que cette liberté s'annule comme auto-interdiction d'entrer dans la loi. L'homme s'est baissé pour voir à l'intérieur, ce qui laisse supposer que pour l'instant il est plus grand que la porte ouverte, et cette question de la taille nous attend encore. Après qu'il eut observé plus attentivement le gardien, il se décide donc à attendre une permission à la fois donnée et différée mais dont le premier gardien lui laisse anticiper qu'elle sera indéfiniment différée. Derrière le premier gardien il y en a d'autres, en nombre indéterminé; peut-être sont-ils innombrables, de plus en plus puissants, donc de plus en plus interdicteurs, forts de pouvoir différer. Leur puissance est la différance, une différance interminable puisqu'elle dure des jours, des 'années' et finalement jusqu'à la fin de l'homme. Différance jusqu'à la mort, pour la mort, sans fin parce que finie. Représenté par le gardien, le discours de la loi ne dit pas 'non' mais 'pas encore', indéfiniment. D'où l'engagement dans un récit à la fois parfaitement fini et brutalement interrompu, on pourrait dire primitivement interrompu.

Ce qui est retardé, ce n'est pas telle ou telle expérience, l'accès à une jouissance, à quelque bien, fût-il souverain, la possession ou la pénétration de quelque chose ou de quelqu'un. Ce qui est à jamais différé, jusqu'à la mort, c'est l'entrée dans la loi elle-même, qui n'est rien d'autre que cela même qui dicte le retard. La loi interdit en interférant et en différant la 'férance', le rapport, la relation, la référence. L'origine de la différance, voilà ce qu'il *ne faut pas* et ne se peut pas approcher, se présenter, se représenter et surtout pénétrer. Voilà la loi de la loi, le procès d'une loi au sujet de la-quelle on ne peut jamais dire 'la voilà', ici ou là. Et elle n'est ni naturelle ni institutionnelle. On n'y arrive jamais et au fond de son avoir-lieu originel et propre, elle n'arrive jamais.

Le récit (de ce qui n'arrive jamais) ne nous dit pas quelle espèce de loi se manifeste ainsi dans sa non-manifestation: naturelle, morale, juridique, politique? Quant au genre sexuel, il est grammaticalement neutre en allemand, *das Gesetz*, ni féminin ni masculin. En français le féminin détermine une contagion sémantique qu'on ne peut pas plus oublier qu'on ne peut ignorer la langue comme milieu élémentaire de la loi. Dans *La folie du jour* de Maurice Blanchot, on peut parler d'une *apparition* de la Loi (avec une majuscule), et c'est une 'silhouette' féminine: ni un homme ni une femme mais une silhouette féminine venue faire couple avec le quasi narrateur d'une narration interdite ou impossible (c'est tout le récit de ce non-récit). Le 'je' du narrateur effraye la Loi. C'est la Loi qui semble avoir peur et battre en retraite. Quant au narrateur, autre analogie sans rapport avec *Devant la loi*, il raconte comment il a dû comparaître devant des représentants de la loi (policiers, juges ou médecins), des hommes, eux, qui exigeaient del lui un récit. Ce récit, il ne pouvait le donner mais il se trouve être celui-la même qu'il propose pour relater l'impossible.

Ici, *das Gesetz*, on ne sait pas ce que c'est ni qui c'est. Et alors commence peut-être la littérature. Un texte philosophique, scientifique, historique, un texte de savoir ou d'information n'abandonnerait pas un nom à un non-savoir, du moins ne le ferait-il que par accident et non de façon essentielle et constitutive. Ici, on ne sait pas la loi, on n'a pas à elle un rapport de savoir, ce n'est ni un sujet ni un objet *devant* lesquels il y aurait à se tenir. Rien ne (se) tient devant la loi. Ce n'est pas une femme ou une figure féminine, même si l'homme, *homo* et *vir*, veut y pénétrer ou la pénétrer (c'est là son leurre, justement). Mais la loi n'est pas davantage un homme, elle est neutre, au-delà du genre grammatical et sexuel, elle qui reste indifférente, impassible, peu soucieuse de répondre oui ou non. Elle laisse l'homme se déterminer librement, elle le laisse attendre, elle le délaisse. Et puis neutre, ni au féminin, ni au masculin, indifférente parce qu'on ne sait pas si c'est une personne (respectable) ou une chose, qui ou quoi. [...]

Il serait tentant, au-delà des limites de cette lecture, de reconstituer ce récit sans récit dans l'enveloppe elliptique de la *Critique de la Raison Pratique*, par exemple, ou dans *Totem et Tabou*. Mais si loin que nous puissions aller dans ce sens, nous n'expliquerions pas la parabole d'un récit dit 'littéraire' à l'aide de contenus sémantiques d'origine philosophique ou psychanalytique, en puisant à quelque savoir. Nous en avons aperçu la nécessité. La fiction de cet ultime récit qui nous dérobe tout événement, ce récit pur ou récit sans récit se trouve impliqué aussi bien par la philosophie, la science ou la psychanalyse que part ladite littérature. [...]

Nous sommes devant ce texte qui, ne disant rien de clair, ne présentant aucun contenu identifiable au-delà du récit même, sinon une différance interminable jusqu'à la mort, reste néanmoins rigoureusement intangible. Intangible : j'entends par là inaccessible au contact, imprenable et finalement insaisissable, incompréhensible, mais aussi bien ce à quoi nous n'avons pas le *droit* de toucher. C'est un texte 'original', comme on dit : il est interdit ou illégitime de la transformer ou de le déformer, de toucher à sa forme. Malgré la non-identité à soi de son sens ou de sa destination, malgré son illisibilité essentielle, sa 'forme' se présente et se performe comme une sorte d'identité personnelle ayant droit au respect absolu. Si quelqu'un y changeait un mot, y altérait une phrase, un juge pourrait toujours dire qu'il y a eu transgression, violence, infidélité. Une mauvaise traduction sera toujours appelée à comparaître devant la version dite originale qui *fait référence*, dit-on, autorisée qu'elle est par l'auteur ou ses ayant-droit, désignée dans son identité par son titre, qui est son nom propre d'état civil, et encadrée entre son premier et son dernier mot. Quiconque porterait atteinte à l'identité originale de ce texte pourrait avoir à comparaître devant la loi. Cela peut arriver à tout lecteur en présence du texte, au critique, à l'éditeur, au traducteur, aux héritiers, aux professeurs. Tous, ils sont donc à la fois gardiens et hommes de la campagne. [...]

Si nous soustrayons de ce texte tous les éléments qui pourraient appartenir à un autre registre (information quotidienne, histoire, savoir, philosophie, fiction, etc., bref tout ce qui n'est pas nécessairement affilié à la littérature), nous sentons obscurément que ce qui *opère et fait oeuvre* dans ce texte garde un rapport essentiel avec le jeu du cadrage et la logique paradoxale des limites qui introduit une sorte de perturbation dans le système 'normal' de la référence, tout en *révélant* une structure essentielle de la référentialité. Révélation obscure de la référentialité qui ne fait pas plus référence, ne réfère pas plus que l'événementialité de l'événement n'est un événement.

Que cela fasse oeuvre néanmoins, c'est peut-être un signe vers la littérature. Signe peut-être insuffisant mais signe nécessaire: il n'est pas de littérature sans oeuvre, sans performance absolument singulière, et l'irremplaçabilité de rigueur appelle encore les questions de l'homme de la campagne quand le singulier croise l'universel, comme doit toujours le faire une littérature. L'homme de la campagne avait du mal à entendre la singularité d'un accès qui devait être universel, et qui en vérité l'était. Il avait du mal avec la littérature.

Comment vérifier la soustraction dont je parlais il y a un instant? Eh bien cette contre-épreuve nous serait proposée par *Le Procès* lui-même. Nous retrouvons le même *contenu* dans un autre cadrage, avec un autre système de limites et surtout sans titre propre, sans autre titre que celui d'un volume de plusieurs centaines de pages. Le même contenu donne lieu, du point de vue littéraire, à une oeuvre tout autre. Et ce qui diffère, d'une oeuvre à l'autre, si ce n'est pas le contenu, ce n'est pas davantage la *forme* (l'expression signifiante, les phénomènes de langue ou de rhétorique). Ce sont les mouvements de cadrage et de référéntialité.

Ces deux oeuvres alors, sur la ligne de leur étrange filiation, deviennent l'une pour l'autre les interprétations métonymiques, chacune devenant la partie absolument indépendante de l'autre, une partie chaque fois plus grande que le tout.

Cela ne suffit pas encore. Si le cadrage, le titre, la structure référentielle sont nécessaires au surgissement de l'oeuvre littéraire comme telle, ces conditions de possibilité restent encore trop générales et valent pour d'autres textes auxquels nous ne songerions pas à reconnaître quelque valeur littéraire. Ces possibilités générales assurent à un texte le pouvoir de *faire la loi*, à commencer par la sienne. Mais cela à la condition que le texte lui-même puise comparaître *devant la loi* d'un autre texte, d'un texte plus puissant, gardé par des gardiens plus puissants. En effet le texte (par exemple le texte dit 'littéraire', singulièrement tel récit de Kafka) devant lequel nous, lecteurs, comparaissons comme devant la loi, ce texte gardé par ses gardiens (auteur, éditeur, critiques, universitaires, archivistes, bibliothécaires, juristes, etc.) ne peut faire la loi que si un système de loi plus puissant le garantit, et d'abord l'ensemble des lois ou conventions sociales autorisant toutes ces légitimités.

Si le texte de Kafka dit tout cela de la littérature, l'ellipse puissante qu'il nous livre n'appartient pas totalement à la littérature. Le lieu depuis lequel il nous parle *des* lois de la littérature, de la loi sans laquelle aucune spécificité littéraire ne prendrait figure ou consistance, ce lieu ne peut être simplement intérieur à la littérature.

C'est qu'il y a lieu de penser *ensemble*, sans doute, une certaine historicité de la loi et une certaine historicité de la littérature. Si je dis 'littérature' plutôt que poésie ou belles-lettres, c'est pour marquer l'hypothèse selon laquelle la spécificité relativement moderne de la littérature comme telle garde un rapport essentiel et étroit avec un moment de l'histoire du droit. Dans une autre culture, ou en Europe à un autre moment de l'histoire du droit positif, de la législation (explicite ou implicite) sur la propriété des oeuvres, par exemple au Moyen Age ou avant le Moyen Age, l'identité de ce texte, son jeu avec le titre, avec les signatures, avec ses bordures ou celles d'autres corpus, tout ce système de cadrage fonctionnerait autrement et avec d'autres garanties. Non pas qu'au Moyen Age il n'eût pas compté avec une protection une veillance institutionnelles. Mais celle-ci réglait tout autrement l'identité des corpus, les livrant plus facilement à l'initiative transformatrice de copistes ou d'autres 'gardiens', aux greffes pratiquées par des héritiers ou d'autres 'auteurs' (anonymes ou non, masqués ou non sous des pseudonymes, individus ou collectivités plus ou moins identifiables). Mais quelle que soit la structure de l'institution juridique et donc politique qui vient à garantir l'oeuvre, celle-ci surgit toujours devant la loi.

Elle n'a d'existence et de consistance qu'aux conditions de la loi et elle ne devient 'littéraire' qu'à une certaine époque du droit réglant les problèmes de propriété des oeuvres, de l'identité des corpus, de la valeur des signatures, de la différence entre créer, produire et reproduire, etc. En gros, ce droit s'est établi entre la fin du XVIIè siècle et le début du XIXè siècle européens. Il reste que de concept le littérature qui soutient ce droit des oeuvres reste obscur. Le lois positives auxquelles je me réfère valent aussi pour d'autres arts et ne jettent aucune lumière critique sur leurs propres présuppositions conceptuelles. Ce qui m'importe ici, c'est que ces pré-suppositions obscures sont aussi le lot des 'gardiens', critiques, universi-taires, théoriciens de la littérature, écrivains, philosophes. Tous doivent en appeler à une loi, comparaître devant elle, à la fois veiller sur elle et se laisser surveiller par elle. Tous ils l'interrogent naïvement sur le singulier et l'universel, aucun d'eux ne reçoit de réponse qui ne relance la différance: plus de loi et plus de littérature.

En ce sens, le texte de Kafka dit peut-être, aussi, l'être-devant-la loi de tout texte. Il le dit par ellipse, l'avançant et le retirant à la fois. Il n'appartient pas seulement à la littérature d'une époque en tant qu'il est lui-même devant la loi (qu'il dit), devant un certain type de loi. Il désigne aussi obliquement la littérature, il parle de lui-même comme d'un effet littéraire. Par où il déborde la littérature dont il parle.

Mais n'y a-t-il pas lieu, pour toute littérature, de déborder la littérature? Que serait une littérature qui ne serait que ce qu'elle est, littérature? Elle ne serait plus elle-même si elle était elle-même. Cela aussi appartient à l'ellipse de *Devant la loi*. Sans doute ne peut-on parler de la 'littérarité' comme d'une *appartenance* à *la* littérature, comme de l'inclusion d'un phénomène ou d'un objet, voire d'une oeuvre, dans un champ, un domaine, une région dont les frontières seraient pures et les titres indivisibles.

La littérature est peut-être venue, dans des conditions historiques qui ne sont pas simplement linguistiques, occuper une place toujours ouverte à une sorte de juridicité subversive. Elle l'aurait occupée pour un certain

Jacques Derrida

temps et sans être elle-même de part en part subversive, bien au contraire parfois. Cette juridicité subversive suppose que l'identité à soi ne soit jamais assurée ou rassurante. Elle suppose aussi un pouvoir de produire performativement les énoncés de la loi, de la loi que peut être la littérature et non seulement de la loi à laquelle elle s'assujettit. Alors elle fait la loi, elle surgit en ce lieu où la loi se fait. Mais dans des conditions déterminées, elle peut user du pouvoir légiférant de la performativité linguistique pour tourner les lois existantes dont elle tient pourtant ses garanties et ses conditions de surgissement. Cela grâce à l'équivoque référentielle de certaines structures linguistiques. Dans ces conditions la littérature peut *jouer la loi*, la répéter en la détournant ou en la contournant. Ces conditions, qui sont aussi les conditions conventionnelles de tout performatif, ne sont sans doute pas purement linguistiques, bien que toute convention puisse à son tour donner lieu à une définition ou à un contrat d'ordre langagier. Nous touchons ici à l'un des points les plus difficiles de cette problématique, quand on doit retrouver le langage sans langage, le langage au-delà du langage, ces rapports de forces muettes, mais déjà hantées par l'écriture, où s'établissent les conditions d'un performatif, les règles du jeu et les limites de la subversion.

Dans l'instant insaisissable où elle joue la loi, une littérature passe la littérature. Elle se trouve des deux côtés de la ligne qui sépare la loi du hors-la-loi; elle divise l'être-devant-la loi, elle est à la fois, comme l'homme de la campagne, 'devant la loi' et 'avant la loi.' Avant l'être-devant-la loi. Mais dans un site aussi improbable, aura-t-elle eu lieu? Et y aura-t-il eu lieu de nommer la littérature? [. . .]

Philosophical Autobiography: St Augustine and John Stuart Mill[1]

MARTIN WARNER

> In autobiography we encounter the highest and most instructive form of the understanding of life (Wilhelm Dilthey).

> A confession has to be a part of your new life (Ludwig Wittgenstein).

I (i). Philosophical

Many classic philosophical debates converge on the twin questions 'What is man?' and 'What is his place in nature?', in the sense that taking up a position in those debates normally commits one to a certain range of answers to these questions. Such answers typically lie near the centre of one's web of belief, deeply entrenched in the structure of one's concepts, and thus remain remarkably resistant to the standard techniques of confirmation and refutation.

This resistance has led many contemporary philosophers who are attached to these techniques near despair. For example, in his discussion of the appraisal of rival conceptual systems Professor Ayer is led to the conclusion that

> so long as it is free from inner contradiction, it is hard to see how any philosophical thesis can be refuted, and equally hard to see how it can ever be proved.

If, he claims, we do not accept such a thesis (the example he gives is that of physicalism), then in arguing with an adherent

> our only hope . . . is to make the interpretations appear so strained that the assumptions on which they rest become discredited (Ayer, 27).

But the criteria by reference to which we are to determine the degree of 'strain' turn out to be remarkably elusive.

---

[1] My thanks are due to Dr R. A. Gekoski for many valuable discussions about these matters. The epigraphs are taken from Dilthey, 214, and Wittgenstein, 18e.

This is not a new problem. More than a century ago, Newman wrote of a pattern of argument involved in metaphysical thinking which is

> the culmination of probabilities, independent of each other, arising out of the nature and circumstances of the particular case which is under review; probabilities too fine to avail separately, too subtle and circuitous to be convertible into syllogisms, too numerous and various for such conversion, even were they convertible (Newman, 288).

Recently, Professor Mitchell has invoked Newman in his attempt to clarify these elusive criteria by use of the notion of a 'cumulative case'. He points out that the humanities generally, not just philosophy, frequently lack procedures which satisfy strict deductive and inductive canons, but are not on that account to be dubbed 'irrational'. Ayer's term 'interpretation' has a home in the field of literary criticism, and in this context it does not follow that because a number of alternative interpretations of a text are logically possible and none are decisively refuted by empirical evidence, that all are equally good; sound judgment in a scholar consists precisely in the trained capacity to adjudicate in such controversial issues. Similar considerations apply in the field of historical controversy; in both cases the elusive notion of 'making the best sense' of all the evidence available plays a key role, for

> there is a continuous tension between the individual bits of evidence and the overall interpretation, such that (a) the overall interpretation has to make sense of the evidence, neither ignoring nor distorting it, (b) the evidence has to square with all the other evidence.

In such cases the different considerations to which one appeals may properly be said to 'reinforce one another', and thus there are

> cases in which an argument which does not purport to be a proof or to rely on strict probability is capable of providing reasonable grounds for a conclusion about a matter of fact (Mitchell, 53, 57).

It is argued that similar considerations apply in the sciences (use is made of the Lakatos/Kuhn debate), and also in metaphysics—specifically in arguments about the truth of Christianity, with all the attendant consequences for our beliefs about man and his place in nature.[2]

---

[2] There is a marked resemblance between this pattern of argument and that based on the convergence of circumstantial evidence in the law courts. Jonathan Cohen has recently argued that there are major difficulties in the way of construing the latter in terms of the classic probability calculus, with its inbuilt requirement that prior probabilities be determined (Cohen, 93–115, 277–281). Unfortunately, his alternative axiomatization seems ill-suited to the cases under discussion, because of its requirement that the items of evidence said to 'con-

These extensions have met resistance. Acceptable 'cumulative' arguments in literary criticism and history operate within frameworks provided by those disciplines in terms of which their canons of acceptability can be defended; it has to be shown that such defences also apply outside those contexts in the philosophical appraisal of Professor Ayer's 'conceptual systems', for

> no form or mode of argument can be said to be rational irrespective of the type of context in which it appears (Durrant, 1).

The force of this type of consideration should not be over-estimated, however, for if it is once conceded that in certain contexts cumulative arguments may properly be regarded as rational, the burden of argument rests with those who claim that in metaphysics only those arguments which conform to the requirements of deductive proof or strict probability are rationally acceptable. One's judgment here should turn on the strength of the analogies between the kinds of interpretation Ayer discusses and those in the less problematic cases, and on whether there is good reason for making a sharp break at some point on Mitchell's spectrum from critical exegesis and historical judgment, through the sciences, to metaphysics. Part of the evidence is provided by arguments in fact used and widely thought to be telling in the various cases, and in particular on the extent to which the type of 'culmination of probabilities' of which Newman writes plays a significant role in the appraisal of rival conceptual systems.

In this context a number of autobiographical works by philosophers of high repute but very different persuasions are instructive. For here we have authors who have written accounts of their own lives which are informed by their overall understanding of man and the world. Part of the aim in each case has been to clarify, fill out, and render plausible that understanding by showing how it illuminates the writer's own life, and how his experience has provided what looks suspiciously like part of the appropriate cumulative case for it.

I (ii). Autobiography

The most fully developed of such works are those in which the story told is significantly reflexive. It is when the central concern is with the author's own life and its attendant experiences, with how it seemed then and how it seems now, that the genre's possibilities and pitfalls become fully apparent. To the extent that what is presented as 'autobiography' approximates on the one side to 'memoir' and on the other to 'novel', the

---

verge' be strongly independent. Such independence is often not to be found even in historical controversy, let alone in exegesis or metaphysics (despite Newman's suggestion to the contrary), and it may reasonably be doubted whether it is so frequent in the law as Cohen would have it.

potentialities and dangers shift away from those with which I am primarily concerned.

The word itself is of comparatively recent manufacture, and there is no general agreement about the precise limits of the genre. But for present purposes it is convenient to follow an influential recent taxonomy where, with autobiographies firmly distinguished from diaries and letters, it is suggested that

> in the autobiography proper, attention is focused on the self, in the memoir or reminiscence on others . . . Memoir concerns itself with public events, reminiscence with private relationships (Pascal, 5).

Although there are problems attendant upon using the notion of attention being 'focused on the self' as part of the definition of 'autobiography' —what, for example, of the status of Sartre's *Words* where a pivotal claim is that 'I had no true self'? (Sartre, 69)—the proposal is useful as a first approximation.

Within the genre thus broadly specified there is a further discrimination to be made about the quality of this 'attention', between more and less 'external' treatments of that self. The term 'autobiography' was constructed as a modification of the older 'biography'; it is a biography written by the protagonist, and the effects of this distinguishing feature can vary widely. At one extreme there are autobiographical writings where extensive recourse is made to publicly available material in order to secure accuracy, and there is little but the use of the first person singular to distinguish the material from that written by a sympathetic and well-informed biographer. To the extent that an autobiography aspires, in this way, to the condition of biography, we may say that the treatment of the self in it is 'external'. At the other extreme we have examples of the old-fashioned 'confession', where the central focus is on self-examination and judgment, with the status of the narrator, together with his grasp on the values he acknowledges and employs, indissolubly connected with the figure whose life is charted. In this sense both Augustine and Rousseau are fundamentally 'inward' in their autobiographical writings; the latter, indeed, goes so far as to preface his *Confessions* with the epigraph 'Intus, et in cute' ('Inwardly, and under the skin'). Mill provides an intermediate case; although the author's present position is seen as won by the striving and self-interrogation of the protagonist, it would be grotesque to find the work entitled *The Confessions of John Stuart Mill*!

For present purposes it is the inward and intermediate cases that are the most significant. But they give rise to a classic problem of autobiography in its most acute form—the problem of truth. The less weight given to those aspects of one's life which are publicly checkable, the more difficult it becomes to be sure that one's memory is reliable. For this reason some commentators seek to cut the link with fact altogether:

The value of an autobiography depends ultimately on the quality of spirit of the writer . . . One demands from the best more than an account of personalities, events, and circumstances. These must become the framework, in some sense the embodiment, of the personality of the writer . . . , and one must be set free from them as historical facts, and from the concern with their accuracy as historical documents, in order to savour the quality of the central personality. . . . Each man constructs out of his world a unique framework of meaningful events, and . . . the deepest purpose of autobiography is the account of a life as a projection of the real self (we call it personality but it seems to lie deeper than personality) on the world (Pascal, 19–20, 45).

But this will hardly do as it stands. A propensity to deceive oneself or lie to others bears directly on a man's 'quality of spirit', and historical facts may be of decisive importance here. Further, if one has no concern with the accuracy of autobiographies 'as historical documents' it is unclear how one is to distinguish between the projection of a 'real self' and that of an idealized self upon the world. Again, the concern with inwardness of the confession very easily spills into the preoccupations of the apologia, where the tendency of self-justification to distort the narrative is notorious.

On the other hand, one should not allow insistence on historical fact-uality to be simple-minded. In the first place, what is to count as a fact may well be one of the questions at issue in an autobiography; the very criteria a historian is liable to use in concluding that Rousseau was deluded in many of his disputes with contemporaries, are themselves under attack in his *Confessions*. Second, we can very often tell through the quality of the writing when an author is beginning to idealize himself or otherwise lose touch with reality; Rousseau again provides excellent examples—consider the discussions of his treatment of his children, and the clear signs of paranoia at the start of the seventh book. Third, an author may deliberately recast the history of some inwardly significant episode in order to throw what he believes to be the essential lineaments of the ex-perience into sharper relief; often close reading will in such cases reveal oddities of chronology as a result, but a painstaking reconstruction of events in the light of such clues may achieve chronological accuracy at the cost of human significance—Mill's account of his mental crisis is a case in point.[3] And, finally, it is common for distorted memories of what has happened or what has been told to shape subsequent behaviour much more powerfully than the reality; if an author presents himself as a man who acted honourably (or dishonourably) because the circumstances were thus and so, the judgment may remain unaffected by the discovery that circumstances were otherwise, particularly if the protagonist's mis-understanding was not culpable.

[3] See, for example, the discussions in Cumming and Thomas.

Nevertheless, none of these considerations enable us to dispense entirely with questions of historical fact in assessing an autobiography, and when such a work provides a vehicle for the author's model of man they become if anything more pressing. For whereas a certain shrillness of tone tends to characterize the inauthentic apologia, when it is not so much the self as a doctrine which is being defended the greater distance between advocate and defendant may make distortion more difficult to detect. Further, so long as the theory is wide-ranging and coherent, it is liable to provide a persuasive framework which includes its own criteria for selection and interpretation of material, thus facilitating circular self-justification—the autobiographical analogue of Ayer's problem. External evidence of suppression or amplification, carefully handled, can thus be of decisive importance. In the philosophical autobiography, design and truth may be in significant tension.

I (iii). Philosophical Autobiography

'The autobiography of a man whose business is thinking', wrote Collingwood, 'should be the story of his thought' (Collingwood, v). His own follows this austere prescription, omitting virtually all experiences that do not directly bear on that story. Against this injunction, however, it is worth placing Nietzsche's aphorism:

> Almost all Europeans confound themselves with their role when they advance in age . . . Their characters have actually evolved out of their role, nature out of art (Nietzsche, V, 356).

For those who do not identify themselves with their 'business' to the extent Collingwood did, other ways of relating philosophy and autobiography are permissible.

Of these, the most central cases appear to be those where personal and philosophical development are presented together, with one informing the other, where the model of man involved is explicit, where the story covers the period up to and including the adoption of the writer's perspective, and where it is intended both to enact that model and thereby to lend some support to it.

Other possibilities are available. Sartre's main story, for example, ends long before adulthood, and the concluding pages do not so much bring the story up to date in the manner of Mill's final chapter as express the fragility of the present standpoint through multiple layers of controlled irony; the 'story' reveals the difficulties of authenticity and hence, by extension, puts in question the authenticity of the entire work. *Words* exploits the traditional conventions of autobiography in an attempt to display their futility. It has been mentioned that we should reserve the term 'philosophical autobiography' for cases such as this where the author, in writing about himself according to the canons of 'historical autobiography' exposes the inadequacy of those canons by revealing his own self-identity as insecure, in the light of the uncertain nature of the self.[4] But this proposal seems merely to reflect the prejudice that the only philosopher worth the name is a sceptical one, and I have preferred to count as genuinely 'philosophical' those central cases by reference to which the sceptics set their course.

The two examples I have chosen are both in their own ways seminal. Augustine is generally regarded as the father of autobiography, and both the Romantic tradition of confession as exemplified by Rousseau, and the sceptical reaction as typified by Sartre, define themselves by reference to the Augustinian precedent. Mill represents a very different approach, widespread in the Anglo-Saxon world where his work is often cited as the very model of what a philosophical autobiography should be, which is clearly distinct from the confessional mode. But despite the differences, it is proper to ask of each work what sort of support (or the reverse) the story of the author's life gives to his account of man and his place in nature. The divergent answers which must be given in the two cases throw considerable light on what is involved in attempting to support a philosophical theory in this way.

II. The *Confessions* of St Augustine

To drive so sharp a wedge between philosophy and theology that objection is raised to calling his *Confessions* 'philosophical' would be un-Augustinian. It would be not only to ignore the role they have played in subsequent philosophical debate, but also the subtle manner in which the work attempts to develop a positive relation between Neoplatonism and Christianity. There would be more point in objecting to the word 'autobiography', for only the first nine books recount the story of the author's life, and the precise relation of these to the remaining four remains a well-worn point of controversy.

The most sustained recent attempt to resolve this conundrum maintains that we should interpret the work as having a tripartite structure. In the first nine books there is a sharp distinction between converted narrator and unconverted protagonist; the former stands on the secure ground of eternal truth from which vantage point the latter's activity can be seen as both sinful and fruitless. In the next three this distinction

---

[4] For an explicit defence of this position see the first and third chapters of Spengemann.

collapses, and the author is found to be himself enmeshed in ignorance, sin and temporality, a discovery which places the whole first part under question. Finally, in the concluding book,

> having discovered that he can neither fix the mind and hold it fast while remembering the past, nor follow its movement to a point where movement stops, he terminates his inquiry and turns to a third mode of confession: an impassioned avowal of his belief that the truth exists even though he cannot know it and that faith in its existence is tantamount to full knowledge of it. In effect, this protestation of the faith that is knowledge *imagines* the absolute that the memory could not hold and the intellect could not reach (Spengemann, 31).

If this analysis were correct, we would have here a case in which reflection on an autobiographical narrative, far from lending support to its integral model of man, fatally undermines both it and the credentials of the central mode of autobiography itself; Professor Spengemann, indeed, appears to draw this conclusion.

Instructive as this would be, I fear that the reading is badly flawed. It is certainly correct to insist on the complex interdependence of the different parts of the work, but these interconnections are stronger than the above account allows. The questioning mode is set up from the outset, where the ignorance and sinfulness of the narrator is acknowledged, and there are many indications in the narrative sections that even the unconverted protagonist may properly be seen as on pilgrimage, with God 'doing good to my soul' (Augustine (1), IV, 3); thus it is misleading to draw so sharp a distinction between narrator and protagonist in the autobiographical books that the subsequent discussions fatally undermine it. Again, it is not the truth of the doctrine of the last book that Augustine puts in question, but only whether Moses intended to teach that doctrine; he does not purport to 'imagine' anything, but only

> to choose one meaning, which, by your inspiration, I shall see to be true, certain, and good, even though many other meanings may occur to me, since many others are possible (XII, 32).

Finally, Augustine himself did not read his work in this way. In his *Retractations* he divides the work into two sections, not three, and only the first ten books are described as 'written about myself'; the other three he characterizes as 'about Holy Scripture'. (Augustine (2), II, 32).

The proposed interpretation over-emphasizes one of two elements which are held in tension by Augustine. On the one hand it notices the sense of self-discovery that permeates the work. Augustine remarks elsewhere that 'I have learned many things by writing' (Augustine (3), III, Preface), a phenomenon elaborated by Montaigne in an autobiographical context with his 'I have no more made my book, than my book has made me' (Montaigne, II, 18). The writing is itself a spiritual exercise, part of a new life, with its concern for self-examination and an ever-deepening understanding of the relation between creature and Creator, and the final sentences of the text triumphantly answer the questions with which it opens.

But this last feature points to the other element; the self-discovery is under very tight controls, both rhetorically and otherwise. The work is written from the standpoint of a man who has learnt in his own experience that life does not stop with conversion, that the ideals of perfection (grounded in the classical model of the *sapiens*) with which he retired to Cassiacum were unrealistic, and the whole narrative of the first nine books is written in this knowledge.[5] It is this very recognition which accounts for the radical innovations he introduces into the classical literary forms, which were adequate for the self-description of the Stoic sage but not for the Pauline man of faith—aware of his own ignorance and of the springs of sin within himself. The fragility of one's life and present perceptions, which is a leading theme of the later books, forms an essential part of the model of man that the narrative enacts. It is not for nothing that Augustine learnt literary control in some of the most exacting schools there have ever been.

And of course he is articulately self-conscious about this training. Always ready to make use of secular arts when they can be put to worthy ends,[6] he criticizes various aspects of his rhetorical education but also makes good use of it. Further, he is also self-conscious about the status of his work. The early criticisms of secular literature, and of the study of literature for its own sake, employ a number of criteria by reference to which the final judgment is made; in the first instance they are presented as approving Scripture while rejecting Vergil, but they also provide touchstones by reference to which Augustine expects his own composition to be judged and interpreted.

True to his Platonic heritage, several of these criteria relate to questions of truth, and in the context of a confession truth and sincerity are interdependent. Here the most obvious surface feature of the work, that it takes the form of an address to God, becomes relevant. In Rousseau's *Confessions* the appeal to God is little more than a conventional figure, but in Augustine it is meant with all seriousness; the work is primarily addressed to God, and only secondarily to the edification of men and of himself. Insincerity in this context is of such momentous consequence that it is

---

[5] A sensitive account of the development of Augustine's thinking between his conversion and the writing of the *Confessions* is given in the fifteenth chapter of Brown.

[6] So far as rhetoric is concerned, the issue is fully discussed in the fourth book of Augustine (4).

an ever-present concern, the full resources of Christian traditions of self-examination are called into play to combat it, and it is a constant prayer that his writing—not least his selection from the storehouse of memory—will be under the control of the Divine truth. No doubt self-deception remains possible, even in the most intense and carefully controlled of spiritual exercises, but not in its cruder forms.

This 'truth' which he presents is not such as to be easily accepted by his contemporaries. Again and again the text confronts objections with which no doubt he had had to wrestle himself, but which are also foreseeable responses from those both inside and outside the Church. For his is fundamentally a revisionary rather than descriptive metaphysic. So far as his model of man is concerned, much of it centres round the notion of 'sin', conceived not as primarily an epistemological matter (freely choosing to do what one believes or knows to be wrong) but as at root an ontological one; it is exemplified by the child crying at the breast long before issues of knowledge, belief and choice are in question. Wittgenstein's echo of this vignette is thoroughly Augustinian:

> Anyone who listens to a child's crying and understands what he hears will know that it harbours dormant psychic forces, terrible forces different from anything commonly assumed. Profound rage, pain and lust for destruction (Wittgenstein, 2e).

On this account, ordinary notions of 'responsibility' are not central to the analysis of sin; the infant is only 'responsible' for his behaviour in a somewhat extended sense. Sinful behaviour is typically consequent upon sinful state. The Kantian 'Ought implies can' neatly encapsulates a leading strand of the Protestant pietistic tradition in which Kant was reared, but it is not a logical truth and Augustine will have none of it. Much of the narrative is designed to show why, in any simple form, such a thesis is false. His experience is seen as helping him to perceive the truth about these matters, culminating with the scene in the eighth book when he cannot bring himself to do what he knows he ought; fallen into sin he cannot do what is right, and only the freely given grace of God can rescue him. This perception is summarized in the celebrated slogan which dominates the latter part of the tenth book: 'Da quod jubes et jube quod vis' ('Give what thou commandest and command what thou wilt' (X, 29, 31, 37)), which Pelagius rightly saw to be the pivot on which the whole Augustinian position turned. His counter-attack on behalf of human responsibility and perfectibility split the Church. Thus until Pelagianism was finally declared heretical, we find the proponents of two rival metaphysical schemes using as the touchstone for their differences Augustine's account of his own life.

Repeatedly, in this account, Augustine applies to himself the parable of the prodigal son (I, 18; III, 6; IV, 16; VIII, 3), and even at the most superficial level this provides a felicitous structure for one who was brought up a catechumen of the Church, apostatized, and returned to the fold. Further, the figure of the elder brother is aptly exemplified by those conservative exegetes, suspicious of Augustine's Platonizing tendencies, with whom he pleads in the latter part of Book XII. But by the time the discussion has progressed this far, it has become clear that the parable's imagery has a far more universal significance; the father's house is eternity and the far country temporality (XII, 11)—and all men are ultimately to be understood as in the prodigal's condition. Thus we find that knowledge of God is discovered in the recesses of memory, that all have fallen from the eternal Jerusalem and seek to return to it, and—by an amazing exegetical *tour de force*—that the Psalmist's reference to the 'heaven of heavens' provides scriptural warrant for this analysis. More generally, the assertions of Book VII about the value of Neoplatonism as a guide to truth are subtly embodied both in the narrative and in the exegetical sections, effecting a harmony between *Enneads* and Scripture that the philosophical reader is expected to discern. Not only are the doctrines of pre-existence and reminiscence part of the sub-text, but the otherwise surprising use of St John's *triplex concupiscentia* to provide the fundamental categories for the analysis of sin falls into place when we realize that they correspond to the three faults to which Plotinus ascribes the fall of the soul. In all this, the ground is being prepared for an integration between Plotinus' account of the Fall and that of *Genesis*. Here, of course, we have the extended sense in which the infant is responsible for its state of sin; Platonic accounts of pre-existence give philosophical teeth to the Pauline doctrine that we are all involved in Adam's fall.[7]

The *Confessions*, in short, represent a finely wrought integration of the different strands picked out in the autobiographical books as affecting him most significantly; but the integration is acknowledged to be a fragile and provisional one—as it must be if his analysis is correct, for he is still a sinner, still seeing 'through a glass darkly', for all the grace and light that he believes to have been granted him. In some cases the integration is achieved by absorbing into the work intellectual defences of the Faith against key assaults of those whose teaching he had rejected; for example, the analysis of time in Book XI is in part designed to demolish a stock Manichee objection to the *Genesis* creation story. In other cases, Augustine accepts and supplements what he had been taught in the days of his apostasy, thus Neoplatonic teaching is supplemented by the psychological analysis of our bondage to habit and need for help to which the story of his double conversion (both of intellect and of will) gives concrete expression. Further, once one has grasped the doctrine it becomes clear how apt the confes-

---

[7] For this whole complex matter see O'Connell (1) and (2), together with the literature there cited.

sional mode is to its exploration. God is to be found not by looking outward but inward, toward 'the eternal in the depths of the internal' ('internum aeternum' (IX, 4). It is in probing the innermost part of the soul, one's true self, that one finds God (VII, 10) who, to change the spatial metaphor, is 'above the summit of my soul' (X, 7). So far as mankind is concerned, the inwardness by means of which we glimpse the eternal is essentially temporal, thus the 'seat of the soul ("animi") itself' is in the memory (X, 25); hence not only the careful analyses of memory and temporality,[8] but also the very enterprise of the *Confessions*. For here we have an attempt to display the deep things of God through the medium of the story of a soul by an author who, through his memory, is equipped to look most deeply into its inwardness—the protagonist himself.

But however finely wrought and integrated, no autobiographical account can of itself be conclusive. Whether the interpretation an author places on his life is acceptable depends also on such matters as theoretical coherence, compatibility with other beliefs and experiences, and the overall plausibility of the embodied metaphysic—in assessing which the autobiography can never play more than a part in a cumulative case. This was recognized well enough by both Augustine and Pelagius; although the *Confessions* may have provided the spark which set the Church ablaze, their debates over freedom and grace soon spread far beyond that work—with both sides claiming to be able best to account for the psychological phenomena the narrative describes.

In assessing the acceptability of such autobiographical interpretations even matters of simple scholarly accuracy can properly play a significant role. We have seen that the exegetical final books play an important part in clarifying, universalizing and grounding in scriptural authority the overall interpretation. But a better grasp of Hebrew than Augustine possessed would have told him that the long exegesis of the 'heaven of heavens', which is used to integrate the heavenly Jerusalem of Christian hope with the creation story and prenatal memory, is fundamentally misguided.[9]

---

[8] Much more careful than is often realized. For example, Augustine is standardly presented as a simple-minded upholder of the Representative theory of memory on the basis of X, 8, and criticized for not making important distinctions (e.g. Locke, Ch. 1–3). A glance at X, 9 *et seq.*, should set the record straight. Wittgenstein's reported admonition (Malcolm, 71) about Augustine's view of language that 'the conception *must* be important if so great a mind held it' is salutary.

[9] It is true that some unease about his procedures here leads Augustine to provide himself with the escape hatch of an ingeniously 'modern' theory of hermeneutics (XII, 14–32), but use of this theory to evade the force of the linguistic argument would seriously undermine the credibility of the whole attempted integration.

But perhaps most important of all, not long after writing the *Confessions*, Augustine himself came to reject one of its main Neoplatonic elements: the belief in the soul's pre-existence. Although he had been distressed by the Origenist controversy, when once Origenism had been decisively condemned by the Church he accepted the authority of Council and Pope, rethinking his faith in the light of their ruling. Thus in his treatise *The Trinity* he replaces the doctrine of reminiscence with an affirmation of the mind's natural affinity for the intelligible world (Augustine (3), XII, 15), and in *The City of God* he mounts his famous attack on Origen's Neoplatonizing doctrine of the fall of pre-existing souls (Augustine (5), XI, 23). But this intellectual shift renders far less universally compelling the dominant image of the prodigal son, together with the accounts of the origin and nature of sin, of God as found in the memory, and hence of God himself; with this element abandoned, the whole web starts to unravel. At the theoretical level, of course, Augustine painstakingly set about reweaving the fabric of his faith, but he made no such attempt at the autobiographical one.

All of which points a rather simple moral. A powerful and successful philosophical autobiography can certainly render the author's model of man 'plausible', in the sense that it may show how one can live and imagine coherently in terms of that model, accounting for relevant phenomena in ways that 'place' them in dynamic terms, thereby enabling one to see life steadily and see it whole. Nevertheless, such works cannot of themselves be probative. If the theory is inadequate at a theoretical level, appeal to the authenticity and imaginative plausibility of the vision is not a final defence.

But there is another side to the coin which may not be so simple. If an author fails to interpret his own life convincingly in terms of his preferred model of man, that very fact may help to undermine the model. Which brings us to Mill.

III. The *Autobiography* of John Stuart Mill

To test this latter possibility we need once again to take a classic case, one which is widely taken to be a principal example of the genre and which purports to carry lessons of universal scope. Mill's *Autobiography* fits the prescription admirably.

In the final draft of the work three purposes are acknowledged. To show how much more than is usually thought can be taught to the young, to display 'the successive phases' of a mind which was 'always pressing forward', and 'to make acknowledgment of the debts which my intellectual and moral development owes to other persons' (Mill (1), 3). Underlying all three projects we find a distinctive picture of the human mind which is empiricist, associationist, and developmental. Education can add one element to another in accordance with certain principles, language associated with 'progress' is preferred to that of an Augustinian pilgrimage, and the main debts are successive in that those incurred later are to those who have provided what was missing in the influence of earlier mentors. A rival '*a priori* view of human knowledge' which sees the human mind as informed by innate principles known by 'intuition' is explicitly rejected (134, 162–163), and we are informed that Carlyle's writings, imbued with such 'German metaphysics', were of value to the author 'not as philosophy to instruct, but as poetry to animate' (105).

The story told is more of an imaginative reconstruction than a strict chronological record, and for that very reason has a memorable shape. Educated intensively by his father along associationist lines, he found himself at the age of twenty with a highly developed intellect but seriously deficient in qualities of feeling. He discovered in his own case that 'the habit of analysis has a tendency to wear away the feelings', and was led to believe that although 'favourable to prudence and clearsightedness' it was nevertheless 'a perpetual worm at the root both of the passions and of the virtues', a perception which lay at the heart of his mental crisis (83). He was rescued from this crisis by the stimulation of his feelings; in the first instance by associating himself with the emotions of the son in Marmontel's *Memoirs* on the occasion of the death of the father, and later by the discovery of Wordsworth's poetry. As a result of this experience, Mill tells us, 'the cultivation of the feelings became one of the cardinal points in my ethical and philosophical creed' (86). The Benthamite influence of his early years was now superseded by that of the Coleridgeans whom he sought out, until his meeting with Harriet Taylor who 'was more a poet' than Carlyle and 'more a thinker than I' (106) and eventually became his wife. The one-sided father who dominated his boyhood is now replaced by one who combines both the intellectual and the passionate sides of human nature in an exemplary degree, and by this time 'the only actual revolution which has ever taken place in my modes of thinking, was already complete' (114).

This thoroughly mythical account of his wife as embodying the unification of the two major influences on his life, which by themselves represent but half-truths, provides a narrative enactment of what Mill elsewhere upholds as a theoretical ideal. In his essays on Bentham and Coleridge, favourably noticed in the *Autobiography*, he writes that

> In every respect the two men are each other's 'completing counterpart': the strong points of each correspond to the weak points of the other. Whoever could master the premises and combine the methods of both, would possess the entire English philosophy of his age (Mill (3), 102).

It is this emphasis on the combination of the two strands which is central to his analysis of the human condition in the *Autobiography* itself:

> I had now learnt by experience that the passive susceptibilities needed to be cultivated as well as the active capacities, and required to be nourished and enriched as well as guided. I did not, for an instant, lose sight of, or undervalue, that part of the truth which I had seen before; I never turned recreant to intellectual culture, or ceased to consider the power and practice of analysis as an essential condition both of individual and of social improvement. But I thought that it had consequences which required to be corrected, by joining other kinds of cultivation with it. The maintenance of a due balance among the faculties, now seemed to me of primary importance (Mill (1), 86).

'Joining' and 'balance', these are the watchwords; 'cultivation of the feelings' as well as 'intellectual culture'. He tells us of how certain types of poetry helped redress the balance:

> I needed to be made to feel that there was real, permanent happiness in tranquil contemplation. Wordsworth taught me this . . . And the delight which these poems gave me, proved that with culture of this sort, there was nothing to dread from the most confirmed habit of analysis . . . The result was that I gradually, but completely, emerged from my habitual depression, and was never again subject to it (89–90).

Earlier he has told us that 'the analysing spirit' needs 'its natural complements and correctives'; in his experience he has learnt how these may be provided by 'the cultivation of the feelings' (83, 86). He is thus ready to come under the influence of Harriet, 'a woman of deep and strong feeling, of penetrating and intuitive intelligence, and of an eminently meditative and poetic nature ' (111–112), thereby winning a great 'prize in the lottery of life', a 'companion, stimulator, adviser, and instructor of the rarest quality' (157). The desiderated balance, it seems to be implied, has been achieved, and the mind of the opening paragraph which was 'always pressing forward' now recounts its story from a position of mature though essentially open-ended 'intellectual and moral development'.

But has it and could it? Although Mill makes stringent criticisms of his father's educational programme, the complaint is that it was incomplete rather than misconceived. Indeed, the first purpose of the work is said to be to show 'how much more than is commonly supposed may be taught, and well taught, in those early years which, in the common modes of what is called instruction, are little better than wasted' (3). There is no withdrawal of this encomium, nor any claim that the partial nature of the early education rendered him incapable of 'joining other kinds of cultivation with it'; indeed, the reverse is implied. The associationist model of the mind which he is working facilitates this optimism;[10] one association can be used to balance another, so it is always in principle possible to provide 'complements and correctives'. Mill is convinced that 'intellectual culture' is an essential condition of 'individual improvement', which merely needs to be 'corrected' by 'joining other kinds of cultivation with it'; he has no intention of 'turning recreant'. But the text puts in doubt the adequacy of the doctrine to which he shows such loyalty.

For Mill's self-revelation displays little of that cultivation of the feelings the narrative leads us to expect. There is, significantly, far less concern with inwardness than in Augustine or, indeed, in Wordsworth. The opening sentence refers to it as a 'biographical sketch' and a 'memorial'; the second denies any interest in the narrative 'as being connected with myself'; and in the second paragraph (which was the actual opening of the early draft) he places himself in a markedly 'external' fashion as being born 'the eldest son' of 'the author of the History of British India'. We seem at the outset to be confronted with an autobiography aspiring to the condition of biography.

Of course memories soon intrude, and attempts have been made to show how their presence displays areas of inwardness not available to the biographer.[11] But attention to those portions of the text where memory is most intimate only serves to underline the paucity of Mill's emotional cultivation. For example, the account of his early reading, and walks with his father discussing it, is certainly imbued with references to feeling rather different from those provided by modern biographers, but they seem forced rather than relived. He writes of 'my earliest recollections of green fields and wild flowers', but leaves it at that; the experience is not particularized or imaged in any way, existing at a level of generality which deadens it.[12] The same is true of the references to 'my greatest delight' and 'intense and lasting interest'; the word 'delight', indeed, is used four times within the space of the one paragraph, as if the rhetoric were attempting to enforce a recapturing of, or belief in, childish delight whose memory is not genuinely present to the writer (6–7). It is rare that there is any apparent recapturing of some previous intensity, and when it occurs it is usually in the context of a painful experience; the most vivid examples, indeed, are in the leaves of the early draft which were later suppressed, apparently because they were not under sufficient control.[13] His 'adviser

[10] The *Autobiography* has, indeed, been described as 'an associationist tract'. (Thomas 356). For Mill's mature version of the associationist model see his preface and notes to Mill (9).

[11] Most recently in McDonnell.

[12] Compare Shumaker, 143: 'Rarely, outside technical treatises, is it possible to find an equal number of pages so nearly devoid of imagery'.

[13] See particularly the passages on his physical awkwardness and on the role of fear in his education, reprinted as footnotes in Mill (1), 23–24, 33–34.

and instructor of the rarest quality' ensured that they were struck out, with some reason.

It is also noteworthy that it was Mill's original intention to divide the work into two parts, the first covering his life before he met Harriet, and the second opening with that meeting; his editor suggests that one reason for abandoning this plan may have been 'because the two parts were of considerably disproportionate lengths (121 *v.* 24 leaves)' (Mill (2), 4), and this brings out a matter which is still noticeable in the final draft. Given the assertion that his acquaintance with Harriet 'could not but have a most beneficial influence on my developement' (Mill (1), 113), there is remarkably little about this development at any but the intellectual level. We should expect the chapter which opens with 'the friendship which has been the honour and the chief blessing of my existence' (III) to enact the new vision of balanced maturity for which the previous chapter on the mental crisis has prepared us, but it does nothing of the sort. Far from showing a progressive development in the life of feeling, partnering the onward movement of the intellect, the chapter is far less emotionally revealing than its predecessor. And the long concluding chapter which immediately follows is even less helpful, being more chronicle added to bring the story up to date than an account of integrated development. We are told much about the importance of the life of feeling, but are given virtually no account of it in Mill's own case after the age of twenty-four.

Worse, the account of Harriet as enacting his ideal of maturity displays notorious signs of emotional immaturity. Readers have had great difficulty in crediting the description he gives of her, and contemporaries lend it little support. She is, indeed, presented as a focus of aspiration rather than a particularized woman, and there is a revealing religious strain in Mill's depiction of her. He is 'admitted' into her 'circle', discovering that 'she possessed in combination the qualities which in all other persons whom I had known I had been only too happy to find singly' (112). Having extolled Carlyle extravagantly, he describes her as 'one greatly the superior of us both . . . whose own mind and nature included his, and infinitely more' (106). Again, he writes of the benefits of being 'admitted into any degree of mental intercourse with a being of these qualities' (113). Having fully taken in that it is his wife to whom he is referring, it comes as no surprise to find that after her death 'her memory is to me a religion, and her approbation the standard by which, summing up as it does all worthiness, I endeavour to regulate my life' (145).

Addressing God at the opening of his *Confessions* Augustine had written 'our hearts are restless until they can find peace in you', thereby indicating the central theme of the work. He might with some justice claim that for all Mill's supposition that his secular education had led him to look upon religion 'as something which in no way concerned me' (28), the 'biographical sketch' unintentionally lends much more support to his own portrayal of the soul as pilgrim than to Mill's developmental one. After Harriet's death there is apparently complete stasis so far as the culture of the feelings is concerned, as the whole set of attributes is shifted from mother to daughter and Helen becomes the new 'instructor of the rarest quality' (157).

All of which casts considerable doubt on the underlying model of the human mind as a nexus of associations where one form of 'cultivation' can be 'joined to' and 'balanced by' others, which thereby provide 'complements and correctives', and by such additions enable the mind to press forward through 'successive phases' (86, 83, 3). Instead of an account of the human condition categorizable in such additive terms, the underlying narrative seems to point to more organic models of the sort favoured by Mill's intuitionist opponents—where one can use as informative analogies such phenomena as trees growing in the manner they were bent as saplings. It may be significant that, despite the wide range of his writings and his unique experience, Mill wrote remarkably little on the topic of education—as if he were unclear how to relate his theoretical model of the mind to the subject.[14] His failure to complete the long planned project on ethology, 'the science which corresponds to the art of education' (Mill (4), VI, v, 4) lends weight to this suggestion.[15]

Of course, such considerations do not invalidate the model in question. No doubt it can be modified to take account of the long-term damage done by the deficiencies in Mill's early education, without any recourse to innate principles or internal dynamic of the sorts Augustine was concerned to display and of which the Coleridgeans wrote. But Mill's lack of self-awareness prevents his *Autobiography* from adding any plausibility to that model, and the way he is able to use it to hide from himself his own

---

[14] References to education are frequent in Mill's writings, but his only extended discussion of the topic does not address itself to the problems I have been raising. It is a Rectoral address and 'the feelings . . . are, in the main, beyond the sphere and inaccessible to the control of public education' (Mill (8), 39).

[15] In 1859 Mill describes ethology as 'a subject I have long wished to take up . . . but I have never yet felt myself sufficiently prepared' (Mill (5), I, 226, 14th November, Letter to Bain), and in the same year admits that 'attempts of the Association psychologists to resolve the emotions by association, have been on the whole the least successful part of their efforts' (Mill (6), 132). A few years later he describes the phenomenon of self-consciousness as an 'inexplicable fact' and 'true incomprehensibility' (Mill (7), XII); in the light of the centrality of this phenomenon to his mental crisis this represents a significant concession. Robert Cumming argues that 'Mill never repaired the foundation on which his life was constructed; he never found a place for self-consciousness in a psychological theory. Instead he satisfies the claims of his self-consciousness by gathering up, in his memory and in his *Autobiography*, the series of feelings he had experienced when this foundation had fallen down' (Cumming, 242).

deficiencies encourages the thoughtful reader to ask, respectively, how far he could use such a model in telling the truth about his own life; Mill's 'memorial' provides only negative help, and goes some way towards bringing out the difficulty of so doing. It is because Mill's *Autobiography* is an expression of his new and officially 'balanced' life that we are led to query the very notion of 'balance'.

IV. Story and Theory

Philosophers from Parmenides to Nietzsche have used the genres associated with imaginative literature to articulate and support their theories. Similarly, 'literary' authors as diverse as Dante and D. H. Lawrence have sought to enact and render plausible philosophical theses in their imaginative works. Clearly, there are many points of contact between such endeavours and the efforts of philosophical autobiographers. But in the latter case the generic requirement that story be related to fact provides a check on the imaginative impulse.

In constructing a fictional universe where Zarathustra descends the mountain, the author can take care that those features of our quotidian world which fit but uneasily into the vision are suppressed. Often in autobiography the selecting process of which Augustine writes, together with supplementations of memory to make a coherent narrative, are similarly used to liberate the imagination—and with it the underlying model of man—from mundane factual shackles; but that is not the end of the story. Here, alleged historical facts are often checkable; Rousseau, for example, did *not* spend much time alone with 'Maman'. Again, the image of man embodied can be checked both against independent theoretical argument and the reader's own experience. Further, an Augustine may not only have considerable insight into himself, but be under strong compulsion to tell the truth. The strengths and limitations of the genre are to be looked for in the cases of authors with some integrity and perception, hence the examples I have used. Augustine is writing before God in the belief that 'there is nothing in me that I could keep secret from you, even if I did not want to confess it' (Augustine (1), X, 2), and his psychological insight is legendary. While in the case of Mill, it is his very integrity that allows the limits of his self-understanding to shine through.[16]

---

[16] If Mill is deceived about himself it is not so much through a lack of integrity as through a blindness fostered by the intellectual blinkers he wears. It has recently been suggested that we should distinguish between deceiving oneself, which may be innocent, and self-deception, where the latter notion is understood as involving 'dishonesty within oneself' (Champlin, 92). In order adequately to assess Mill's *Autobiography* we appear to need some such distinction.

It is in relation to this notion of 'integrity', together with the associated one of 'distortion', that the distinction from more wholly imaginative genres becomes important in exploring the relation between story and theory. The author's vision of man and his place in nature, together with his own remembered or ascertainable past, provide crucial controls on the imagery, selection of incidents, and overall organization of the auto-biography. However much the author may be convinced that he remembers 'how it seemed then', the presentation will always be that of the adult mind remembering. Thus a narration of the life in terms of developing awareness, without constant reference to the present perspective, is liable to provide an internally coherent fiction which is more akin to a novel than to either of the two texts I have considered, and in which the temptation to fill the gaps 'as it must have been' is very strong; self-deception and distortion are here most difficult to avoid. The recurrent sense one has in reading Sartre's *Words*, of a shaping adult mind of great sophistication and irony involved in the very presentation of how a child thought and felt, reflects the work's major weakness considered as a challenge to the central auto-biographical tradition. It may be a fair riposte to Rousseau, who is certainly one of those in Sartre's sights; if the work is really a type of novel, as Sartre claimed, then so, perhaps, are Rousseau's *Confessions*. But Augustine and Mill cannot be dismissed so easily.

The latter are not writing novels in which imaginative flights have a range limited only by the anchorage of a few ascertainable facts; rather, they are attempting to analyse themselves in the light of their present memories. Augustine is as usual the more explicit; the constant placing of each selected episode in the context of present belief, together with complete openness about both the fact of and the criteria governing this placing, distances the work from mere fiction. It is the very requirement of this mode of autobiography that authors endeavour to tell the truth without distortion, and to render clear the intellectual model used to determine what counts as distortion, that enables the relation between story and theory to have the complex potential for illumination, support and undercutting that we have found in the cases of Augustine and Mill.

An autobiography of this sort presents us with a model of man which is integrated with the author's perception of his own self in the light of past experience. This integration provides a point of reference for under-standing that experience, and hence may constitute a significant element in any cumulative case which seeks to defend (or attack) the model in question. The connection between the old adage 'Know thyself' and one's overall metaphysical standpoint may not be so dated as is sometimes thought, and there is point in Dilthey's (doubtless exaggerated) claim that 'In autobiography we encounter the highest and most instructive form of the understanding of life'.

Bibliography

(Except where translation and original have been given together, renderings of foreign language texts have been taken from the editions here listed.)

Augustine (1): *The Confessions of St Augustine*, trans. Rex Warner (New York: Mentor Books, 1963).

Augustine (2): Saint Augustine, *The Retractations*, trans. Sister Mary Bogan (Washington: Catholic University of America Press, 1968).

Augustine (3): Saint Augustine, *The Trinity*, trans. Stephen McKenna, (Washington: Catholic University of America Press, 1963).

Augustine (4): Saint Augustine, *Christian Instruction*, trans. John Gavigan (Washington, Catholic University of America Press, 1950).

Augustine (5): Saint Augustine, *The City of God*, trans. John Healey, R. V. G. Tasker (ed.), 2 vols. (London: Everyman, 1945).

Ayer: A. J. Ayer, 'Philosophy and Language', in his *The Concept of a Person and Other Essays* (London: Macmillan, 1963).

Brown: Peter Brown, *Augustine of Hippo: A Biography* (London, Faber and Faber, 1967).

Champlin: T. S. Champlin, 'Self-Deception: A Problem about Autobiography', *Proceedings of the Aristotelian Society*, suppl. vol. liii, 1979.

Cohen: L. Jonathan Cohen, *The Probable and the Provable* (Oxford: Clarendon Press, 1977).

Collingwood: R. G. Collingwood, *An Autobiography* (London: Oxford University Press, 1939).

Cumming: Robert D. Cumming, 'Mill's History of His Ideas', *Journal of the History of Ideas* **xxv** (1964).

Dilthey: W. Dilthey, *Selected Writings*, ed. & trans. H. P. Rickman (Cambridge: Cambridge University Press, 1976).

Durrant: Michael Durrant, 'Cumulative Arguments in Theology', *Sophia* **xv** (1976).

Locke: Don Locke, *Memory* (London: Macmillan, 1971).

Malcolm: Norman Malcolm, *Ludwig Wittgenstein: A Memoir* (London: Oxford University Press, 1962).

McDonnell: James McDonnell, 'Success and Failure: A Rhetorical Study of the First Two Chapters of Mill's *Autobiography*', *University of Toronto Quarterly* **xlv** (1975–76).

Mill (1): John Stuart Mill, *Autobiography* (ed.) Jack Stillinger (London and Oxford: Oxford University Press, 1971).

Mill (2): *The Early Draft of John Stuart Mill's Autobiography*, Jack Stillinger (ed.) (Urbana: University of Illinois Press, 1961).

Mill (3): *Mill on Bentham and Coleridge*, F. R. Leavis (ed.) (London: Chatto & Windus, 1950).

Mill (4): John Stuart Mill, *A System of Logic Ratiocinative and Inductive*, 8th edn., London, Longmans Green Reader and Dyer, 1872.

Mill (5): *The Letters of John Stuart Mill*, ed. Hugh S. R. Elliot, 2 vols., London, Longmans Green & Co., 1910.

Mill (6): John Stuart Mill, 'Bain's Psychology', in his *Dissertations and Discussions*, vol. III, London, Longmans Green Reader and Dyer, 1867.

Mill (7): John Stuart Mill, *An Examination of Sir William Hamilton's Philosophy and of the Principal Philosophical Questions Discussed in his Writings*, London, Longman Green Longman Roberts and Green 1865.

Mill (8): John Stuart Mill, 'Inaugural Address: Delivered to the University of St. Andrews', in *Mill's Essays on Literature and Society*, ed. J. B. Schneewind New York, Collier Books, Macmillan, 1965.

Mill (9): James Mill, *Analysis of the Phenomena of the Human Mind*, John Stuart Mill (ed.), 2 vols. (London: Longmans Green Reader and Dyer, 1869).

Mitchell: Basil Mitchell, *The Justification of Religious Belief* (London: Macmillan, 1973).

Montaigne: *The Essays of Michel Eyquem de Montaigne*, trans. C. Cotton, W. Carew Hazlitt (ed.) (Chicago, London and Toronto: William Barton, 1952).

Newman: John Henry Cardinal Newman, *An Ewsay in Aid of a Grammar of Assent* (Westminster Md.: Christian Classics Inc., 1973).

Nietzsche: Freidrich Nietzsche, *Joyful Wisdom*, trans. Thomas Common, Kurt F. Reinhardt (ed.) (New York: Frederick Ungar, 1960).

O'Connell (1): Robert J. O'Connell, S.J., 'The Plotinian Fall of the Soul in St Augustine'. *Traditio* **xix** (1963).

O'Connell (2): Robert J. O'Connell, S.J., 'The Riddle of Augustine's *Confessions:* A Plotinian Key', *International Philosophical Quarterly* **iv** (1964).

Pascal: Roy Pascal, *Design and Truth in Autobiography* (Cambridge Mass.: Harvard University Press, 1960).

Rousseau: *The Confessions of Jean-Jacques Rousseau*, trans. J. M. Cohen (London: Penguin Books, 1953).

Sartre: Jean-Paul Sartre, *Words*, trans., Irene Clephane (London: Penguin Books, 1967).

Shumaker: Wayne Shumaker, *English Autobiography: Its Emergence, Materials, and Form* (Berkeley and Los Angeles: University of California Press, 1954).

Spengemann: William C. Spengemann, *The Forms of Autobiography: Episodes in the History of a Literary Genre* (New Haven and London: Yale University Press, 1980).

Thomas: William Thomas, 'John Stuart Mill and the Uses of Autobiography', *History* **56** (1971).

Wittgenstein: Ludwig Wittgenstein, *Culture and Value*, trans. Peter Winch, G. H. von Wright (ed.) (Oxford: Basil Blackwell, 1980).

Philosophy, Interpretation and *The Golden Bowl*

PETER JONES

In the first part of this lecture I aim to characterize the moral dimensions of Henry James's novel *The Golden Bowl*; in the second part, and for the purposes of comparison with my interpretation as well as for their intrinsic interest, I outline some of James's theoretical reflections about novels and the nature of experience, supplementing them with quotations from the work of William James.

It may be helpful to begin with a reminder of the plot, especially as some discussion of the novel has focused on precisely what, in the broadest sense, happens in it. The story is of an immensely rich American widower and his young daughter, who now live in London amidst their almost priceless collections. The daughter marries a young Italian Prince, and her father marries her own oldest friend. Both father and daughter gradually become aware that the Prince and the friend are old lovers, and that their affair has continued after their marriages. The novel ends with the father, Adam Verver, returning to America with his wife, thus leaving behind his own daughter and grandson, and his wife's lover; his daughter, Maggie, prepares to pursue her marriage with the Prince in a more positive manner than previously, armed with a knowledge of his past and an awareness of her own capacities and responsibilities.

The Golden Bowl was published in 1904.[1] Five years later James wrote a Preface to it, for the New York edition of his novels. Several features of the book struck him, he claims, on reading it again at that time. There is a 'certain indirect and oblique view' of the action, a preference for seeing the story from the standpoint of 'an imagined observer'; in addition, he claims that 'the whole thing remains subject to the register . . . of the consciousness of but two of the characters'[2]—the Prince and Maggie. The plan was to show each of these characters through the vision of the other, and the remaining characters through the interests of those two. James also asserts that

as the whole conduct of life consists of things done, which do other

[1] Page references to *The Golden Bowl* are to the Penguin Modern Classics edition (Harmondsworth, 1966).

[2] *The Art of the Novel: Critical Prefaces by Henry James*, R. P. Blackmur (ed.) (New York: 1962), 327, 328, 329. Page references to Prefaces will all be to the versions in this edition.

things in their turn, just so our behaviour and its fruits are essentially one and continuous and persistent and unquenchable. . . . to 'put' things is very exactly and responsibly and interminably to do them. Our expression of them, and the terms on which we understand that, belong as nearly to our conduct and our life as every other feature of our freedom; these things yield in fact some of its most exquisite material to the religion of doing.[3]

The opening book of the novel is dominated by metaphors from economics—money, price, profit, assets. Adam Verver, and to a lesser extent his daughter Maggie and her suitor Prince Amerigo, are shown as treating people as things, to be bartered for and acquired. These characters show no imagination on behalf of others, and other beings, invariably kept at a distance, are rarely taken as factors to be considered. Verver is described as a consummate collector of things and, as a consequence, 'a taster of life, economically constructed'; we are told that he applied 'the same measure of value to such different pieces of property as old Persian carpets, say, and new human acquisitions' (160). He 'was mostly, as a purchaser, approached privately and from afar' (95); when he and Charlotte Stant visit a dealer Verver takes as little notice of him as the Prince takes of the shopkeeper who tries to sell Charlotte the cracked golden bowl. Money is 'power' (39), and like all forms of power, it can be used for good or ill. Verver envisaged a museum which would be 'a monument to the religion he wished to propagate, the exemplary passion, the passion for perfection at any price' (125). What 'he best liked' was a life that was 'deliciously dull' (161), which meant an undisturbed existence, free from the need to think or act, and thus, he hoped, free from duties and responsibilities. Verver's aim was to ensure that 'the complications of life kept down, the bores sifted out' (314), and success in this aim, coupled with his vast wealth, combined to give his country house, Fawns, the impression of being 'out of the world' (170; cf. 508). Fanny Assingham, one of two minor characters who act as an ironically unreliable chorus (the other is her husband), remarks of Verver and his daughter that 'they don't know *how* to live' (289). The force of this remark will emerge later. Maggie declares that in her father's eyes the Prince rates 'as part of his collection . . . an object of beauty, an object of price', and later we are told that 'the particular sharpened appetite of the collector, had fairly served as a basis of his acceptance of the Prince's suit' (35, 121). Verver even admired his daughter for her quality of resembling 'the perfect felicity of the statue', and she herself welcomed a description of her as resembling a nun (154; cf. 466). He took her primness, no doubt, as ensuring an even tenor in his existence; certainly the things they both disliked were 'flights of brilliancy, of audacity,

[3] Ibid., 347.

of originality' (303). Even towards the end of the story, when Maggie admits to trying 'to wake up', both father and daughter find it easier to 'avoid . . . the serious', and to 'stand off . . . from the real' (475, 472).

Any account of the moral dimensions of *The Golden Bowl* must first record the emphasis on the nature, and consequences of knowledge. The Prince is initially shown as understanding little of the Anglo-American society he finds himself in (42, 120), and as little inclined to dispel his ignorance in any effective way (e.g. 94). When things went well he typically never asked why; he liked explanations 'rather for ornament and amusement' than 'for use' (120, 135). He is admired for his taste, but his aesthetic attitude functions as a substitute for, and not alongside, moral sensitivity. In this novel, as in *The Portrait of a Lady*, we can discern the view that in a hierarchy of values the aesthetic falls below the moral, and that, on occasion, it can be immoral to restrict oneself to aesthetic responses, even though such responses, in themselves, be non-moral.[4] The Prince claimed to know 'by instinct' that the golden bowl was cracked (109), without bothering to ask himself whether such knowledge might not have been grounded in, and tested by, experience. In any case, he neither claimed nor revealed such subtlety in his understanding of Charlotte and Maggie, for example, and he even took 'refuge' in a 'generalized view of his father-in-law' (245; cf. 223). His recognition that 'knowledge' was not one of the 'needs' of Verver and his daughter, and his detection of their 'extraordinary substitute for perception' (251), express a dim awareness of his own false position rather than insight into the minds of his wife and her father.

The second book of the novel traces Maggie's growing awareness of the world about her, of her responsibilities, and of the extent of her former ignorance. Fanny Assingham, although herself unable to distinguish between mere speculation and justified belief, rejoices at Maggie's 'beginning to doubt', (283), that is, to question her previously unquestioned assumptions. Through the long years of passive submission to her father's whims, in a relationship, she realized, which struck others as that of 'husband and wife' (471), Maggie not only denied herself the pleasure of going to balls, but even allowed her capacity to think to lapse: 'her faculties had not for a good while been concomitantly used' (304). Her first self-conscious gropings revealed the necessity of putting thoughts 'to the proof', because her new perceptions were inevitably unfocused: 'they were like a roomful of confused objects, never as yet "sorted"' (305, 309). Once possibilities began to occur to her, as a result of her 'quickened sensibility',

---

[4] See my 'Pragmatism and *The Portrait of a Lady*', in *Philosophy and Literature* **5** (1981). There is no opportunity here to discuss the parallels between *The Portrait of a Lady* and *The Golden Bowl*. Earlier versions of my discussions of the two novels were delivered in the University of Edinburgh, 1976.

everything seemed capable of bearing meaning, and she soon came to the view that 'sentiment too would have motives and grounds' (320, 372). 'Her grasp of appearances' was 'out of proportion to her view of causes', but it occurred to her 'that if she could only get the facts of appearance straight', 'the reasons lurking behind them' would not be able 'to help showing' (335). She is mistaken, of course, in the hope that causes or traces of them necessarily manifest themselves in their effects, but at this interim stage of her understanding where she is still relying on the passive accumulation (309) of appearances, she begins to see the importance of basing descriptions of events on knowledge of their causes. Sometimes the clue needed to solve a puzzle was provided by a single word: 'the word that flashed the light, was that they were *treating* her . . . by a plan that was the exact counterpart of her own' (328). More commonly, however, understanding was to be reached by a gradual process of gathering and sifting evidence in the light of testable and disposable hypotheses (341). The loneliness she felt 'during the first shock of complete perception' (330) referred less to the practical impossibility of sharing it with anyone within her very small group of family and friends, than to recognition that everyone would be affected by knowing of her new awareness. So alarming was the prospect of having to cope with the consequences of knowledge, that Maggie at times repressed inquiry (371). It is understandable that Maggie should occasionally yearn for 'her own simple certainty' of former times, especially when she recognizes 'the number of *kinds* of relation' that can exist between persons (423, 429). Even if knowledge is often 'the outbreak of the definite' (415), it rarely emerges without positive effort by the inquirer.

Along with the value of approaching people and events with an idea, that is, with a provisional interpretative framework, and of having 'some imagination of the states of others' (441, 473), Maggie comes to see the general significance of expression as a condition of knowledge. To interpret other people it may be necessary to revise or extend one's notion of what counts as expression. It occurred to Maggie, for example, that the Prince's apparent 'blankness' might itself 'have a meaning' (310) if he suspected her discovery of his past. When it is a matter of inference to determine the meaning of what we perceive, we must try to establish the legitimacy of the inference; that, notoriously, Fanny Assingham failed to do. Colonel Assingham was right to ignore 'a large proportion' of her 'meanings' precisely because she multiplies them indiscriminately—hence the irony of her claim to think too much (417). Lacking the wealth of the Ververs to collect what they collect, Mrs Assingham collects and hoards ideas in order to savour them aesthetically. At first, Maggie is also unable to choose between the possibilities her imagination generates, but she comes to see the need for 'intelligent comparison' and the importance of seeing other persons on their terms as well as on one's own (502, 516).

Persons, unlike things, are capable of thought, and that fact must be taken into account as a condition of response to someone *as* a person. Amerigo and Charlotte, Maggie believes, failed at just this point in their dealings with her (523). Indeed, as we have seen, because Amerigo had formerly guided his life by taste, he discovered that when faced by moral decisions 'taste, in him, as a touchstone, was now all at sea'; and the thought occurs to him that 'taste by itself, the taste he had always conformed to, had no importance whatsoever' (531). In respect of their attempt to conduct life according to the dictates of aesthetic taste, there is a family resemblance between Gilbert Osmond in *The Portrait of a Lady* and Amerigo, for whom 'not to be flurried was the kind of consistency he wanted, just as consistency was the kind of dignity' (60). Even when training, specialized knowledge and discriminating perception are required for the exercise of taste, the typical objects of taste are treated as inorganic and static, calling for no constant modification in our responses. On such a view taste is contemplative, generous in its capacity to reflect with equal attention on very diverse presentations, and in no way forced to make exclusive choices prior to action. To this extent the objects of aesthetic contemplation resemble the mere possibilities generated by our creative imagination. By contrast, however, a properly moral response is active, not passive, and to act is to actualize some possibilities and discard others; it involves thought, and choice, and thus change, and denial.

In the first book of *The Golden Bowl* most of the characters are shown as submerged, with varying degrees of complacency, in a passive state. The Prince, in his own eyes, felt the need 'only to wait' in order to be 'in the right' (61); Colonel Assingham 'could deal with things perfectly, for all his needs, without getting near them' (73); Verver enjoyed 'a flattered, passive state' (170)—never was anyone further from fervour; and Charlotte observed to the Prince that as a 'well meaning, perfectly passive pair', they had 'to "do" nothing in life at all' (221; cf. 225, 230). Charlotte, in particular, emphasizes the fact that the Prince's life is 'passive . . . not active' (229), although, like Anna and Vronsky in *Anna Karenina*,[5] her own grasp of these notions is sadly inadequate. Verver regarded his own 'doing', in a vulgar sense, as past, even though, as a result of it, he now exercises power to be active on a higher level: his 'being able to "do", would have no ground if he hadn't been, to start with . . . provably luxurious' (115). The force of remarks such as these is felt only in Book Second.

At the beginning of that book we read that 'it had been a step, distinctly, on Maggie's part, her deciding to do something', albeit that her first steps 'were small variations and mild manoeuvres' accompanied 'with an infinite sense of intention' (305). She views her life with her father at

---

[5] See my discussion of *Anna Karenina*, in *Philosophy and the Novel* (Oxford, 1975).

home, 'the large ease of the home preserved', as due to the fact that 'others held the field and braved the weather'; but she also recalled Fanny Assingham's old judgment of them 'as not living at all, as not knowing what to do or what might be done for them' (314). Initially, Maggie sees one of her problems as maintaining the 'equilibrium' of their lives and their relations to others, partly because she fears 'the loss of balance' whch might result from any move on her part (349, 366; cf. 326). But she comes to realize that her appeal to equilibrium is often an appeal to inertia and the *status quo*. Moreover, on moral issues equal weight ought not to be accorded to good and ill, and whatever is meant by 'balance' it can be, and sometimes ought only to be, achieved by mutually adjusting forces. Inevitably she is disorientated by her sense of 'action quite positively for the first time in her life', and she feels herself unprepared with reasons should she be challenged to explain her new behaviour (322). Although, like Charlotte, Maggie had admired the Prince for his 'large and beautiful ease, his genius . . . for life', her judgment is askew because she is ignorant of genuine expressions of life. Maggie's own capacity to act grows in tandem with her capacity to detect and sympathize with the subtle actions and responses of others; for example, it was obvious that the Prince was watching her, 'as if thinking, waiting, deciding; yet it was still before he spoke that he, as she felt it to be, definitely acted' (338). And the physical coercion he attempted, and to which she felt herself to be normally so vulnerable, was no real surprise to her and, accordingly, ineffective.[6] Gradually Maggie brings Verver to an admission of his passive existence, so that he wonders whether they have all not been 'perhaps lazy, a wee bit languid—lying like gods together, all careless of mankind'. He adds that 'there's something haunting —as if it were a bit uncanny—in such a consciousness of our general comfort and privilege'; but he qualifies his apparent resolve to change with the thought that 'the beauty of it is, at the same time, that we *are* doing; we're doing, that is, after all, what we went in for' (361). Only by expunging the self-deception from that thought can Verver himself achieve fully moral agency; successful pursuit of goals merits no praise where they are reprehensible.

The numerous references to fear, in *The Golden Bowl*, echo those in *The Portrait of a Lady*, and typically occur when Maggie discovers her ignorance and succumbs to indecision.[7] 'Knowledge was a fascination as

---

[6] Compare with Goodwood, in *The Portrait of a Lady*, or Vronsky, in *Anna Karenina*.

[7] Among other things, Isabel Archer is said to fear herself, and her mind; various possibilities conjured up by her imagination; appearing narrow-minded; Goodwood, Mme Merle, Countess Gemini, sex: apart from her unspecified or undiagnosed fears, Maggie is said to fear herself, and her ideas; knowledge, freedom, change; being alone with her father and with the Prince; sex.

well as a fear' (395) to her because she had to face the problem of escaping from possession by others, and thus of disturbing the apparent calm of their corporate existence:

> what it came to was that seeing herself finally sure, knowing everything, having the fact, in all its abomination, so utterly before her that there was nothing else to add—what it came to was that, merely by being *with* him there in silence, she felt, within her, the sudden split between conviction and action. They had begun to cease, on the spot, surprisingly, to be connected; conviction, that is, budged no inch, only planting its feet more firmly in the soil—but action began to hover like some lighter and larger, but easier form, excited by its very power to keep above ground (426).

Maggie perceives, however, that 'what would condemn' action 'to the responsibility of freedom' was that her husband would have 'a new need of her', arising from the changed situation, and his own recognition of that change. In the earlier part of the novel all the main characters express inadequate views of freedom. For example, the Prince saw himself as 'free to feel and yet not to formulate', and Verver, who admired himself as free (essentially, financially free), saw his 'freedom to see' as growing (41, 128); Maggie tells her father that they are as 'free as air', and Charlotte and the Prince see themselves as enjoying together extraordinary freedom (146, 220). 'Charlotte's own judgment was, always, that they were ideally free', and when Colonel and Mrs Assingham join the house party at Matcham they are said to feel afresh 'the convenience of a society so placed that it had only its own sensibility to consider' (242, 249). All the characters typically take freedom to be independence from others, and exemption from responsibilities towards them. A later thought of Maggie's reveals her changing conception, as well as some nostalgia for the past:

> the loss, more than anything else, of their old freedom, their never having had to think, where they were together concerned, of anyone, of anything but each other (354).

In their attempts to shift responsibility to others, both Amerigo and Charlotte declare that Fanny Assingham made their marriages (41, 256); they explicitly disclaim responsibility for the consequences, as if they were the victims of some thoroughly deterministic force, and as if they were in no way parties to the arrangements (233). Fanny herself claims responsibility for 'it all' (283), but this melodramatic masochism and pathetic claim to influence others, only serves to highlight the entirely random propriety of her judgments.

In the light of all this the self-centredness of the characters hardly needs underlining. Charlotte tells Verver that 'it's the last folly ever to care, in an anxious way, the least particle more than one is absolutely forced', and Verver himself acknowledges to Maggie that even if they are 'tremendously moral . . . for each other', such an attitude amounts to selfishness (188, 361). Some of the factors constituting a fully moral response to life should now be apparent. The central point is that knowledge is a condition of, and an integral element in, moral action, properly understood. That is why Fanny Assingham is right to assert that 'stupidity pushed to a certain point *is* . . . immorality' (87). But if the attainment of knowledge is a duty, knowledge itself gives rise to duties, not least because it is a power to its possessors. Knowledge without action is essentially aesthetic in its function; and although a contemplative attitude is not in itself morally reprehensible, and is sometimes appropriate, the fundamental practical question which confronts every human being is how to act morally in a world of constant change. Moreover, morality is the highest and all-embracing category; according to its tenets one can not be selectively moral. The complexity of the changing contexts we find ourselves in resists the imposition of simple solutions, or appeal to simple formulae; and even the most considered and considerate action may have unforseen and undesired consequences. One cannot please, or be pleased by, all of the people all of the time. But the possibility of further revising one's present beliefs in the light of future information is no sufficient ground for postponing action on the basis of the best available evidence; indeed, the possibility of mistake is a necessary condition for classifying a claim as empirical, not a sufficient condition for judging such a claim to be false.

It is here instructive to turn our attention back to *The Portrait of a Lady*, written more than twenty years earlier. A reader of that novel is expected to conclude that there is an essential social dimension to knowledge and its acquisition, and that morally responsible behaviour requires directed thought about others, based on concern for them and an effort to transcend any natural egoism. Furthermore, the recipe for avoiding disasters of the kind described in the novel, which stem from untested and self-centred ideas, urges recognition of the open-endedness of all enquiry, the provisional nature of empirical claims, the multiplicity of possibly fruitful viewpoints, the inter-relation of our knowledge claims, and, of course, their fallibility.

It is not at all surprising that the same general views re-appear in *The Golden Bowl*. Verver, as we have seen, reduces all relationships to a matter of possession; by acquiring ownership or control of everything that might disturb his own existence, he aims to be immune to the world, and thus immune to the need to change in response to it. His achieved passivity is the antithesis of moral agency, and even his fondness for Maggie is essentially proprietary—no reader can ensorse the Prince's admiration for Verver's moral integrity. Maggie's own submission to her father entailed that she never learned to think; when, under external pressure, she is forced to start, she lacks guidance and criteria and, like Isabel Archer, she is isolated from others who are essential to the enterprise. Maggie's own aim for consistency and smoothness reveal her attempt to avoid challenge, decision, adjustment, displacement of established attitudes and beliefs; her wish not to hurt others cannot be finally dissociated from her wish not to be disturbed, even by the adverse judgment of others. Initially, Maggie is unable to distinguish the source of her beliefs, her father, from their truth or propriety; and his thought that she had never 'been wrong for more than three minutes' (187) carries the double implication that she is merely the mirror of his own virtue, and that, more importantly, her avoidance of error was only a consequence of her avoidance of action. The test of a moral character lies in what a person does; moreover, the moral worth of knowledge lies in what a person does with it. No merit attaches to the mere acquisition or possession of knowledge, as such, just as no moral virtue attaches to the mere acquisition of beautiful things. The world of beauty is, perhaps, a timeless domain and aesthetic contemplation is the mode of apprehending it; but man lives in a world of constant change, and responsible agency requires a grasp of the particular situation in which action must take place, and possibilities actualized. In reflecting on the relations between the moral and the aesthetic, a reader of Henry James must also reflect on the roles of principle and particular in each domain. A writer who wishes to establish the primacy of the particular case needs to convince readers of the many ways in which general principles fail us in particular cases, and of the ways, nevertheless, in which each case can be adequately met. There is no substitute for the elaboration of detail in this enterprise, and it is no accident, accordingly, that the serious novels of Henry James are so long. In addition, the detailed presentation of a particular case, itself counts as the representation of the philosophical view; and in this respect James's philosophical novels can be distinguished from the bare statement of moral precepts or insights, by writers such as Pascal or La Rochefoucauld, and from the analysis of arguments and concepts, by writers such as Hume and Kant.

It is here appropriate to underpin my interpretation of *The Golden Bowl* by reference to remarks in James's Prefaces, and also to the philosophical work of his brother, William James. Two passages can serve as a transition to that discussion. At the beginning of the novel, Mrs Assingham, reflecting on the arrival in London of Charlotte Stant, comments that 'it was a situation with such different sides . . . and to none of which one could, in justice, be blind'; at the end of the novel, when Maggie confronts Charlotte in the garden at Fawns, we are told that 'the full significance . . . could be no more, after all, than a matter of interpretation, differing always for a different interpreter' (74, 464). Such passages themselves require interpretation, of course, not so much for their compatibility as for the possibility that the second might be taken to express an extreme relativism which further inhibited fruitful thought and responsible action. James's remarks from the Preface to *The Golden Bowl* on the nature of freedom and action—'the religion of doing', in his phrase—have already been quoted at the beginning of this paper. They can now be usefully amplified by quotation from two other Prefaces written at the same time. Reflecting on the nature of experience and its representation in art, in the Preface to *The American*, James derides the thought that anyone could intelligently 'expect at once freedom and ease! That silly safety is but the sign of bondage and forfeiture.' He declares that 'the real represents to my perception the things we cannot possibly *not* know, sooner or later, in one way or another'. Life, itself, involves risk; indeed, 'the panting pursuit of danger is the pursuit of life itself, in which danger awaits us possibly at every step and faces us at every turn'.[8] On such a view, to cushion oneself against danger would be to cushion oneself against life, like Verver. In the Preface to *The Princess Casamassima* James observes that 'the agents in any drama, are interesting only in proportion as they feel their respective situations; since the consciousness, on their part, of the complication exhibited forms for us their link of connexion with it'. He adds that 'the interest of the attitude and the act would be the actor's imagination and vision of them, together with the nature and degree of their felt return upon him.' 'Experience', James suggests, 'is our apprehension and our measure of what happens to us as social creatures'. It must be insisted that there is no sharp distinction 'between doing and feeling'; on the contrary, 'what a man thinks and what he feels are the history and the character of what he does'.[9] There are 'degrees of feeling', and the highest degree is 'to be finely aware and richly responsible':

> It is those moved in this latter fashion who 'get most' out of all that happens to them and who in so doing enable us, as readers of their record, as participators by a fond attention, also to get most.[10]

James contends that the most general state about which stories are told is 'the state of bewilderment', and that 'by so much as the affair matters *for* some such individual, by so much do we get the best there is of it'.[11] On other occasions he had urged that 'there is our general sense of the way things happen—it abides with us indefeasibly, as readers of fiction, from the moment we demand that our fiction shall be intelligible'. Furthermore, James takes close attention to the text 'absolutely' for granted, not least

---

[8] *The Art of the Novel*, 30, 31, 32.
[9] Ibid., 62–63, 64, 66.
[10] Ibid., 62.
[11] Ibid., 66, 67.

because the enjoyment of a work of art is greatest when a work asks for such attention.[12]

In a much quoted letter of 1905 William James complained to his brother about the narrative method of *The Golden Bowl*:

> But why won't you, just to please Brother, sit down and write a new book, with no twilight or mustiness in the plot, with great vigor and decisiveness in the action, no fencing in the dialogue, no psychological commentaries, and absolute straightness in the style?[13]

Henry replied, in mock horror, that he would write such a book, 'on that two-and-two-make-four system on which all the awful truck that surrounds us is produced', adding that his brother seemed 'condemned to look at it from a point of view remotely alien to' his own in writing it.[14] In fact, however, William James had for a long time expressed general views consonant with those Henry expressed in his works. The short Preface to *The Will to Believe* (1897), for example, alone gives some indication of the parallelism. 'To the very last', William James asserts, there are 'various "points of view" which the philosopher must distinguish in discussing the world; and what is inwardly clear from one point remains a bare externality and datum to the other.'[15] Above all, 'there is no possible point of view from which the world can appear an absolutely single fact'. Mankind's 'cardinal weakness is to let belief follow recklessly upon lively conception, especially when the conception has instinctive liking at its back'. A purely passive attitude is no way to 'steer safely between the opposite dangers of believing too little or of believing too much'. 'What *should* be preached', he contends, 'is courage weighted with responsibility'—and he adds, almost as an after-thought, that 'the most interesting and valuable things about a man are his ideals and over-beliefs'.[16] Two remarks from within the volume itself, dating respectively from 1896 and 1882, are worthy of quotation in the present context. In the first, he argues that 'our non-intellectual nature does influence our convictions'; indeed,

> our passional nature not only lawfully may, but must decide an option between propositions, whenever it is a genuine option that cannot by its nature be decided on intellectual grounds.[17]

---

[12] Ibid., 34, 304.

[13] Reprinted in *Henry James: The Critical Heritage*, R. Gard (ed.) (London, 1968), 392.

[14] Ibid., 393.

[15] William James, *The Will to Believe and Other Essays in Popular Philosophy* (New York, 1956), viii.

[16] Ibid., ix, x, xi, xiii.

[17] Ibid., 11.

The second remark concerns the nature of moral choice:

> To eat our cake and have it, to lose our soul and save it, to enjoy the physical privileges of selfishness and the moral luxury of altruism at the same time, would be the ideal. But the real offers us these terms in the shape of mutually exclusive alternatives of which only one can be true at once; so that we must choose, and in choosing murder one possibility.

James adds that ' "facts" are the bounds of human knowledge, set for it, not by it'.[18]

Of equal interest to us in our attempt to characterize the moral dimensions of *The Golden Bowl* is the 'general sketch' that William James offers of man's consciousness in *The Principles of Psychology* (1890). In that work James argues that in order to understand a man's mind one must understand the context in which it functions. A central tenet is that 'consciousness is at all times primarily *a selecting agency*'; accordingly,

> *My experience is what I agree to attend to.* Only those items which I *notice* shape my mind—without selective interest, experience is an utter chaos.[19]

The following passage, originally published in 1884, is especially revealing when juxtaposed with the Preface to *The Princess Casamassima*, already quoted:

> the difference between thought and feling thus reduces itself, in the last subjective analysis, to the presence or absence of 'fringe' . . . once allow that fringes and halos, inarticulate perceptions, whereof the objects are as yet unnamed, mere nascencies of cognition, premonitions, awareness of direction, are thoughts *sui generis*, as much as articulate imaginings and propositions are; once restore, I say, the *vague* to its psychological rights, and the matter presents no further difficulty.

> And then we see that the current opposition of Feeling to Knowledge is quite a false issue.[20]

William James held that initial experience is 'one great blooming, buzzing confusion', which is later differentiated. 'The mind', he maintained, 'is at every stage a theatre of simultaneous possibilities. Consciousness consists in the comparison of these with each other, the selection of some, and the suppression of the rest by the reinforcing and inhibiting agency of attention.'[21]

[18] Ibid., 269, 271.
[19] William James, *The Principles of Psychology* (London, 1890), I, 139, 402; cf. II, 619. James records that the book was completed in 1885 (II, 686).
[20] Ibid., I, 478 n.
[21] Ibid., I, 488, 288.

When he turns to moral issues, James insists that 'the essential achievement of the will . . . when it is most "voluntary", is to ATTEND to a difficult object and hold it fast before the mind'; the difficulty of right action, indeed, is 'mental; it is that of getting the idea of the wise action to stay before our mind at all'. For this reason he asserts that '*to think is, in short, the only moral act*'.[22] A second point is that in a hierarchy of conscious values the aesthetic lies below that of ethics, essentially because moral choices determine the manner of being an agent will attain; 'one sign of intelligence', James claims, is 'never to mistake' 'the world of aesthetics' for the actual world of 'outer experience'.[23] A third point concerns the nature of the contexts in which moral choice is called for:

> The most characteristically and peculiarly moral judgments that a man is ever called on to make are in unprecedented cases and lonely emergencies, where no rhetorical maxims can avail, and the hidden oracle alone can speak.

James adds that 'life is one long struggle between conclusions based on abstract ways of conceiving cases, and opposite conclusions prompted by our instinctive perception of them as individual facts'; 'we can give no general rule for deciding when it is morally useful to treat a concrete case *sui generis*, and when to lump it together with others in an abstract class'.[24]

The juxtaposition of these reflections by William James with the quotations from his brother can serve, perhaps, not only to lend substance to what I claimed to be the moral dimension of *The Golden Bowl*, but also to remind us that what counts as philosophy varies greatly over time and between different groups of people. The methods of philosophy are as varied as its objects of concern, and its results, but the sharp distinctions that we draw for certain purposes have a curious magnetism, and attach themselves to us long after those purposes have been served. Some contemporary philosophers, for example, distinguish between moralists, who advocate policies by whatever persuasive devices they deem appropriate, but without all the supporting arguments and theories that can be provided, and moral philosophers who are concerned precisely with the nature and validity of such arguments.[25] And in an attempt to separate their own activities from the undefined activities of science and literature, they define philosophy itself as the reflective and systematic analysis of concepts, arguments and theories. But such restricted definitions exclude so many writers, and inhibit one's grasp of so many historical and cultural continuities and differences, that their disadvantages almost at once outweigh

[22] Ibid., II. 561, 563, 566.
[23] Ibid., II. 639.
[24] Ibid., II. 672, 674.
[25] *Philosophy and the Novel*, 68.

their value. All of this is by way of saying that our classifications of texts as novels, or as works of philosophy, reflect the conventions and traditions of a given culture, together with various needs and purposes which those conventions serve. Certainly the conventions are often backed by theories, presuppositions and judgments about the matters in hand, and others deemed relevant, but neither the conventions nor the categories associated with them need be thought of as eternal, immutable or irreplaceable. There should be no embarrassment, therefore, in asking ourselves for the force of the term 'philosophical' if we apply it to *The Golden Bowl*.

In an essay published in 1899, entitled 'The Future of the Novel', Henry James describes the novel, that is, the serious novel which alone merits and rewards the attention of an 'acute and mature' critical mind, as a 'prose picture' which appeals to us because it gives us 'knowledge abundant yet vicarious', and which we can afford to neglect only if we have 'a rare faculty, or great opportunities, for the extension of experience—by thought, by emotion, by energy—at first hand'.[26] A few years later, in 1905, James remarks that a novelist 'rewards consideration' in so far as he 'offers the critical spirit this opportunity for a certain intensity of educative practice'; the presence of such writers, in their works, 'causes our ideas, whether about life in general or about the art they have exemplified in particular, to revive and breathe again, to multiply, more or less to swarm'.[27] Twenty years earlier Henry James had insisted that the novelist 'has at once so much in common with the philosopher and the painter'; he resembles the painter in that the novel is 'everywhere an effort at *representation*'—'the only reason for the existence of a novel is that it does attempt to represent life'.[28] But life is 'all inclusion and confusion', whereas art is 'all discrimination and selection'; 'literature is an objective, a projected result; . . . life . . . is the unconscious, the agitated, the struggling, floundering cause'.[29] But how does the novelist resemble the philosopher? At least in respect of the 'truths he brings home' which, presumably, first must be identified, and then accepted as truths.[30] Even if the novelist's problem is to interfuse 'a picture and an idea',[31] part of a reader's problem must concern the possibility of re-formulating that idea. At this point, and as readers with a general interest in philosophy, we must ask whether, in *The Golden Bowl* in particular, we are offered or can find anything more than occasional thoughtful observations about life and our experience

---

[26] Reprinted in *The House of Fiction: Essays on the Novel by Henry James* L. Edel (ed.) (London, 1957), 54, 53, 51.

[27] Ibid., 61.

[28] Ibid., 26, 76, 25.

[29] *The Art of the Novel*, 120; *The House of Fiction*, 64.

[30] *The House of Fiction*, 79.

[31] Ibid., 155.

of it, from which, if we are so minded, we can construct a few generalizations? Is it a strange accident that the author himself submitted his work to the public as a novel, and a perverse coincidence that for more than seventy years no one has seen fit to discuss it as philosophy?

It is certainly very easy to state, in a thoroughly banal way, a series of philosophical generalizations that have not, as such, been stated within the novel; but banal statements are not the exclusive preserve of novel readers—the conclusions of the greatest thinkers can readily be stated in a banal fashion. Philosophers, typically, are often seen as presenting considerations and arguments with the aim of establishing a specific point or an identifiable conclusion, and as indicating the ground on which they are prepared to be challenged. Novelists, on the other hand, sometimes can be said to present a picture, the elements of which are distinguished and classified, if at all, only by an individual reader; it is often only the reader who *says* what has been *shown* in a novel. However these notions of showing and saying should be formally defined, it is clear that showing is identical with neither saying nor arguing, any more than the giving of examples is the same as the giving of reasons. But whilst arguments can themselves be argued with, it is not clear what modes of response are possible or appropriate towards the presentation of pictures. Furthermore, several philosophers in the Western tradition, including Cicero and his eighteenth-century heirs, but most notably in modern times Wittgenstein, have urged that *showing* constitutes an essential part of philosophy itself; and not only when the giving of reasons comes to an end, but also when we have no conventions for saying what can been seen if certain items are juxtaposed for comparison. It is often unclear what the relations are between the events in a novel, grouped and described in certain ways, and an overall thesis, whether that thesis be deemed explicit, implicit, or inferred from the text. But we should remember that the notion of evidential support is not very well understood in philosophy itself, and counter-examples, notoriously, are not always admitted as undermining the validity or diminishing the value of a thesis.

We have already seen that Henry James himself thought of novels as pictures of life, in which ideas would be essentially embodied; the pictures are designed to reward consideration and cause readers to detect and endorse the truths embodied, and to generate relevant thoughts and actions of their own. Detection of the embodiment must be a precondition of a reader pursuing such thoughts on his own, of course, in whatever manner or direction he may carry that pursuit. And here there is no difference between a novelist and a more traditional philosopher inviting readers to test ideas in their own experience. But there is a tradition of assuming that a philosopher's medium and a novelist's message are alike discountable, if not dispensable, in any proper assessment of their achievements; that is, one searches for a philosopher's message, however it has been expressed and, indeed, as if it is precisely expressible in countless different ways, whereas one's attention is largely confined to a novelist's expression, and extends to a message only, if at all, so far as it can be identified through that unique expression. Views such as these, however, themselves have a history, and a theoretical backing that can be challenged. Here it need only be insisted that literary works from different periods and *genres* do not all and necessarily evoke only contemplative responses, and philosophical works do not all and necessarily arouse readers to action; moreover, it is false that every idea is uniquely expressible, and equally false that every idea is expressible in countless ways. To the extent that James saw himself as embodying ideas which competent readers could recognize, he presumably did not envisage a necessary connection between the idea and its expression in the novel;[32] moreover, he did not expect a reader, in detecting the established truth, to learn something previously unknown. Rather, a reader might be expected to *realize*, quite literally, the experiences of the characters and the propriety or impropriety of their responses: 'What befalls us is but another name for the way our circumstances press upon us—so that an account of what befalls us is an account of our circumstances.'[33] It might be held that in seeking to provide a reader with surrogate experience James is really subscribing to the view that having is a necessary condition of knowing. The accusation is too quick, however. Firstly, James readily accepts that recognition, that is re-cognition, of ideas within a novel presupposes a prior grasp of them outside the novel in real life; he is not committed to holding that a novel provides new experiences to which a reader's prior concepts have no application. Secondly, although he thinks that, typically, a good novel brings about a reader's realization of a particular mode of perception or response, he does not claim that it necessarily has this effect; an exceptional reader might have achieved such realization by other means. A further point concerns James's view that 'criticism is the only gate to appreciation', and his utter condemnation of 'passive consciousness'.[34] Although he insists that no human being 'is under the smallest positive obligation to "like"' any work of art, James allows a normative element to appreciation which

[32] But in 1884 James did argue for something like a necessary connection, although it must be stressed that he later used a different notion of 'idea': 'This sense of the story being the idea, the starting-point, of the novel, is the only one that I see in which it can be spoken of as something different from its organic whole; and since in proportion as the work is successful the idea permeates and penetrates it, informs and animates it, so that every word and every punctuation-point contribute directly to the expression, in that proportion do we lose our sense of the story being a blade which may be drawn more or less out of its sheath' (*The House of Fiction*, 39).

[33] Ibid., 81.

[34] Ibid., 60, 48.

separates it from mere understanding;[35] and this might suggest that a reader would generally be unable to realize those fictionally represented experiences which typically conflict with his own mode of consciousness. This aside, James does see critical appreciation—'the lucid report of impressions received, of estimates formed, of intentions understood, of values attached'[36]—as subject to public scrutiny by the small minority of readers qualified to judge. We have to learn what counts as an appropriate response to a particular work at a given time, even though the limits of propriety may take time to determine, and may change.

James frequently refers to the delicate relation between the typical in art, and the particularity of each work. 'Art is essentially selection, but it is a selection whose main care is to be typical, to be inclusive', and 'as people feel life, so they will feel the art that is most closely related to it'; accordingly, 'in proportion as in what [fiction] offers us we see life *without* rearrangement do we feel that we are touching the truth'.[37] Only if a novelist successfully represents the particularity of experience can a reader *realize* it for himself or herself; but equally, only if the typical is represented can there be any re-application of the responses realized, the truths recognized. James is not committed to an extreme form of particularism which precludes the possibility of reasons, and ultimately thought. His sympathy with pragmatism of the kind espoused by his brother leads James to distrust absolutes, formulae, rigid distinctions, not because they can never serve useful ends, but because they are traps which cut off thought and blind us to their limited value. He would agree that '*to think* is . . . the only moral act', because a person has being and can be characterized only in terms of thought or consciousness; and the processes of awareness that we are invited to realize, in reading *The Golden Bowl*, are designed to enable us to grasp, not what it would be *like* to be Maggie but, what it *is* to *be* Maggie.

The contributors to this series were asked to explore the question: 'What are the important issues involved in the relationship between philosophy and literature?'—a question, incidentally, to which no self-respecting English-speaking philosopher would have given much time twenty-five years ago. In the first part of my lecture I offered a brief interpretation of what I called 'the moral dimensions' of *The Golden Bowl*; in the second part I have referred to Henry James's reflections in the Prefaces to his novels and to some of his theoretical claims about novels; in addition, some of William James's philosophical tenets were outlined, for comparison with what his brother said and with the interpretation of the novel. In conclusion it may

---

[35] Ibid., 52; cf. 80–81.
[36] Ibid., 60.
[37] Ibid., 38.

be helpful simply to list some of the problems, which I take this lecture to have raised.

If we say that an interpretation is offered from a particular viewpoint, for example, from a philosophical viewpoint, how is such a viewpoint to be properly characterized, distinguished from others, judged for appropriateness, or understood as controlling an interpretation? By what principles or general theories are interpretations of the kind offered warranted: by what means is it proper to adjudicate between different interpretations? Some of Henry James's remarks, as we have seen, seem to envisage the novel as *dulce et utile*; it is an author's aim to provide enjoyment that, in part, leads him to offer his text to the public as a 'novel', rather than as 'philosophy'. But when is it legitimate to study a novelist's thoughts alongside an attempt to interpret his novel? What kinds of response are appropriate to a text which a reader takes to be a form of philosophy? James did not expect a reader with an active, critical intelligence merely to determine and acquiesce in the content of the novel; rather a reader was expected to re-formulate in his own terms whatever he found, explore its implications and, in brief, to *argue* with it. Such a view presents a challenge to those critics of literature who never discuss ideas, or who regard the notions of literary response and argument as mutually exclusive. These last attitudes have one source in the institutional separation of philosophical and literary studies, and the specialized nature of those studies; only recently have there been attempts to diminish misunderstanding between the two camps and broaden the approaches of each.

The Golden Bowl, I suggest, does represent one way of doing philosophy, notably in the showing and comparing of carefully delineated particular cases; the showing is intended to elicit certain responses, and ultimately to cause action of certain kinds—it is not intended to be a mere display, of a take-it-or-leave-it variety. Typically, the method of showing omits detailed explanation, or statements, for example, of presuppositions, and here a reader encounters problems which he cannot solve as a partner in a dialogue. James's own explicit philosophical reflections, along with his theoretical remarks about the novel, themselves require analysis and elaboration. An adequate discussion of these, however, together with a fuller interpretation of *The Golden Bowl*, must await another occasion. One thing is clear: a writer cannot legitimately challenge readers to test his ideas in their own experience, and then claim immunity to criticism and argument; it would be regrettable if the notion of a philosophical novel encouraged such a view.[38]

[38] All readers of Henry James should study Martha Craven Nussbaum's forthcoming article in *New Literary History*, 'Flawed Crystals: James's *The Golden Bowl* and Literature as Moral Philosophy'. I am most grateful to Professor Nussbaum for sending me a typescript of her discussion.

Notes on Contributors

Hywel D. Lewis is Professor Emeritus of King's College, London, and Chairman of the Council of the Royal Institute. He is the author of many books, including his Gifford Lectures, *The Elusive Mind* (1969), and *The Elusive Self* (1982), and of many articles in *Philosophy* since 1972.

Stewart Sutherland is Professor of the Philosophy of Religion at King's College, London. He is the author of *Atheism and the Rejection of God: Philosophy and Literature in* The Brothers Karamazov (1977) and of *God, Jesus and Belief* (1984) and *Faith and Ambiguity* (1984). He is a member of the Council of the Royal Institute.

Renford Bambrough, Fellow and sometime President of St John's College, Cambridge, is the Editor of *Philosophy*. His latest book is *Moral Scepticism and Moral Knowledge* and he has contributed to three other volumes in this series; he wrote the introduction to the Royal Institute Conference volume, *Reason and Religion*. He contributed several articles to *Philosophy* before he became its Editor.

J. P. Stern is Professor of German at University College, London. He is the author of *A Study of Nietzsche* (1979) and *Hitler: The Führer and the People* (1984).

R. W. Beardsmore is Lecturer in Philosophy at University College, Bangor. He has written many articles on morals and aesthetics, and *Moral Reasoning* (1969), *Art and Morality* (1972).

Stein Haugom Olsen, of the University of Oslo, published his *The Structure of Literary Understanding* in 1978. He is the author of many articles on aesthetics in learned journals.

İlham Dilman is Reader in Philosophy at University College, Swansea. He has written many books on a wide range of philosophical and literary topics: the latest, *Quine on Ontology, Necessity and Experience* (1984). He has contributed to *Philosophy* and to the seventh volume of this series, *Understanding Wittgenstein* (1974).

Jacquelyn Kegley is Professor in the Department of Philosophy and Religious Studies at the California State College, Bakersfield. She has written, mainly on American philosophy, in various learned journals, and is author together with Charles W. Kegley of *Introduction to Logic* (1978).

John Casey is Fellow of Gonville and Caius College, Cambridge. He published *The Logic of Criticism* in 1966, and edited *Morality and Moral Reasoning* (1971). He was a contributor to the volume of Royal Institute lectures for 1971–72.

Frank Cioffi is Professor of Philosophy at the University of Essex. He was a contributor to the fourth volume of this series, *The Proper Study* (1971) and has written on Freud, on Wittgenstein, and on aesthetics.

Jacques Derrida is Professor at the Ecole Normale Superieure in Paris. Among his many works are *Of Grammatology* and *La Carte Postale*.

Martin Warner is Lecturer in Philosophy at the University of Warwick, a member of the Council of the Royal Institute, and a member of the editorial board of *Philosophy and Literature*. He has published in the learned journals.

Peter Jones is Reader in Philosophy at the University of Edinburgh. His *Philosophy and the Novel* was published in 1975 and *Hume's Sentiments* in 1982. His numerous articles include contributions to *Philosophy*.

Index of Names

Adkins, A. W. H., 29 and ff.
Allen, Walter, 85
Amis, Kingsley, 85
Aristophanes, 5
Aristotle, 29ff, 135, 137, 138, 141, 150, 152
Aquinas, St. Thomas, 136, 137
Arnold, Matthew, 88
Atwood, Margaret, 1
Austen, Jane, 150–151
Ayer, A. J., 189, 190, 194

Bakhtin, M. M., 17
Bambrough, R., 71, 73
Barth, John, 115–134
Barth, Karl, 19, 22
Benn, Gottfried, 45
Bentham, Jeremy, 69, 202
Berkeley, G., 37
Berryman, John, 169
Blake, William, 79, 83, 89
Bluestone, Gregory, 117
Bourget, Paul, 165
Bradley, F. H., 67
Bramhall, N., 37
Brown, Peter, 197
Burke, E., 152
Burroughs, E. R., 64

Calvin, J., 33
Cary, Joyce, 73
Camus, A., 96
Carlyle, Thomas, 202, 205
Cherry, Christopher, 171
Cicero, 225
Cohen, Jonathan, 191n
Coleridge, S. T., 145, 202
Collingwood, R. G., 194
Conrad, Joseph, 5, 107
Coulson, Jessie, 16n, 24n
Croce, B., 138
Cumming, R. D., 193

Dante, 206
Defoe, Daniel, 63
Denniston, J. D., 30
Dickens, Charles, 85, 92
Diderot, D., 142, 170
Dilthey, William, 168, 189, 208
Doblin, Alfred, 54
Doderer, Hermito von, 54
Dostoyewsky, Feodor, 95–114
Drury, M., 95
Dryden, J., 149
Ducasse, S., 62, 64
Durrant, M., 191

Edwards, Christopher, 153
Elgar, Edward, 138
Eliot, George, 44, 67, 95, 159
Eliot, T. S., 48, 51, 144

Faulkner, W., 60, 70
Fielding, Henry, 151
Flaubert, G., 165
Fleming, I., 64
Ford, Ford Madox, 72
Forster, E. M., 115
Frazer, J., 155ff.
Freud, S., 37, 95–96, 155–156
Froude, J. A., 29 and ff.

Galsworthy, J., 67
Gardner, John, 1
Gaskell, Elizabeth, 84
Gekoski, R. A., 189n
George, Stefan, 45
Gibbon, Edward, 166
Goethe, J. W. von, 42
Goldberg, S. L., 150n, 153n
Golding, William, 5
Gombay, A., 63
Grimm, Jacob and Wilhelm, 42n, 46
Guseva, P. Ye., 16n

Index of Names

Hardy, Thomas, 46
Hare, R. M., 40, 59, 63, 64
Hegel, G. W. F., 43, 44, 45, 139, 142
Heidegger, M., 168
Heller, Erich, 50
Heraclitus, 30, 44
Hertz, Heinrich, 157
Hesse, Hermann, 54
Hippocrates, 56
Hitler, A., 46
Hobbes, Thomas, 37
Hofmannstal, H., 45
Homer, 31
Hopkins, G. M., 167
Hopkins, L., 153
Hulme, T. E., 82
Humboldt, W. von, 48
Hume, David, 135, 136, 141, 146

Ibsen, H., 92

James, Henry, 217–228
James, William, 219, 221, 223
Jesus, 13
Johnson, Samuel, 32, 35
Jones, Ernest, 112
Jonson, Ben, 143
Joyce, James, 137
Jünger, Ernst, 45
Juvenal, 144

Kafka, Franz, 45, 53
Kamenka, E., 59
Kant, Immanuel, 7, 42, 48, 136
Kaplan, Chaim, 159
Klein, Melanie, 105

Lawrence, D. H., 9, 56, 67, 72, 206
Leavis, F. R., 144
Lessing, G., 42
Lesky, Albin, 38
Longinus, 136
Lukacs, George, 130
Luther, Martin, 37, 47
Lutyens, E., 138

McLintock, David, 41
Mahler-Werfel, Alma, 55n

Malcolm, N., 65
Mankowitz, Wolf, 80
Mann, Thomas, 45
Marvell, A., 143, 152
Marx, Karl, 33
Mauriac, F., 64
Merleau-Ponty, M., 131
Meyer, R. W., 42n
Mill, J. S., 69, 192ff
Mitchell, Basil, 190
Machulsky, K., 16, 24
Moore, G. E., 67, 155, 156, 158
Mujuskovic, Ben, 5
Mundle, C. W. K., 59
Musil, Robert, 45, 52–54

Nagel, Thomas, 85
Newman, J. H., 190, 191
Nietzsche, Friedrich, 41, 44–49, 55, 57, 96, 138, 142, 194, 206
Nussbaum, Martha Craven, 228

O'Hara, John, 2
Ohmann, Richard, 115, 117
Origen, 201
Ortega y Basset, J., 16, 8
Orwell, G., 62

Page, Denys, 30
Parmenides, 206
Pascal, Roy, 192, 193
Paskins, B., 61
Pelagius, 198, 200
Pepys, Samuel, 167
Plato, 5, 42, 43, 45, 71, 73, 89
Plutarch, 146, 149
Pound, Ezra, 81–83
Powys, J. C., 168
Proust, 5

Radford, C., 60
Rahv, Philip, 96
Ramsey, Frank, 156
Reimarus, H. S., 42
Renoir, F., 66
Rhees, Rush, 109, 169
Richards, I. A., 156
Rilke, R. M., 45, 49–52

Robson, W. W., 86
Rousseau, J. J., 192ff
Royce, Josiah, 131–134
Russell, Bertrand, 9, 72
Ryle, Gilbert, 6

Sartre, Jean Paul, 40, 64, 115, 120, 125,
   129, 130–134, 139, 141, 165, 192,
   194, 195, 207
Schiller, J. C. von, 42, 44
Schroder, A. A., 42n
Shakespeare, 44, 64, 143ff
Shumaker, W., 204
Solovyev, Vsevolod, 21
Snodgrass, W. D., 98, 102
Spender, Stephen, 37
Spengemann, W. C., 195–196
Spinoza, Benedict de, 29 and ff.
Steiner, George, 159
Steiner, J. F., 159
Sterne, L., 151

Talgeri, Pramod, 44n
Tauler, H., 42, 44
Taylor, Harriet, 202ff.
Thomas, William, 193
Thucydides, 152
Thurneyson, Edward, 19–25
Tolstoy, L., 64, 95, 164

Trakl, Georg, 45
Trilling, Lionel, 90, 95n, 110, 115, 142,
   143
Tynan, K., 66

Wagner, Fred., 41
Waller, Chris, 57
Warnock, Mary, 129
Weil, Simone, 98, 108, 110
Werfel, Franz, 54–55
Welleck, René, 96n
Willey, Basil, 165
Wilson, Dower, 112–114
Wilson, Edmund, 3
Winch, P., 59
Winckleman, J., 141
Wisdom, John, 95, 105
Wittgenstein, Ludwig, 64–66, 72, 139,
   155ff, 189, 196, 200, 225
Wolff, A., 66
Wolfe, Thomas, 5
Wolff, Christian, 42
Woolf, Virginia, 115
Wootton, Barbara, 11
Wordsworth, W., 204

Vivas, Elisea, 96

Yeats, W. B., 143